Beyond Establishment

Beyond Establishment

*Resetting Church–State
Relations in England*

Jonathan Chaplin

scm press

© Jonathan Chaplin 2022
Published in 2022 by SCM Press
Editorial office
3rd Floor, Invicta House,
108–114 Golden Lane,
London EC1Y 0TG, UK

www.scmpress.co.uk

SCM Press is an imprint of Hymns Ancient & Modern Ltd
(a registered charity)

Hymns Ancient & Modern® is a registered trademark of
Hymns Ancient & Modern Ltd
13A Hellesdon Park Road, Norwich,
Norfolk NR6 5DR, UK

British Library Cataloguing in Publication data

A catalogue record for this book is available
from the British Library

978-0-334-06173-1

Typeset by Regent Typesetting
Printed and bound by
CPI Group (UK) Ltd

Contents

Acknowledgements

I am much indebted to Paul Barber, Malcolm Brown, Daniel DeHanas, Doug Gay, Jenny Leith, David McIlroy and Julian Rivers for many valuable comments on earlier drafts of this book. It is a better book for their input, but their being named here does not imply agreement with everything in it, even its central thesis. Any errors of fact or judgement remain my own. Although I was privileged to enjoy the status of Associate Fellow of Theos while writing the book, it was not the product of my association with them and I do not speak on their behalf on this issue. Chapter 2 draws on material first appearing in 'Can nations be "Christian"?', *Theology* (November/December 2009), pp. 410–24, and I am grateful to the editor for permission to use it here. Warm thanks to David Shervington and all involved at SCM Press for their professionalism and good cheer. It has again been a pleasure to work with them.

Some of my intellectual debts are evident in the references. But I would, unusually, like to dedicate the book to three people I have never met but who have been among the most articulate and principled advocates of disestablishment in my lifetime and whose writings have inspired my own. The first is Bishop Colin Buchanan, the leading Evangelical advocate of disestablishment over the last 40 years. He is author of *Cut the Connection: Disestablishment and the Church of England* (1994), which lovingly lambasted the Church for meekly accepting the persistence of state supervision of its affairs. The second is the late Fr Peter Cornwell, former Vicar of St Mary's University Church, Oxford. Fr Cornwell was author of *Church and Nation* (1983), a theologically rich and generous-spirited statement of the Anglo-Catholic case for disestablishment, and a dissenting member of the Chadwick Commission (1970). The third is the late Professor Valerie Pitt, the only woman on the Chadwick Commission and also a dissenting Anglo-Catholic member. She was author of some of the most penetrating and eloquent critiques of Establishment in the last half century. I regret only discovering Fr Cornwell's work on disestablishment in 2021, shortly after his passing. I also regret missing the chance to meet Professor Pitt in 1996 at a conference on Establishment to which I was invited but which my employer declined to grant me leave to attend. I hope their family and friends might take satisfaction from the fact that their work is still inspiring readers today. There are, in fact, few arguments in this book that were not already anticipated in the writings of these three authors. At times seen as mavericks, their aim was only to summon the Church to greater theological clarity, integrity and courage in its relation to society and nation. If my book does no more than remind the Church of England of the continuing importance of these unheeded saints, it will have been worth the effort.

All Saints' Day 2021

Introduction
Awakening 'the dog that didn't bark'

According to one constitutional expert, the established status of the Church of England is 'a vital part of how our current society constructs its political identity in ways that make sense to all citizens'.[1] That will come as a surprise to those in the churches or wider society for whom the question never crosses their mind.[2] Could it really be that the arcane workings of one of the most ancient and seemingly ineffectual parts of the British constitution actually matters to contemporary British – or at least English – citizens?[3]

Establishment hardly seems the most pressing issue at stake in the larger question of the place of faith in British society.[4] The business of the Ecclesiastical Committee of Parliament, for example, which few British citizens will even know exists, seems light years away from much more pressing questions of public religion, such as whether the latest iteration of the 'Prevent' programme stigmatizes Muslims, or what are the religious motivations of Extinction Rebellion protestors who shut down Westminster Bridge for several days in 2019. Yet the established status of the Church of England – the church 'by law established' – continues to arouse animated responses from both the Church and sections of wider society, in spite of the fact that it is a shadow of what it was 50 years ago.[5] In classifications of church–state regimes, English Establishment is typically placed well into the category of 'weak' establishments on account of the relatively modest obligations it imposes on Church and state.[6] The Church of England is not the state's lapdog. It is not a 'state church', defined by Paul Avis as existing where there is a confluence of national and church government within a confessionally uniform nation.[7] Such a state of affairs has not existed in Britain since the late seventeenth century.[8] The state does not own the Church, order it around or subsidize it.[9] A chief aim of twentieth-century Church reformers (mostly aristocratic Anglo-Catholics) was effective self-government for the Church in matters of doctrine and liturgy, while retaining the status of a 'national Church'. This was largely achieved in 1969 with the creation of General Synod and in the subsequent Worship and Doctrine Measure 1974.[10] As a result, many observers doubt that it is worth expending any significant energy on Establishment. A report of the Evangelical Alliance in 2006 concluded that 'government and churches should not divert significant resources to [wholesale disestablishment]'.[11] Or, as Oliver O'Donovan put it more crisply in a submission to that report, 'If it ain't broke, don't fix it!'[12]

Yet the issue is resurfacing again today with renewed vigour, for at least three reasons. First, the accelerating secularization and pluralization of British society, combined with a precipitate decline in membership of the Church, is making it decreasingly plausible for the Church to present itself as 'the Church of the nation', still less to sustain the myth that England is a 'Christian nation'.[13] It is hard to disagree with Robert Morris's blunt assessment that 'the weight of evidence about the state of religious belief and its plurality beyond Christianity render the surviving late seventeenth-century settlement in principle indefensible even if its increasingly emaciated formal remnant may stagger on.'[14] Second, escalating conflicts over the place of religion in the public square seem to be reinforcing the resolve both of defenders of Establishment to protect it and of secularist critics to terminate it.[15] The unedifying, if at the time unavoidable, conflict between Church and state over same-sex marriage in 2013 is a painful recent case.[16] To many on the state's side, the Church was simply digging in to defend an obviously reactionary position. To many on the Church's side, it was yet another example of a state-led campaign to impose an ideologically driven regime of egalitarian rights on social organizations generally.[17] Third, the imminent prospect of having to revise the coronation service for a new monarch is the most time-sensitive factor concentrating minds (and events may already have overtaken us by the time this book appears). Revisiting a national Christian ceremony in the light of the momentous cultural changes over the 70 years since it was last held will inevitably thrust Establishment as a whole back into public debate. The issue of Establishment does, after all, retain the potential to touch a deep nerve of constitutional and spiritual anxiety in the British body politic.

Writing as a lifelong Anglican, I argue in this book that Establishment is not simply an idea whose time has long gone but an arrangement that has always been theologically problematic, and that it continues to be distracting and compromising both for English Anglicanism and for the British state. The book calls for a planned sequence of steps towards 'disestablishment' – the severance of the special legal ties binding Church and state. It also proposes that the Church should not wait on events, or dither around until the state comes knocking at its door with proposals framed by its own interests, but take the initiative itself towards disestablishment.

I happen to think progress towards disestablishment could bring net, if modest, practical benefits for both state and Church. Yet I do not adopt a consequentialist approach to the question, weighing up a series of pragmatic losses or gains for either institution. For example, whether life beyond Establishment puts the survival of the Crown in doubt, makes the Church's pastoral or outreach tasks easier or harder or enables the government to enlist 'faith communities' in the policy process more or less easily, will not be decisive concerns. I offer occasional reflections on such questions but no sustained assessment of them. Rather I argue that English Establishment has always amounted to an improper blurring of the jurisdictional boundaries of Church and state and that today it continues to confer unwarranted (if minor) privileges and burdens on the

Church and cede an unwarranted (if also minor) role for the state over certain matters that fall within the Church's unique sphere of authority. Establishment should end irrespective of empirical consequences like those listed.

Such a 'principled' approach to constitutional change will be seen by some as un-British (or at least un-English), given that, it might be claimed, such changes take place quite satisfactorily in the UK in an ad hoc or 'organic' fashion without resort to fundamental constitutional, still less theological, principle. Yet two of the latest incremental steps in that direction should give them pause. The decision taken in 2007 by Gordon Brown that the Prime Minister should no longer play an active role in making senior ecclesiastical appointments is an example of how constitutional conventions can be changed on the hoof by sitting politicians without proper consultation.[18] A few years later, Parliament was, according to Robert Morris, 'bounced' into passing the Succession to the Crown Act 2013, allowing an heir to the throne to marry a Roman Catholic, following a hasty consultation at a Commonwealth Heads of Government meeting in 2011.[19] This is not good stewardship of something as important as a nation's constitution, even if one agrees with the outcome in any particular case (as I do in these).

What is needed is a theologically principled reconsideration of the proper jurisdictional spheres of Church and state. This is required not only for the sake of the British constitution but also to help the Church better clarify its own understanding of its role in the life of a nation that has largely turned its back on it. This is a theological question because it is a question of mission. Critics have observed that the Church's own reports on Establishment over the last century have been strong on legal detail but weak on theological principle. The only traces of theology in the last one, the Chadwick Report of 1970, which ran to 125 pages, appear in the dissenting contributions of Valerie Pitt and Peter Cornwell.[20] The Church has not put its official theological mind to the question for well over half a century.[21] The outcome of this neglect is that while Establishment remains the default stance for most Church leaders, compelling theological arguments for it are thin on the ground. As Jeremy Morris has put it, 'contemporary support for Establishment lacks confidence in the authenticity of the Anglican Church's apprehension of its truth, resting its case finally on pragmatism.'[22]

Anglican proponents of disestablishment (at least those willing to make a case for it) have, however, always been in a small minority, never able to muster sufficient support to compel a sustained inquiry into first principles. For most of the last century, the cause has rarely won the backing of more than a handful of outliers.[23] Apart from during the 'Prayer Book Crisis' of the late 1920s, when the House of Commons shocked the Church by twice brusquely vetoing its considered recommendations for liturgical reform, campaigners have failed to keep the issue on the Church's agenda for any length of time. As one historian has put it, disestablishment has been 'the dog that didn't bark'.[24] Official bodies set up to address the question have been dominated by defenders of Establishment, even while proposing important modifications to existing machinery. In the decades after the 1960s, the default support for Establishment in the dominant Liberal Catholicism of the time was classically, and loftily, expressed in John Habgood's book, *Church and Nation in a Secular Age*, which reflected the assumption of a close convergence between Christian values and those of the nation as a whole.[25] General Synod, the Church's most representative body, voted in 1994 firmly against a Private Member's motion, put by redoubtable disestablishmentarian Bishop Colin Buchanan, calling for an end to a state role in episcopal appointments and in Church legislation.[26] He repeated his call regarding episcopal appointments in 2002 during what turned out to be a controversial process for appointing a successor to Archbishop George Carey, but with the same result.[27] Given the overwhelming predominance of the Establishmentarian stance in the Church's leadership and the paucity of formidable recent critiques of it, it is thus hardly surprising that the latest academic collection on the subject, *The Established Church: Past, Present and Future* (2011), while containing theologically serious contributions, included among its 11 chapters only one call for significant change, and that only as far as the Church of Scotland model.[28]

Newly assertive defences of Establishment are also coming from the Church's own engine room. In 2019, Malcolm Brown, the Church's Director of Mission and Public Affairs, mounted a renewed theological case for Establishment, urging the Church to be 'more robustly committed to its established status, not on grounds of self-interest but as a huge potential contribution to the common good'.[29] Establishment, he proposed, 'captures some important truths about what a good society might look like', while 'disestablishment is often an idea founded in deeply questionable assumptions', by which he meant those based in 'political liberalism'.[30] The special issue of *Ecclesiastical Law Journal* in which this article appeared contained no contribution explicitly arguing a disestablishmentarian case. Campaigners, then, are running against powerful centres of institutional and scholarly resistance (or, at least, inertia).

Given the factors noted above, the time is ripe for the case for disestablishment to be put again. The last robust advocacy of it was Theo Hobson's *Against Establishment: An Anglican Polemic*, published in 2003, the most provocative and entertaining book on the subject I have come across. Hobson frames his argument for disestablishment against the widespread collapse of support for the Church of England resulting from late twentieth-century secularization. While I share many of his sympathies, my book attempts a more forensic treatment of legal and political issues. It is an argument from political theology presented to the Church, although I hope curious outsiders will take a look at it too. The book is an attempt to recharge a debate that continues to get kept off the Church's agenda by what are thought to be more pressing concerns of the moment. While some of the issues are legally complex, I have tried to keep secondary details out of the main text (the book is not written primarily for lawyers), so as to allow the shape of the larger argument to remain in focus.

Chapter 1 explains what 'Establishment' means today and

defines what 'disestablishment' could amount to. It distinguishes the senses in which I shall use these terms from other usages with which they are often conflated. These conflations feed ongoing confusions on which the case for the defence of the status quo too easily trades. The chapter then defines the scope and limits of the book.

Chapter 2 presents a 'theology of disestablishment'. It argues that Establishment is, and always was, theologically unjustifiable. This is so even when all mitigation is allowed for the complex historical circumstances that gave it birth and shaped its evolution. Establishment today still amounts to a damaging confusion of the proper spheres of jurisdiction of Church and state, in ways that still matter to both. It both compromises the autonomy of the Church and breaches the principle of the religiously impartial state, which mandates a stance of even-handedness on the part of the state towards diverse religious adherents and organizations present in society. An influential version of this principle is central to 'political liberalism', but I present a different, theological rendition of it. This rendition requires a critique of often unexamined theological notions at work in most versions of establishment – the idea that there can be a 'Christian nation' and that such a nation needs a 'Christian state'. I argue that these claims are theologically invalid. I then point to an important statement of how the jurisdictions of Church and state might be better understood. The statement lies surprisingly close to hand, ironically attached to an Act of Parliament – the Church of Scotland Act of 1921, to which is appended the Articles Declaratory of the Constitution of the Church of Scotland in Matters Spiritual. I suggest that, as English Anglicans develop a suitable post-Establishment theology of church–state relations, they can draw inspiration from this historic document produced by one of their closest neighbours.

Chapters 3 and 4 'deconstruct' Establishment, by which I mean not some deep postmodern unveiling, but simply 'taking it apart' in order to offer a critical overview of its remaining central components. They show how each component, even today, breaches the principles of Church autonomy and state impartiality in ways that Church and state should care about. Chapter 3 explores the most important ways in which the constitutional ties between Church, Crown and government breach these principles. Under discussion here are Royal Supremacy, Protestant succession, the coronation and accession oaths and crown appointments. Chapter 4 addresses the relation between Church and Parliament. The chapter exposes the Church's continuing dependence on parliamentary approval of its own legislation, assesses the problematic role of bishops in the House of Lords and calls for an end to parliamentary supervision of the Church Commissioners.

Chapters 5 and 6 seek to 'dispute' Establishment by exposing the flaws in three influential defences of it. These defences prove surprisingly tenacious in spite of what I regard as their implausibility. The first is the 'concession to secularism' defence: disestablishment would 'send the wrong signal' to society by suggesting a public retreat of faith from the public square. The second is the 'anti-neutrality' defence: given that states cannot be religiously neutral, disestablishment would open the field to some other privileged public confession, such as 'secular liberalism'. The third is the 'national mission' defence: disestablishment would amount to the abandonment by the Church of its sense of responsibility for the spiritual welfare of the nation as a whole. This third defence comes in two parts: one argues that disestablishment would mean relinquishing the Church's pastoral openness to all comers; the other is that it would signal the Church's retreat from national political engagement. Chapter 5 addresses the concession to secularism defence, the anti-neutrality defence, and the first part of the national mission defence. Chapter 6 explores the second part of the national mission defence. These distinct issues are often conflated in the writings of defenders of Establishment. I disaggregate them and show how all are invalid. The book proposes that the principles of Church autonomy and state religious impartiality, together with the weakness of these three defences, cumulatively point to the need for a deliberate severance of the Church's remaining privileged legal ties to the British state.

Moves towards English disestablishment would be more complex than parallels in Ireland (1871) and Wales (1920)[31] because of the scale and depth of the church–state ties involved.[32] The legislation required will also be more complex than the Church of Scotland Act 1921, which neither established nor disestablished that church but rather ratified its long-standing jurisdictional autonomy from the British state. Notionally, the Church of Scotland remains 'established', in the sense that it is officially recognized, if only symbolically, as Scotland's 'national church'.[33] Yet the Church of Scotland is in legal substance a voluntary association, thus realizing the chief objective of a disestablished church anyway. I will suggest (following a long line of commentators) that the Scottish model might inform the Church of England's own thinking, yet without having to be emulated in every detail. But before we get immersed in constitutional blueprints, we need theological clarity on the issues at stake and the necessary moral courage to contemplate leaving current arrangements behind. Both will be substantial challenges for the Church of England. This is because it lacks an adequate contemporary theology of church–state relationships and because its attentions are currently distracted by a series of divisive and draining internal challenges set to absorb its energies for years to come.[34]

If the Church is to reflect intelligently and confidently on its established status, it must reset and deepen its theology of church–state relations. To do that it must honestly engage with all sides of the debate instead of simply assuming that Establishment needs no rigorous defence. A complacent 'anti-disestablishmentarianism-by-default' will no longer do. Nor can the Church leave itself entirely vulnerable to the changing enthusiasms of the state (or lack of them). Robert Morris reported in 2008 that the Labour government's default stance at that point was that it was up to the Church to take the initiative in proposing reform.[35] In 2011, however, a Conservative member of the Coalition government declared that the government remained 'absolutely committed' to Establishment.[36] In any event, the Church should heed Morris's warning that it 'cannot depend on bottomless government benignity or a willingness to continue only at a pace which suits the Church'.[37] The current stance in much of the Church's leadership seems to be, 'if there is to be disestablishment it should come at the behest of the state not the Church'.[38] But this suggests a body that does not know its own mind on the matter or lacks the courage to declare it. If it were properly prepared, it could then go on the front foot and generate a strategically important opportunity for the public explanation of its identity and mission. The larger purpose of this book is to provoke better reflection on that missional question.

Notes

1 R. M. Morris, ed., *Church and State in 21st Century Britain: The Future of Church Establishment* (Basingstoke: Palgrave Macmillan, 2009), p. 14. This is the most comprehensive recent survey of Establishment and I make extensive use of it.

2 Ben Clements reports survey evidence from 2011 suggesting that 'The status of the Church of England as the established church is rarely a leading item of political debate, nor does it represent a "bread-and-butter" issue for members of the public.' Fifty-four per cent of respondents did, however, favour retaining the status quo ('Attitudes Towards the Disestablishment of the Church of England', *British Religion in Numbers*, www.brin.ac.uk/figures/attitudes-towards-the-disestablishment-of-the-church-of-england/, accessed 11.10.2021).

3 The ambiguities arising from the fact that the Church of *England* occupies a unique place in the *British* constitution will be remarked on at several points in the book.

4 In the book, 'Establishment' refers to the establishment of the Church of England, while 'establishment' or 'established' refer to the concept generally.

5 In the book, 'Church' is shorthand for Church of England, while 'church' or 'churches' refer to churches generally.

6 Thomas K. Sealy and Tariq Modood, 'The United Kingdom: Weak Establishment and Pragmatic Pluralism', in Anna Triandafyllidou and Tina Maggazini, eds, *Routledge Handbook on the Governance of*

Religious Diversity (Abingdon: Routledge, 2021). J. Christopher Soper,
Kevin R. den Dulk and Stephen V. Monsma speak of England as a case
of 'restrained establishment' (*The Challenge of Pluralism: Church and
State in Six Democracies*, 3rd edn (Lanham, MD: Rowman & Littlefield, 2017), ch. 6).

7 Paul Avis, *Church, State and Establishment* (London: SPCK,
2001), p. 19.

8 It ended with the Toleration Act 1689, which granted freedom
of worship to most Nonconformists. Active parliamentary control over
the Church of England nevertheless continued until the late nineteenth
century (e.g. the Public Worship Regulation Act 1874). From 1880 to
1913, 217 Church of England bills were introduced into Parliament, of
which 33 passed with government assistance (Morris, *Church and State
in 21st Century Britain*, pp. 22, 29).

9 The last direct state subsidy was in 1824, though the Church
continued to benefit from tithes and rates. Direct benefit from tithes
ended in 1836 (they were finally abolished in 1936), while rates lasted
until 1868 when they became voluntary. See Julian Rivers, *The Law of
Organized Religions: Between Establishment and Secularism* (Oxford:
Oxford University Press, 2010), p. 22; Morris, *Church and State in
21st Century Britain*, pp. 64–7. In spite of *laïcité*, some of the French
Roman Catholic Church's buildings receive state subsidy as historical
monuments, suggesting that non-established status is not necessarily
financially disadvantageous.

10 For overviews of twentieth-century developments, see Jeremy
Morris, 'The Future of Church and State', in Duncan Dormor, Jack
McDonald and Jeremy Caddick, eds, *Anglicanism: The Answer to
Modernity* (London: Continuum, 2003), pp. 161–85; Colin Podmore,
'Self-Government without Disestablishment: From the Enabling Act to
the General Synod', *Ecclesiastical Law Journal* 21 (2019), pp. 312–28.

11 Evangelical Alliance, *Faith in the Nation: Report of a Commission of Inquiry to the UK Evangelical Alliance* (London: Evangelical
Alliance, 2006), p. 168.

12 'Establishment', submission to the Commission of Inquiry on
Faith and Nation of the Evangelical Alliance (2006), p. 6.

13 For statistics up to 2015, see Grace Davie, *Religion in Britain: A
Persistent Paradox* (Chichester: Wiley Blackwell, 2015), ch. 3. Indeed,
since 1662, the presence of Nonconformists has meant that Anglican
primacy in defining English national identity has been contested.

14 Morris, *Church and State in 21st Century Britain*, p. 206.

15 A leading critic of Establishment is the National Secular Society
(NSS). See *Separating Church and State: The Case for Disestablishment*
(London: NSS, 2017); *Rethinking Religion and Belief in Public Life:*

A Manifesto for Change (London: NSS, 2016), ch. 6; Keith Porteous Wood, 'The National Secular Society', in R. M. Morris, ed., *Church and State: Some Reflections on Church Establishment in England* (London: UCL Constitution Unit, 2008), pp. 59–73.

16 Archbishop Justin Welby reported later to General Synod that 'opposition to the Bill was utterly overwhelmed ... [and] there was noticeable hostility to the view of the churches' (Sam Jones, 'Archbishop uses first address to warn of sexual revolution', *Guardian*, 6 July 2013, www.theguardian.com/uk-news/2013/jul/06/archbishop-canterbury-welby-sexuality-revolution). Tim Stevens (Bishop of Leicester) argued that same-sex marriage placed Establishment in question ('Gay Marriage is One of the Worst Threats in 500 Years Says Church of England', *The Independent*, 12 June 2012, www.independent.co.uk/news/uk/home-news/gay-marriage-is-one-of-worst-threats-in-500-years-says-church-of-england-7836852.html). See also Church of England, 'A Response to the Government Equalities Office Consultation, "Equal Civil Marriage"' (London: Church of England, June 2012); Javier Garcia Oliva and Helen Hall, 'Same-Sex Marriage: An Inevitable Challenge to Religious Liberty and Establishment?', *Oxford Journal of Law and Religion* 3.1 (2014), pp. 25–56.

17 Joan Lockwood O'Donovan levelled such a charge in 2011 in 'The Liberal Legal Legacy of English Church Establishment: A Theological Contribution to the Legal Accommodation of Religious Plurality in Europe', *Journal of Law, Philosophy and Culture* 6.1 (2011), pp. 17–45. In fact, the churches' liberty to decline to solemnize same-sex marriages was secured in the 2013 legislation.

18 *The Governance of Britain* (Government Paper Cm 7170), paras 57–66.

19 Robert Morris, 'Half-Opening Cans of Worms: The Present State of "High"' Establishment', *Law and Justice* 172 (2014), p. 11.

20 *Church and State: Report of the Archbishops' Commission* (London: Church Information Office, 1970). On the paucity of theology in this and earlier reports, see Anthony Dyson, '"Little Else But the Name" – Reflections on Four Church and State Reports', in George Moyser, ed., *Church and Politics Today: The Role of the Church of England in Contemporary Politics* (Edinburgh: T&T Clark, 1985), pp. 282–312.

21 The Methodist Church, however, has done, producing *A Report on Church, State and Establishment* (Peterborough: Methodist Church, 2004), occasioned by the need to explore the implications of Establishment for the 2003 Anglican-Methodist Covenant.

22 'Future of Church and State', pp. 176–7.

23 In the nineteenth century, most Nonconformists opposed Estab-

lishment on account of the serious civil disadvantages it imposed on them. An Anti-State-Church Society (later called the 'Liberation Society') was founded in 1844 but had fizzled out by the end of the century when the most serious of those grievances had been addressed. See Timothy Larsen, *Friends of Religious Equality: Nonconformist Politics in Mid-Victorian England* (Milton Keynes: Paternoster, 1999), ch. 3.

24 Matthew Grimley, 'The Dog that Didn't Bark: The Failure of Disestablishment Since 1927', in Mark Chapman, Judith Maltby and William Whyte, eds, *The Established Church: Past, Present and Future* (London: T&T Clark, 2011), pp. 39–55. For a summary of the debate up to 2003, see Theo Hobson, *Against Establishment: An Anglican Polemic* (London: Darton, Longman and Todd, 2003).

25 John Habgood, *Church and Nation in a Secular Age* (London: Darton, Longman and Todd, 1983).

26 Andrew Atherstone, 'Gospel Opportunity or Unbiblical Relic: The Established Church through Anglican Evangelical Eyes', in Chapman, Maltby and Whyte, *The Established Church*, p. 92. A series of bishops lined up against it, all appealing to the pragmatic and pastoral advantages of Establishment and none addressing the issue of authority pressed by Buchanan.

27 Hobson, *Against Establishment*, pp. 46–50.

28 Iain McLean and Scot Peterson, 'A Uniform British Establishment', in Chapman, Maltby and Whyte, *The Established Church*, pp. 141–57.

29 Malcolm Brown, 'Establishment: Some Theological Considerations', *Ecclesiastical Law Journal* 21 (2019), p. 340.

30 Brown, 'Establishment', p. 330.

31 The Church in Wales was a new legal creation. What the Welsh Church Act 1914 disestablished was Anglicanism in Wales (the Act came into effect in 1920). It was the outcome of decades of discontent in Welsh Nonconformity at its second-class status in spite of its majority position. In fact, the Church in Wales retains vestigial traces of establishment and has been termed 'quasi-established' (Morris, *Church and State in 21st Century Britain*, p. 124). See Frank Cranmer, 'Disestablishing the Church in Wales – at last?', in *Law & Religion UK*, 15 June 2013, https://lawandreligionuk.com/2013/06/15/disestablishing-the-church-in-wales-at-last/, accessed 11.10.2021.

32 English disestablishment would affect other nations of the UK to a degree that Welsh and Irish disestablishments did not. For example, it would involve amendment of the Act of Union 1707, which requires Protestantism to be upheld in both England and Scotland. It would also have implications for some Commonwealth nations.

33 As Morris writes: 'In Scotland, it is said, the Church and the state are *separate* and *distinct*: in England, even though Parliament has delegated the initiative in legislative functions since 1919 to what is now the General Synod, the Church of England is, save presently for matters of worship and doctrine, *subordinate* to the state' (*Church and State in 21st Century Britain*, p. 78). Emphasis original.

34 For example, the fallout from historic sexual abuse; the reform of the Clergy Discipline Measure; 'Renewal and Reform' (www.church ofengland.org/about/renewal-reform); 'Living in Love and Faith' (www. churchofengland.org/resources/living-love-and-faith); 'Vision and Strategy' (www.churchofengland.org/sites/default/files/2020-11/GS%2021 80%20Vision%20and%20Strategy.pdf; www.churchofengland.org/ system/files/2020-12//A%20vision%20for%20the%20church%20 of%20England%20in%20the%202020s%20-%20commentary%20 by%20Stephen%20Cottrell.pdf).

35 Morris, *Church and State in 21st Century Britain*, p. 194.

36 Chloe Smith, quoted in Morris, 'Half-Opening', p. 12.

37 Morris, *Church and State in 21st Century Britain*, p. 236.

38 The stance goes back to at least 1950 (Grimley, 'The Dog that Didn't Bark', p. 50).

I

Defining 'Establishment'

[Establishment is] ever an elastic term, its meaning often
[being] stretched to accommodate the rhetorical purpose and
policy preferences of particular writers.
(Robert Morris)[1]

To understand what 'disestablishment' would amount to in
England, we first need a workable definition of 'English Establishment'.[2] There is not a single model, called 'establishment',
replicated identically in many different states and entirely absent
in others. In countries where there are special ties between the
state and a church, 'establishment' assumes a wide variety of
forms. In England, what we now speak of as 'Establishment' is
a unique constellation of legal and political arrangements, and
cultural expectations, resulting from a complex and idiosyncratic history reaching back to the Middle Ages.[3] This is one
reason why it has rightly been described as 'a nest of contested
issues and theories that is not easy to disentangle'.[4] The term
ends up being used very differently by rival protagonists in the
debate, making for confusions about the merits and demerits
of disestablishment. For example, in *Church, State and Establishment* a leading defender of Establishment, Paul Avis, offers
a very capacious definition. He sees the 'core' of Establishment
as including four elements:

the principle of partnership in service between Church and
civil society; the national pastoral mission of the Church
that aims to reach the whole community, territorially understood; the State's recognition of the things of God and its

responsibility for the spiritual welfare of its citizens, in preference to a purely secular constitution; the acknowledged role of the Church in the debate over public issues.[5]

Avis claims that the constitutional scaffolding around these elements is what people 'tend to get excited about' but is not the most important aspect of Establishment, only 'the cherry on the cake'.[6] His chief concern is with the four elements, 'the submerged nine-tenths of the iceberg'. I argue in Chapter 2 that the third of those elements – 'the State's recognition of the things of God' – is theologically objectionable if it implies an official confessional preference on the part of the state (as for Avis it does). Then in subsequent chapters I show that, while the other three elements are in one way or another commendable, they do not in any way depend on the constitutional scaffolding that surrounds them. We need a more precise definition.

The Chadwick Report of 1970 defined Establishment as 'the laws which apply to the Church of England and not to other churches'.[7] That is helpful insofar as it draws attention to the unique status enjoyed by the Church of England vis-à-vis other churches. But it is inadequate as it does not convey that such laws confer *advantages* on the Church not enjoyed by other churches (the definition would apply even if the Church were uniquely *disadvantaged* by law). Joan Lockwood O'Donovan offers a more helpful general definition of establishment as a system 'in which a particular church or churches (or more generally, one or more religious bodies) is accorded in public law *special forms of privilege and responsibility* not accorded to other territorial religious bodies'.[8] That is the sense intended in this book. English 'Establishment' refers to the 'special forms of privilege and responsibility' accorded to the Church of England by the British state.[9] Because such forms are particular to England, disestablishment here will also involve a unique trajectory of change.

Nigel Biggar, who defends Establishment, correctly refers to it as the 'public privileging' of the Church of England.[10] We need, however, to specify both the privileges and the responsibilities. One sometimes hears supporters of Establishment opining that it is not first of all a 'privilege' but a 'responsibility', held (long-sufferingly, they imply) on behalf of the nation. Malcolm Brown, for example, rejects as 'secular' the criticism that Establishment 'is primarily about power and privilege rather than service'.[11] William Whyte asserts more bluntly that Establishment 'gives the Church of England all of the responsibilities of being a national Church and very few of the advantages'.[12] But 'privileges' are indeed advantages even if they come bundled up with burdens.[13] For example, Protestant succession and bishops' seats in the House of Lords bring responsibilities but are also privileges, while the Church's role in the coronation can also be seen as both a privilege (it holds it exclusively) and an obligation (it cannot decline it). By contrast, the Crown's role in the appointment of bishops and Parliament's role in approving Church legislation are better described as legal competences exercised by the state over the Church, and thus 'burdens' on Church autonomy.

I will argue that *any* 'special forms of privilege and responsibility' afforded to any church by the state are theologically problematic, even once we have recognized the peculiar histories by which they may have come about. By saying that they are 'afforded by the state', however, is not to suggest that the English state sat down one day, surveyed the options and chose to single out the Church of England for special treatment (even the term 'English state' is problematic). The historical reality is much messier than that. The next two chapters briefly dip into some episodes from the unique history of English Establishment. Their purpose is to understand its evolution, not to assign retrospective blame. We are engaging in a contemporary theological critique of the fruits of a tangled history in which, admittedly, most people at the time thought they were doing the right thing.

I shall understand *disestablishment*, then, broadly as Morris puts it: 'the abolition of all privileged links between the Church of England and the British state to place [it] in the same position as any other religious body in the UK' (with the rider that 'the same position' need not mean 'an identical position').[14] In 1974, a Whitehall committee specified it more fully as 'a complete severance of all obligatory and exclusive official relations between Church and State', creating 'complete freedom for the Church as respects discipline, doctrine, finance, appointments and promotion and general administration' and the 'abolition of any precedence officially accorded at present to the Church at all official, National, civic and legal ceremonies ...'[15] That formulation may send a chill down the spine of some highly placed defenders of the current system, but this book argues that something approximating that state of affairs is the direction in which the Church should intentionally travel. It also argues that we need to ensure that where a disestablished Church 'lands' – what model of state–religion relationships it then enters into – also needs careful reflection if disestablishment is not to be seized on to fuel the wrong sort of secularism.

Wesley Carr draws a useful distinction between 'high establishment' – the larger constitutional architecture of the system – and 'earthed establishment', principally the parochial presence of the Church across the nation.[16] High establishment will be the chief focus of the book, but I do discuss 'earthed establishment' in Chapter 5 under the heading of the Church's sense of pastoral responsibility for the whole nation. Both senses of Establishment involve 'privileges and responsibilities'. Carr is correct that the two senses are linked, but I will argue that this link is, today, thin and largely dispensable. Almost all of what is valuable in earthed establishment could proceed undisturbed by the removal of high establishment.

Disestablishment would restore important elements of self-government to the Church, further shoring up its autonomy from illicit pressures coming from the side of the state. But it is vital to recognize that disestablishment would not be some grand gesture of total severance from the state. Life 'beyond Establishment' would not entirely 'cut the connection' between Church and state (to allude to the title of Colin Buchanan's book).[17] All churches (and other religious bodies) stand in legal relations to the state merely by virtue of, for example, owning (or using) land and property, enjoying charitable status or availing themselves of a wide range of generic associational rights. Such legal relations are determined, finally, by Parliament. And as a Working Party of the Ecclesiastical Law Society put it, 'No Church can be fully "disestablished" so that it is outside the control of Parliament.'[18]

Consider, for example, a landmark case in Scotland, *Percy v Church of Scotland Board of National Mission* (2005), in which Helen Percy charged the Kirk with sexual discrimination in the termination of her employment.[19] The case raised the question whether, notwithstanding the Church of Scotland Act 1921, which recognized the Kirk's legal independence, the Kirk yet fell under general statutory prohibitions on sex discrimination in employment. Percy won her case, showing that the 1921 Act, even while ratifying the principle of the Kirk's autonomy vis-à-vis the state, had not insulated it against all possible state scrutiny. Some might have thought that it did, but it could not have done so. In the 1921 Act, Parliament clearly (and unusually) recognized the limits to its own sovereignty, but the Act could never have implied absolute legal autonomy on the part of the Kirk.

Disputes like *Percy* are indeed disputes over the respective jurisdictions of church and state. But they need to be seen as instances of those arising from the state's general regulatory role towards any non-governmental organization (as in, for example, charity law, health and safety, safeguarding and so forth). Churches cannot, should not and do not seek to be wholly exempt from such regulations. That regulatory authority can, of course, exceed its proper reach. I noted in the Introduction that concerns have been raised over the current tendency of legislators and courts progressively to impose general statutory duties on religious organizations that intrude upon the latter's proper autonomy and compromise their spiritual integrity.[20] In *Percy*, the key issue was whether Percy's sex-discrimination claim against the Church of Scotland counted as a 'matter spiritual' protected under Article IV of the Articles Declaratory and thus an internal matter for the

Kirk, or a 'civil' matter falling within the jurisdiction of the civil courts.[21] Now there is a case to be made that the court should have deferred to the Kirk's own disciplinary decision in this particular case. As Julian Rivers puts it: 'It is part of [a religious] association's right of religious liberty to design the relationship with its ministers as it sees fit, and it is the obligation of the court to translate that relationship into the best legal analogy.'[22] But where courts try to impose standardized norms from employment law on very diverse religious associations,

> there is a danger that as religious diversity increases and religious literacy drops, secular courts and tribunals will lose their sensitivity to the ways in which organized religions conceive of themselves. Instead, they will treat religious bodies as if they were secular organizations operating on some religious equivalent to economic rationality.[23]

However, retaining unwarranted legal privilege is not the way for churches to resist such illicit encroachments by the state. Wherever the respective jurisdictions between churches and the state get defined in specific cases, boundary disputes can never be entirely pre-empted in a society that both values associational autonomy and accords to the state a wide-ranging brief for protecting citizens against many kinds of injustice (such as arbitrary discrimination). Disestablishment would not and should not make the Church of England an 'island of immunity'. But any such conflicts arising from state intervention would no longer be disputes over the defence of ecclesial privilege, and that would be an important gain.

The Church not only stands under the state's broad regulatory role but also benefits from the state's desire to enlist it in public service delivery. The state quite properly invites many religious or other organizations into such a role, such as through funding of schools and hospital chaplaincies or offering tax relief on charitable giving (such as Gift Aid).[24] Especially since 1997, British governments have been keen to enlist faith-based organizations in pursuit of their favoured, if often shifting, public policy goals, such as promoting 'cohesion', building 'social capital', protecting 'security' or curbing 'extremism'. Some critics have attacked such partnerships as amounting to a 'new establishment', in which the identity and values of religious providers are being subtly skewed towards secular state purposes.[25] More recently, critics have charged that Conservative governments have turned to such organizations only in order to compensate for the gaping holes left in public service provision by years of 'austerity'.[26] I will not assess those debates here: such state–church public service partnerships do not depend on the special legal arrangements of Establishment and nor would they disappear if these arrangements lapsed. Certainly, disestablishment would not remotely amount to what David Edwards called 'a unilateral declaration of ecclesiastical isolation'.[27]

Nor, therefore, will I discuss the Church of England's extensive role in education (schools, Church foundation universities, chaplaincies, and more).[28] The vast scale of this provision is certainly a legacy of the pre-eminent historical position of the Church in English society, although it is gradually being reduced relative to that offered by other denominations and faiths, as where formerly exclusively Anglican chaplaincies are now becoming ecumenical or inter-faith in character.[29] If a church's provision of publicly funded schools were thought to qualify a church as 'established', however, the Roman Catholic Church would also qualify. I shall deem education to fall outside the scope of Establishment.

There is little doubt that disestablishment would be weaponized by some in state and society as an opportunity to downgrade the status of religious groups generally in the provision of public services – to further 'secularize' them. There are currently no signs that the present government has any wish to advance such a goal.[30] But given longer-term trends in that direction, however, it is a possibility that has to be confronted.[31] This underlines the importance of coupling a move towards disestablishment with a campaign to place all religious organizations on a more secure legal footing than they currently enjoy. That in turn requires a wider debate about the equity of state–civil society relationships generally.[32] That debate is beyond the scope of this book, but an important assumption underlying the argument I develop here needs to be made explicit. Disestablishment is a negative term, indicating the removal of something. In itself it could be compatible with French-style *laïcité*, in which the state treats all religions equally merely by keeping them all at a safe distance and promoting a thoroughly secularized public realm where religious identity is invisible and religious voices silenced. This is why a case for disestablishment must go together with a positive vision of how the state should engage with religious bodies generally.[33]

I favour an approach that can be termed 'equitable public pluralism'. This is a vision in which the state affirms and supports a wide array of associations, institutions and organizations, relating to them all justly by 'rendering to each their due' (to use a classical definition of justice).[34] These bodies include families and other households, educational institutions, economic organizations such as businesses and trades unions, professional, artistic and charitable bodies, campaigning groups, religious communities and so forth. Equitable public pluralism values these intermediate bodies as indispensable to the growth of rounded and responsible human beings, as vital to the shared pursuit of diverse social purposes and the broader common good, and as necessary to check state overreach.

The precise stance of the state towards such groups will obviously differ according to the nature and needs of the group: families do not need formal public recognition but the British Medical Association (BMA) does, while poorer families may need income support but the BMA does not. Hence the state should relate to them 'equitably' – attending to *their* particular public needs – not necessarily 'equally' in the sense of 'identically'. This will imply, for example, creating appropriate public policy frameworks in which such diverse bodies can flourish (including robust civil liberties, rights to associate, fair taxation and welfare systems); deferring in the first instance to their rights of self-governance, rather than seeing those rights as concessions from the state; and protecting them against being colonized either by overweening market forces or predatory bureaucracies. This is the social world into which a disestablished Church should be released. The Church would possess no significant public privileges denied to other faith-based organizations (religious or secular) but rather enjoy overall public parity with them.[35] As with social bodies in general, so with religious bodies, such parity need not imply *identical* legal relations between them and the state. For example, the Welsh Church Act 1914, the Church of Scotland Act 1921 and the Methodist Church Act 1976 define customized legal relations between these churches and the state, yet without conferring on any of them significant legal privileges denied to others. Other religious organizations might require different customized legal relations, again with the intention of establishing broad public parity of standing.[36]

It is worth noting here that the Church of England is currently the institution of choice used by government to deliver the Near Neighbours programme, an initiative designed to boost inter-faith cooperation on local community-building projects. Funding is administered by the Church of England's Church Urban Fund but distributed to a wide range of faith groups, notably Muslim ones. Yet it has attracted both strong support and pointed criticism from some Muslim leaders – the critics complaining that 'the parish' is not a meaningful entity for Muslims.[37] The debate points to the challenges facing governmental attempts to apply equitable public pluralism in practice. They are not, however, insurmountable.

Such a model of equitable public pluralism underlies the case for disestablishment developed in this book.[38] It is already partially realized in Britain but stands in need of more robust and consistent affirmation by the state. There is important work to do here if disestablishment is not to be placed in service of a confining, reductionist model of state and society. A pluralist vision finds itself increasingly confronting in law and public opinion a demand for what Rowan Williams calls an 'unqualified secular legal monopoly' over all associations.[39] This should be resisted irrespective of the status of the Church of England, but disestablishment might make such resistance more urgent. This is a worry expressed by Julian Rivers, who points out that a model of 'secularism-as-separation' could help safeguard the autonomy of the churches, while a model of 'secularism-as-indifference' would likely threaten it.[40] He observes that the tendency of law since 2000 has been 'desecularizing in the sense of secularism-as-separation, but secularizing in the sense of secularism-as-indifference'.[41] The latter is inadvertently being fed, he claims, by construing the religion–state relationship as reducible merely to the equal right to individual freedom of conscience, to the detriment of the autonomy of religious institutions.[42] However important they are, individual religious rights 'do not represent an adequate grounding of principle for the law of organized religions. They ... distort the underlying social reality, they are inherently weak, and they risk capture by a statist agenda that subjects all of civil society to its own ethos.'[43] A disestablished Church – indeed any church – would not fare well under such an agenda. The case for disestablishment, then, needs to be one plank in a larger pluralist vision of state and society that resists these distorting extremes. The Church needs not only a better theology of church–state relations, but also a fuller and more compelling vision of state–society relationships in which religious organizations, alongside many others, would occupy a respected and secure place.

In order to define more closely the parameters of the book, I now want to comment briefly on four further questions not addressed in detail in subsequent chapters. The first will, for most readers, be esoteric: the implications of disestablishment for the Church's courts. Ecclesiastical courts date back to the medieval period, where they presided over an array of matters that, after the Reformation, became subject to civil law, such as criminal offences against religion and morality, and marriage formalities. Many of the matters they dealt with were then progressively transferred to the civil courts. Their remaining jurisdiction was considerably curtailed in the course of the nineteenth and twentieth centuries.[44] Under the Ecclesiastical Jurisdiction Measure of 1963 this jurisdiction is now confined to internal Church matters, such as church fabric, consecrated land and clergy discipline. Yet one legacy of the history of ecclesiastical courts is that certain matters involving doctrine or ritual can, after all, end up being heard by higher judicial bodies that include members not chosen by the Church and who may not even be Anglicans. Another is that ecclesiastical courts retain High Court powers to compel attendance and submission of documents, enforceable via the contempt process. This is a hangover from a time when the Church enlisted temporal authority to enforce its decisions. I will say no more about these arrangements but it will be clear why I think they should end.

The second question is potentially more momentous. Would disestablishment also imply 'disendowment', a transfer of some of the Church's historic assets to the state (or some other body)? This did occur when Anglicanism was disestablished in Wales and Ireland. The issue in those cases was thought to concern those assets bequeathed to the Church at a time when it was legally bound to fulfil constitutional and pastoral duties to the whole nation. In view of that, it was claimed, the state could assert a right to determine how they might be allocated once that legal obligation had ended.[45] It is not fanciful to assume that the question might be put in the English case. In addition, there would be complex questions arising over what body, if any, actually 'owns' some of the more ancient lands and buildings currently under the control of the Church but where no clear 'title deed' exists. These would need to be resolved in a process of political negotiation if disestablishment were undertaken.[46] I will, however, proceed on the (perhaps optimistic) assumption that the state would not intentionally seek any punitive transfer of assets from a disestablished Church of England.[47] I will touch on the idiosyncratic case of 'royal peculiars' – a small cluster of churches deemed to be under the immediate jurisdiction of the Crown as 'Supreme

Ordinary'.[48] This is potentially significant because one of them is Westminster Abbey, where coronations take place.[49]

The third issue is that the Church of England can only presume to function as a national church *in England*, not in the UK as a whole. It has no standing to represent or speak on behalf of, or to, the other three nations of the UK, nor to speak on behalf of Anglican churches in those other nations. It is not pedantic to point this out, since senior English Anglicans often lapse into just such presumptions.[50] Aware of the charge, Malcolm Brown (in a footnote) defends the Church of England against it. He has the coronation especially in mind, but his point applies generally. The monarch, he acknowledges, 'rules over a nation greater than England':

> But as an extension of the point that there is no position from nowhere, the particular role of the Church of England in the coronation need not be an offence to Scotland, Wales or Northern Ireland unless some invented neutral institution that is not English, Welsh, Scottish or Irish is posited as the only inclusive mechanism to do the job – or if the Church of England were to forget its role of speaking generously for identities beyond its own.[51]

Leaving aside the risk of a lapse of generosity on the part of the Church, there is in fact already such a 'neutral institution'. It is called the United Kingdom, which was 'invented' in 1707 (as the United Kingdom of Great Britain).[52] Such an institution does not occupy a 'position from nowhere', but from, well, the whole territory known as the UK. The question is whether the historically dominant Church in just one of those nations is still entitled to special constitutional recognition by a state that is supposed to embody all of them equally. Brown does not address that question. Nor does he inquire whether the asymmetry of *English* Establishment within a *UK* state indirectly consolidates the long-standing wider domination of the UK by England, a factor now feeding resurgent nationalisms in all three other nations. All that said, I do not think that this asymmetry is in itself a free-standing argument for disestablishment. What it does is to compound the problem of state religious partiality implied by Establishment with a further national religious inequality. Disestablishment would, however, at least afford an opportunity for the UK state to assess how it might engage with faith communities more equitably and constructively across all four nations.

The fourth question that merits mention here is the attitude of England's other faith communities to disestablishment. An influential view among liberal political theorists, and secular humanists, is that establishment inherently amounts to the 'symbolic exclusion' of non-Anglicans from the state. By lending special privileges to one church or religion, a state creates a feeling of 'alienation' in those not identifying with the majority religion and renders them 'second-class citizens'. It thus breaches the core liberal principle of equal treatment. Cécile Laborde, for example, holds that while this kind of 'symbolic establishment' is not necessarily wrong, it is so 'when it constitutes and perpetuates social relations of hierarchy, subordination, and domination'. It might do so when a non-established minority is subjected to disrespect or disadvantage.[53] In the same vein, Tariq Modood and Simon Thompson propose that establishment is unacceptable when it sustains a form of alienation 'in which a number of citizens, given their particular identity, are unable to identify with their national citizenship'.[54] They argue that 'citizens who are not able to identify with their polity are alienated from it, and in effect they are alienated from their national citizenship too'.[55] Establishment risks creating such an effect, declaring that 'it is in virtue of Anglicans' specific religious identity that their privileged status is deserved.' A subordinate religious group thus finds that 'its religious identity is not aligned with that of the state'.[56] Equally, secular humanists might complain that in Establishment 'religious people get something material or symbolic from the state that non-believers do not.'[57]

I am sympathetic to the charge of 'symbolic exclusion'; indeed, I appeal to it at specific points in the book. But the veracity of the general charge of alienation is not essential to my critique of Establishment. That critique has a jurisdictional not a sociological focus. My argument is that, even if *no one* was alienated by Establishment, it would still be illegitimate because it is a conflation of the proper spheres of authority of both state and Church. As it happens, Modood and Thompson claim to have found no credible evidence that significant portions of England's minority faith communities actually *do* feel alienated or symbolically excluded by Establishment.[58] The available evidence, after all, suggests that Establishment is quite widely appreciated by minority faith communities.[59]

This fact is one reason why many Anglicans want to defend it – in itself, a very good reason.[60] Several minority faith leaders claim that it helps secure a place for faith generally in the public realm; and they appreciate what they take to be the 'hospitable' manner in which the Church of England discharges that role. These claims were first widely disseminated in a short volume edited by Tariq Modood in 1997, *Church, State and Religious Minorities*.[61] The volume records positive evaluations of Establishment from representatives of Liberal Judaism, Sikhism, Hinduism and Islam and is (still) often cited by supporters of Establishment. Such supporters, however, do not usually point out that the book also contains pointed critiques of current arrangements. Both the Hindu and Muslim writers complain that the Church needs to work much harder to be inclusive of other faiths. The Buddhist contributor opposes Establishment on principle, observing (correctly, in my view):

> The Christian church is a missionary church, charged, by its founder, with a missionary purpose. In trying to be simply the guardian of religion, rather than the guardian of Anglicanism, the Church has to be both poacher and gamekeeper – a task in which it cannot but fail.[62]

Nonetheless, such a view seems to be held by relatively few members of England's minority faiths. The majority view, summarized elsewhere by Modood, seems to be this:

The minimal nature of Anglican establishment, its proven openness to other denominations and faiths seeking public space, and the fact that its very existence is an ongoing recognition of the public character of religion, are all reasons why it may seem far less intimidating to the minority faiths than a triumphal secularism.[63]

Joan Lockwood O'Donovan claims that the Church has been fulfilling such a hospitality role since the nineteenth century (when important civil disadvantages suffered by Roman Catholics and Nonconformists were removed). By virtue of Establishment, she holds, it has acted as a 'broker and gatekeeper, *prima inter pares*, enabling other Christian denominations and religious communities to access state resources in developing their public ministries',[64] 'a capacity appreciated across the English religious spectrum'.[65] The Queen herself echoed the point in a Jubilee address at Lambeth palace in 2012:

> The concept of our established Church is occasionally misunderstood and, I believe, commonly under-appreciated. Its role is not to defend Anglicanism to the exclusion of other religions. Instead, the Church has a duty to protect the free practice of all faiths in this country. It certainly provides an identity and spiritual dimension for its own many adherents. But also, gently and assuredly, the Church of England has created an environment for other faith communities and indeed people of no faith to live freely. Woven into the fabric of this country, the Church has helped to build a better society – more and more in active co-operation for the common good with those of other faiths.[66]

The academic lawyer Charlotte Smith also proposes that such an arrangement is compatible with, even conducive to, liberal democracy. The Church:

acts as a stakeholder for those who believe that religion and religious views should be seen and heard in the public sphere, and also provides a conduit through which a diverse range of such views can be transmitted and represented in the machinery of state.[67]

It is worth noting here that some faith community leaders do favour an adjustment of the Church of England's privileges in the direction of a new 'plural establishment' in which their communities would approach a position of legal parity with the Church.[68] Bhikhu Parekh, for example, identifies a necessary tension between a state's legitimate desire to recognize the role of a faith in forming its cultural identity and its obligation to treat all faiths equally. In the UK, he says:

> The only way to reconcile the two demands is both to accept the privileged status of Christianity *and* to give public recognition to other religions. Christianity may therefore rightly remain the central part of British collective identity, provided that other religions receive adequate, though not necessarily equal, recognition in the institutions, rituals and ceremonies of the state ... [D]isestablishment is not required by the principle of religious equality.[69]

This would certainly be one way to protect the public place of faith: instead of 'levelling down' the Church of England to the status of other faiths, other faiths could be 'levelled up' towards the status of the Church of England, enjoying certain aspects of establishment if not quite displacing Anglican pre-eminence.[70]

The fear expressed by Anglican (or other Christian) defenders of Establishment, then, is that disestablishment with nothing to replace it would amount to a betrayal of the legitimate desire of other faith communities to shelter under the Church of England's established status in order to protect their possibly more precarious public standing. Grace Davie underlines this concern, quite rightly noting that 'the creation and sustaining of a tolerant and pluralistic society requires creative rather than destructive thinking. What ... do we need to create in order to ensure a healthy pluralism and to give this institutional recognition ...?'[71]

To this I would offer a pragmatic and a theological reply. The pragmatic reply is that a model of equitable public pluralism could indeed grant diverse religious communities public parity in the British state without granting any or all of them special privileges that would be denied to other religious or non-religious groups. This can be secured by, for example, allowing them open access to the public service partnerships noted above, or rights to sit on public consultative bodies. This is already happening (and may be part of what Parekh has in mind). However, it is confusing to call such an arrangement a 'plural establishment', since it should be pursuant to equitable, not privileged, treatment on the part of the state towards a wide range of groups in civil society.[72] The theological reply is that, while the Church must pay careful and respectful attention to the concerns of other faiths, it must make up its own theological mind on its relationship to the state. Christianity has distinctive insights on the relation between religion and the state and it is not surprising if these turn out to differ from those held by other faiths.

The next chapter offers a 'theology of disestablishment' and is the foundation of my larger argument. It makes a theological case for the principles of the religious impartiality of the state and the autonomy of the Church and shows how English Establishment breaches both. I develop the case by means of a critique of a position underlying most defences of establishment, the 'Christian nation' view.

Notes

1 R. M. Morris, ed., *Church and State in 21st Century Britain: The Future of Church Establishment* (Basingstoke: Palgrave Macmillan, 2009), p. 84.

2 For a succinct overview of its core features, see David Torrance, *The Relationship Between Church and State in the United Kingdom,*

Commons Library Research Briefing (28 July 2021) (London: House of
Commons Library, 2021), pp. 6–26.

3 For a succinct overview of the history, see Peter Cornwell, 'The
Church of England and the State: Changing Constitutional Links in
Historical Perspective', in George Moyser, ed., *Church and Politics
Today: The Role of the Church of England in Contemporary Politics*
(Edinburgh: T&T Clark, 1985), pp. 33–54.

4 Martyn Percy, 'Opportunity Knocks: Church, Nationhood and
Establishment', in Mark Chapman, Judith Maltby and William Whyte,
eds, *The Established Church: Past, Present and Future* (London: T&T
Clark, 2011), p. 28.

5 *Church, State and Establishment* (London: SPCK, 2001), p. x.

6 *Church, State and Establishment*, p. x.

7 *Church and State: Report of the Archbishops' Commission*
(London: Church Information Office, 1970), p. 2.

8 'The Liberal Legacy of English Church Establishment: A Theological Contribution to the Legal Accommodation of Religious Plurality
in Europe', *Journal of Law, Philosophy and Culture* 6.1 (2011), p. 17
(emphasis added). By 'public law', Lockwood O'Donovan here means
'the law the land' (of which 'public law' is a special subset). Tariq
Modood and Simon Thompson note that establishment 'comes with
a range of [symbolic and material] benefits for members of the established religion which members of other religions – and non-religious
members of the political community – either do not enjoy to the same
degree or do not enjoy at all' ('Othering, Alienation and Establishment',
Political Studies Online First (January 2021), p. 2).

9 Julian Rivers has pointed out (in personal communication) that
the difference between this status and that enjoyed by other churches or
religious communities can be described as the result of 'uneven decon-
fessionalisation', in which formerly unlawful religions began to be
tolerated, and the nation's official religion became progressively separated from the state. The 'established' status of the Church of England is
thus a 'residue' of that process.

10 'Why the "Establishment" of the Church of England is Good for
a Liberal Society', in Chapman, Maltby and Whyte, *The Established
Church*, p. 1.

11 'Establishment: Some Theological Considerations', *Ecclesiastical
Law Journal* 21 (2019), p. 331.

12 'What Future for Establishment?', in Chapman, Maltby and
Whyte, *The Established Church*, p. 191.

13 John Habgood's justification of Establishment is classically patrician, a version of *noblesse oblige*: 'Mere privilege is to be deplored. But
privilege which comes as the other side of responsibility can only be

avoided by shirking the responsibility' (*Church and Nation in a Secular Age* (London: Darton, Longman and Todd, 1983), p. 100).

14 Morris, *Church and State in 21st Century Britain*, p. 193. This parallels the definition in the Ecclesiastical Law Society's 'Working Party on "Disestablishment" Report' (George Spafford, Roger L. Brown and Ben Nichols, *Ecclesiastical Law Journal* 6 (2002), p. 265, where Julian Rivers is being quoted).

15 Quoted in Morris, *Church and State in 21st Century Britain*, p. 195.

16 'A Developing Establishment', in *Theology* 102 (1999), pp. 2–10.

17 *Cut the Connection: Disestablishment and the Church of England* (London: Darton, Longman and Todd, 1994). For a snappier statement, see Colin Buchanan, 'Disestablishment – The Straightforward Case', in Mark Mills-Powell, ed., *Setting the Church of England Free* (Alresford: John Hunt, 2003), pp. 153–63.

18 'Working Party Report', p. 265.

19 *Percy [AP] v Board of National Mission of the Church of Scotland* [2005] UKHL 73; [2006] 2 AC 28; [2006] 2 WLR 353; [2006] 4 All ER 1354.

20 See Lockwood O'Donovan, 'Liberal Legacy'. For example, in 2001 the Court of Appeal ruled that Parochial Church Councils were 'public authorities' within the meaning of the Human Rights Act 1998, requiring them to apply all its equality and non-discrimination provisions to their churches. This was overturned by the House of Lords in 2003. On the wider issue, see Julian Rivers, 'Is Religious Freedom Under Threat from British Equality Laws?', in *Studies in Christian Ethics* 33.2 (2020), pp. 180–1; Jonathan Chaplin, *Faith in Democracy: Framing a Politics of Deep Diversity* (London: SCM Press, 2021), chs 6 and 7.

21 See Marjorie MacLean, Frank Cranmer and Scot Peterson, 'Recent Developments in Church/State Relations in Scotland', in Morris, *Church and State in 21st Century Britain*, pp. 95–6. The case turned considerably on whether Percy's relation to the Kirk constituted 'employment' (as distinct from 'office-holding') for the purposes of the Sex Discrimination Act 1975.

22 Julian Rivers, *The Law of Organized Religions: Between Establishment and Secularism* (Oxford: Oxford University Press, 2010), p. 119.

23 Rivers, *Law of Organized Religions*, p. 122.

24 Thus, while Avis is right to observe that 'churches, like all institutions in civil society, are inevitably implicated in a relationship to the state', and that 'they need a theology to guide them in this demanding relationship' (*Church, State and Establishment*, p. x), it does not follow that such a relationship should take the form of anything like Establishment.

25 Jenny Taylor, 'There's Life in Establishment – But Not as We Know It', *Political Theology* 5.3 (2004), pp. 329–49; Luke Bretherton, *Christianity and Contemporary Politics: The Conditions and Possibilities of Faithful Witness* (Chichester: Wiley-Blackwell, 2010), p. 36.

26 'Propping up the State? Omnicompetent Faith in a Disorganised World', *William Temple Foundation Blog* (4 May 2016), https://williamtemplefoundation.org.uk/propping-up-the-state-omnicompetent-faith-in-a-disorganised-world/, accessed 18.10.2021. See also Adam Dinham, *Faith and Social Capital after the Debt Crisis* (Basingstoke: Palgrave Macmillan, 2012).

27 Quoted in Andrew Atherstone, 'Gospel Opportunity or Unbiblical Relic: The Established Church Through Anglican Evangelical Eyes', in Chapman, Maltby and Whyte, *The Established Church*, p. 92.

28 In 2018, the Church of England ran about 23 per cent of maintained primary schools in England. Muslims, who constitute 6 per cent of the British population, ran 0.2 per cent of (English) maintained schools (2018 figures).

29 See Grace Davie, *Religion in Britain: A Persistent Paradox*, 2nd edn (Chichester: Wiley-Blackwell, 2015), ch. 6.

30 See, for example, Cabinet Office, *Civil Society Strategy: Building a Future that Works for Everyone* (London: Cabinet Office, 2018); Danny Kruger, *Levelling Up Our Communities: Proposals for a New Social Covenant*, a report to Government by Danny Kruger MP (2020).

31 The National Secular Society has proposed to remove 'the advancement of religion' as a charitable purpose (*For the Public Benefit? The Case for Removing 'the advancement of religion' as a Charitable Purpose* (London: NSS, 2019)). No doubt NSS would seize on disestablishment as an opportunity to press such a case. That would have to be resisted.

32 A classic Anglican pluralist statement of this view is John Neville Figgis, *Churches in the Modern State* (London: Longmans, Green & Co., 1913). Warning against the creeping state monism of his own day, Figgis warned that 'disestablishment of itself would [not] save all risk of inconvenient action on the part of the State' (p. 20).

33 For contemporary articulations of such a vision, see John Inazu, *Confident Pluralism: Surviving and Thriving through Deep Difference* (Chicago: University of Chicago Press, IL, 2016); Rowan Williams, *Faith in the Public Square* (London: Bloomsbury, 2012), chs 2–4; Jeanne Heffernan Schindler, ed., *Christianity and Civil Society: Catholic and Neo-Calvinist Perspectives* (Lanham, MD: Lexington, 2008).

34 See Chaplin, *Faith in Democracy*, ch. 7.

35 State funds channelled through the Church's public service offerings, or granted to its historic buildings, are already allocated via

processes that seek to be impartial as between different faith groups (Morris, *Church and State in 21st Century Britain*, pp. 7, 70 and ch. 5).

36 For example, the General of the Salvation Army and the world-wide leader of the Dawoodi Bohra Muslims are, uniquely in England, 'statutory corporations sole' (Rivers, *Law of Organized Religions*, p. 87).

37 See Therese O'Toole et al., *Taking Part: Muslim Participation in Contemporary Government* (Bristol: Centre for the Study of Ethnicity and Citizenship, University of Bristol, 2013), pp. 48–51; Daniel Nilsson DeHanas, Therese O'Toole and Nasar Meer, 'Faith and Muslims in Public Policy', in Daniel Singleton, ed., *Faith with its Sleeves Rolled Up: A Collection of Essays on the Role of Faith in Society* (London: FaithAction, 2013), pp. 19–36.

38 Scepticism about such a model is expressed by Edward Norman in 'Notes on *Church and State: A Mapping Exercise*', in R. M. Morris, ed., *Church and State: Some Reflections on Church Establishment in England* (London: UCL Constitution Unit, 2008), pp. 9–13.

39 'Civil and Religious Law in England: A Religious Perspective', in Robin Griffith-Jones, ed., *Islam and English Law: Rights, Responsibilities and the Place of Shari'a* (Cambridge: Cambridge University Press, 2013), p. 31. See Jonathan Chaplin, 'Legal Monism and Religious Pluralism: Rowan Williams on Religion, Loyalty and Law', *International Journal of Public Theology* 2.4 (2008), pp. 418–41.

40 *Law of Organized Religions*, ch. 11. I am not, however, persuaded by his judgements that, in certain circumstances, 'special legal regulation [of a church] may be necessary to secure great levels of autonomy' (p. 344), and that British secularism 'would [not] be so accommodating to religion were it not for the constitutionally secure position of the Church of England' (p. 345).

41 *Law of Organized Religions*, p. 333.

42 *Law of Organized Religions*, p. 318–22.

43 *Law of Organized Religions*, p. 322.

44 *Law of Organized Religions*, p. 22.

45 Morris, *Church and State in 21st Century Britain*, pp. 9–10, 115, 121–5.

46 'Ownership' of land or buildings is distinct from 'jurisdiction'. For example, the Crown 'owns' the Royal Chapels. But the Church can exercise jurisdiction over a church apart from ownership. A third issue is who appoints clergy to the said church (e.g. the Ordinary, or the Crown). Paul Barber drew my attention to these distinctions.

47 Disestablishment would likely have to reckon with the fact that much of the property of the Church of England is in the hands of numerous 'corporations sole', not its National Institutions. Welsh and

Irish disendowments involved the transfer of property to a new central common trust. That would be one option for England (Spafford, Brown and Nichols, 'Working Party Report', pp. 265–6).

48 There are other similar cases: Bristol City Council has owned a chapel (St Mark's) as a 'civic peculiar' since 1722. I owe this point to David McIlroy.

49 Henry VIII's statutes, under which the Church of England still operates, simply replaced the jurisdiction of the Pope as Universal Ordinary with the Crown as Supreme Ordinary in England. The most obvious manifestation of this is in royal peculiar jurisdictions where, in the absence of other ecclesiastical jurisdiction, the Crown's jurisdiction is immediate. The Crown's role as Supreme Ordinary also raises wider questions that would need to be resolved if the relevant Henrician statutes were repealed. I owe these points to Paul Barber.

50 This is one of the criticisms levelled by Church of Scotland theologian Doug Gay in his 'Response' to the chapters in *The Future of Brexit Britain: Anglican Reflections on British Identity and European Solidarity*, ed. Jonathan Chaplin and Andrew Bradstock (London: SPCK, 2020), pp. 249–52. A recent example was when Archbishop Justin Welby presumed he was entitled to rebuke the Bishop of St David's when she sent a deprecatory tweet about 'Tories' (quickly deleted). He then apologized to the government. But he has no pastoral authority over her because she is a bishop of the Church in Wales, the Archbishop of which issued his own apology. See 'Archbishop of Canterbury "deeply embarrassed" at bishop's Tory tweet', *BBC News*, www.bbc.co.uk/news/uk-wales-57531927, accessed 18.10.2021.

51 Brown, 'Establishment', p. 338, n. 4.

52 It became the United Kingdom of Great Britain and Ireland in 1801, losing most of Ireland in 1921 at Partition, after which it became the United Kingdom of Great Britain and Northern Ireland.

53 *Liberalism's Religion* (Cambridge, MA: Harvard University Press, 2017), p. 136.

54 Modood and Thompson, 'Othering', p. 6.

55 Modood and Thompson, 'Othering', p. 9.

56 Modood and Thompson, 'Othering', p. 11.

57 Tariq Modood, 'Introduction: Establishment, Reform and Multiculturalism', in Tariq Modood, ed., *Church, State and Religious Minorities* (London: Policy Studies Institute, 1997), p. 14.

58 They rightly point out that we cannot simply *assume* that such groups feel alienated, but must investigate the question. For them this would involve engaging the relevant minority in a 'multicultural dialogue' in which their voices could be truly heard – a commendable proposal ('Othering', p. 11).

59 This is confirmed in relation to the Coronation by survey evidence cited in Nick Spencer and Nicholas Dixon, *Who wants a Christian Coronation?* (London: Theos, 2015).

60 Ian Leigh argues that 'it is a fallacy to assume ... that a secular state is somehow more inclusive because of its professed neutrality between religions; rather, it is equally alienating to people of all religions' ('By Law Established? The Crown, Constitutional Reform and the Church of England', *Public Law* (Summer 2004), p. 272). But that is only so to the extent that religious people bring with them the prior expectation that the state is entitled to favour a religion. I will argue that this is an improper expectation.

61 See Modood, *Church, State and Religious Minorities*.

62 Dharmachari Kulananda, 'A Buddhist Perspective', in Modood, *Church, State and Religious Minorities*, p. 72.

63 'Establishment, Multiculturalism and Citizenship', *The Political Quarterly* 65.1 (1994), p. 72.

64 'Liberal Legacy', p. 20. She expresses regret, however, at the recent 'shift from accommodating church establishment to egalitarian religious pluralism' (p. 20).

65 'Liberal Legacy', p. 22. Rivers notes that from this time, religious groups other than the Church of England were already gradually being 'partially included in the incidents of establishment' (*Law of Organized Religions*, p. 324).

66 'A Speech by the Queen at Lambeth Palace 2012', *Royal*, 15 February 2012, www.royal.uk/queens-speech-lambeth-palace-15-febru ary-2012, accessed 18.10.2012.

67 'Is there a place and role for an established church in a liberal democratic state?', in Theos, *Religion and Law* (London: Theos, 2012), p. 138.

68 Modood is sympathetic to the idea. Tariq Modood, *Essays on Secularism and Multiculturalism* (London: Rowman & Littlefield International/Colchester: ECPR Press, 2019), chs 8, 10.

69 'Religion and Public Life', in Modood, *Church, State and Religious Minorities*, p. 20. Such recognition could include representatives of various faiths in the House of Lords, non-Christian elements of state ceremonies or royal patronage of non-Christian festivals, or a national inter-religious forum or consultative council (Bhikhu Parekh, *Rethinking Multiculturalism: Cultural Diversity and Political Theory*, 2nd edn (Basingstoke: Palgrave Macmillan, 2006), p. 331).

70 Versions of this model exist in, for example, Belgium and the Czech Republic, where public funding is available to multiple officially recognized religions.

71 *Religion in Britain*, p. 97.

72 Another term some have used to refer to this state of affairs is 'concurrent endowment', meaning simultaneous and more or less equitable provision of public funding to diverse religious bodies engaged in some form of public service delivery. This would be one application of the broader idea of an 'equitable public pluralism' I am proposing.

2

A Theology of Disestablishment

Introduction

> Christian faith has been central to the emergence of our nation and its development. We cannot really understand the nature and achievements of British society without reference to it. In a plural, multi-faith and multicultural society, it can still provide the resources for both supporting and providing a critique of public life in this country ... [Christian faith] is necessary to understand where we have come from, to guide us to where we are going, and to bring us back when we wander too from the path of national destiny.
> (Former Anglican bishop Michael Nazir-Ali)[1]

> We are secular judges serving a multicultural community of many faiths sworn to do justice to all manner of people ... We live in this country in a democratic and pluralist society in a secular state, not a theocracy.
> (Sir James Munby, President of the Family Division)[2]

These two assertions crisply capture prominent contrasting stances in the debate over the place of the churches in state and society. The first expresses a central conviction of the 'Christian nation' position, the second a standard formulation of the 'secular neutrality' view. Neither is adequate to the question of this book. In this chapter I will, however, show that it is possible to affirm what is valid in the former statement without setting aside the just concerns of the latter (however imperfectly formulated by Sir James). I offer a theological case in favour of the principles of the religious impartiality of the state and the jurisdictional autonomy of the Church. These principles render English Establishment theologically problematic. But I equally defend the right of Christians – and those of other faiths – to offer what Nazir-Ali calls 'guidance' on the public affairs of the nation, through any democratic forum available in principle to others. I suggest that Anglicans, other Christians and all people of faith may even be in a stronger position to pursue that legitimate goal if the Church of England were to be disestablished.

The view that the state should adopt a posture of impartiality among different religions existing within its territory is a staple of modern liberal democratic thought, although its precise meaning and rationale are much contested.[3] I will offer a theological rationale for the principle. I speak of 'impartiality' rather than 'neutrality'. The advantage of this term is that it helps me distinguish my position from the 'secular neutrality' stance. The disadvantage is that in legal parlance the relevant term is indeed 'neutrality'; when I speak of 'impartiality', it is this legal sense that I will have in mind. 'Impartiality' does not simply mean 'equal treatment', for that could be satisfied where the state were equally hostile or indifferent to religions. As I use it, it means formal institutional separation between the state and religious bodies, but combined with constructive even-handed engagement by the state on the basis of respect for autonomous self-governance by such bodies.

A commitment to state impartiality has assumed a specific shape in contemporary liberal political thought, which has held that the state must be 'neutral' not only with respect to religious beliefs but also with respect to any 'competing conceptions of the human good'. The narrower legal principle of state impartiality is often conflated with this wider liberal claim. The wider claim assumes that the state should, and can, adopt a posture of neutrality in the face of profoundly contending *moral* visions of the human good held in society. Such visions, so the liberal argument goes, might, perhaps, legitimately be brought to bear by citizens in debates about

laws and policies pertaining to many issues – the commence-
ment or ending of human life, the purpose of education, the
value and nature of the family, the use of military force, our
duties to the environment and so forth. But in its law-making
and executive acts on such matters, the liberal state must itself
remain neutral with respect to such moral visions of 'the good'.
It must confine itself to protecting the 'rights' of its citizens,
which can be formulated without invoking notions of 'the
good'. Although I will not argue the point here, the assumption
that such moral neutrality is attainable by the state seems manifestly false. Many liberals now also reject it, conceding that
their theory of the state after all requires at least a 'thin theory
of the good'. Whatever the state or its officials *think* they are
doing when they make laws or policies impinging upon such
matters of fundamental human concern, they *are in fact* necessarily preferring certain controversial moral commitments on
such matters over others.

The legal principle of the religious impartiality of the state
does not assume this liberal theory of the moral neutrality of the
state. The version of the principle I defend makes the narrower
claim that the state *should not assume the competence to decide
what is religious (or ultimate) truth*. As the European Court of
Human Rights succinctly puts it, the state lacks 'any power
... to assess the legitimacy of religious beliefs'.[4] This, in the
first instance, is the fundamental basis of the right to religious
freedom. Because the state has no competence to identify religious truth, or to adjudicate between competing conceptions
of it, it must allow citizens and their organizations to make
their own free choices in the matter. The state is not the sort
of institution that is equipped to render judgement on matters
of religious or other ultimate truth-claims. Such matters are
beyond its proper jurisdiction – although, of course, states frequently *attempt* to render such judgements (often disastrously
so). English courts, for example, are therefore rightly reluctant to adjudicate doctrinal disputes among those who appear
before them (though at times they find themselves having to do
so when religious bodies tie material interests, such as property

claims, to doctrinal questions).[5] The state can, however, recognize religious identity and convictions as vital to some citizens' sense of their public standing, and religious communities as supplying important public goods. Impartiality does not mean blindness to religion as a persisting source of human meaning and social flourishing.

So far, so good, many may think. But acknowledging the religious incompetence of the state has further-reaching implications than defenders of Establishment seem willing to admit. The state's religious incompetence also means that it has no authority to decide that a particular faith or church may stand in a *special* relationship to the state or receive *special* treatment from it in the form of either particular privileges or burdens. As already noted, the state may cooperate with and fund religious organizations insofar as they contribute to one or other public purpose sponsored by the state. But the logic of impartiality means that it should do so on the same terms that it would towards any other social organization, not because it favours or endorses the religious (or indeed secular) beliefs of that body. Thus, if it funds Anglican schools, for example, it should in principle also fund Methodist, Jewish, Hindu or Muslim schools (so long as all adhere to public regulations regarding the conduct of education and otherwise operate within the law). And, in the UK, so it does. State religious impartiality is a necessary condition of equitable public pluralism.

My argument is that for the state to go beyond such equitable engagement with religions (in order to pursue public purposes) exceeds its proper authority. The state may not create any special public privilege or burden for one religious faith or organization denied in principle to others. The state is incompetent to decide, on religious grounds, which of the faiths represented in its society merit such special treatment. If this claim is valid, it rules out *all* cases of religious establishment – not only 'strong' ones like Iran but also 'weak' ones like England. This is so even if, as in England, the established religious body practises complete toleration towards all others, and even if the state secures robust religious freedom for all non-established faiths. The fact that political favouritism is not abused by the body so privileged or by the state offering the privilege does not take away the fact that it is unwarranted.

Notice that I said it was improper for the state to favour a particular faith 'on religious grounds' (such as 'because Christianity is true', or 'because the state stands under God', or some such). Some might counter that decisions to favour a faith are, after all, not made on religious but *cultural* grounds. They would claim that such decisions flow from the state's natural deference to the dominant cultural traditions of the nation, of which its historic religious character may be one. Just as the state may protect a nation's language, enduring values and customs, or architectural patrimony, so it may protect its most formative religion. Now it is true that states can claim the authority to protect central features of the cultural heritage of its majority population, so long as it does not do so in ways prejudicial to those of minority traditions. That could, perhaps, include requiring schools to teach about the majority religion, or supporting religious buildings of great historical worth.[6] But an appeal to cultural protection cannot override the norm of religious impartiality. Endorsing a religious (or secular) faith, whether through establishment or some other means, involves the state in claiming to have knowledge of ultimate truth that exceeds its legitimate remit, however deeply embedded such truth claims are in the culture of the nation(s) over which it presides.

This is an argument about the epistemological and jurisdictional limits of the state. From the side of the church there is another concern. For the church to justify the state's deference to its faith in terms of defending the nation's majority culture, risks hitching the church to the state's own definition of the meaning and value of that faith. For example, in *Lautsi v Italy*, a case eventually ending up in the European Court of Human Rights, the highest Italian court had agreed that it was permissible to display a crucifix in every state school in Italy.[7] But it did so only because it judged that the crucifix had now become merely a general cultural symbol representing

Italian values such as tolerance, respect and freedom of conscience (and so could not be construed as indoctrination or an infringement of students' religious freedom).[8] Such a reductionist reading of a symbol of what Christians hold to be the most momentous event in history is hardly one the church itself should encourage.

I now want to unfold this argument by means of a critical engagement with the 'Christian nation' position, especially its English renditions. Such a position is explicitly or tacitly at work in most defences of Establishment.

The 'Christian nation' position

The Christian nation position I have in mind holds that it is both possible and desirable for a nation to be corporately 'Christian' and that it is part of the mission of the churches to look to the state to defend a Christian nation where one exists and to work towards one where it does not. On this view the state is not at all bound to be religiously impartial between faiths but may, or perhaps should, endorse Christianity as its official faith and confer certain privileges on it. Christianity is seen as the necessary spiritual and moral foundation of social and political order and the state is held to have a solemn duty to acknowledge this foundation and shore it up.

The Christian nation view has re-emerged of late partly as a response to the reassertion of what Rowan Williams has called 'programmatic secularism',[9] a militant stance bent on pushing faith to the margins of public life. The concern is that the public mores and institutions of the British nation will become further secularized in the absence of a core of publicly validated moral commitments. Such commitments are unsustainable in the long term if the underground reservoir of a common Christian (or 'Judaeo-Christian') culture dries up. For many British – or at least English – defenders of the idea of a Christian nation, the establishment of the Church of England is a bulwark against this kind of secularism.[10]

Part of the argument for the Christian nation view is historical: advocates assert that liberal democracy did not arise in Europe by accident but grew organically out of distinctive elements of Christian culture and that its future sustenance depends on contemporary culture being replenished by these Christian sources. As the Roman Catholic theologian Aidan Nichols puts it, the thousand years of Catholic Christianity that preceded the Reformation settlement are:

> responsible for the origins of the English literary imagination, for the principles of the common law, for the concept of a covenanted people under God that permeates the induction of the sovereign, and for the range of virtues that have been commended, and sometimes practised, in English society and culture.[11]

I think such a historical claim could be partly vindicated – core liberal democratic principles can indeed claim significant Christian provenance – but an adequate defence of that claim would require another book.[12] But this historical argument, even if true, would not suffice to justify the retention of Establishment today. Historical provenance does not in itself prove contemporary legitimacy. So I have chosen to focus mainly on the theological argument for the Christian nation view.[13] I will argue that this position harbours two problematic assumptions: first, that nations can legitimately 'confess' a faith – that they can presume to exercise 'corporate religious agency'; second, that the fusion of faith and nationhood in the ancient Israelite polity is still analogically valid even after the coming of Jesus Christ.[14]

It is important to note that advocates of the Christian nation and Christian state positions remain committed to the principle of universal religious liberty. They are among the foremost defenders of religious freedom at home and abroad – often ahead of their secular human rights counterparts who tend to campaign predominantly on other issues and some of whom – lamentably and incoherently – tend to see religious freedom as a 'right-wing issue'. Nazir-Ali argues that religious liberty is itself a gift of the Christian faith and depends for its sustenance on the ongoing public influence of that faith. Defenders of this position rightly affirm that a legally privileged status for Christianity in the public realm is compatible with extensive religious liberty for adherents of other faiths or none.[15]

Nor does anything in the Christian nation view imply 'theocracy' – a thoughtlessly alarmist spectre invoked by Sir James Munby in the quotation at the head of this chapter and by other members of the political establishment.[16] Theocracy literally means 'the rule of God'. But not even the ancient Israelite polity was a literal theocracy, since God's rule was always mediated by some human officeholder, whether a Moses, a Samuel or a David. What is really meant by 'theocracy' is the *rule of the clergy*, which would be more accurately (if less elegantly) termed *clerocracy*. Contemporary Iran is an example of sorts, where a council of senior Islamic clerics functions as a type of supreme court tasked with vetting parliamentary legislation. English Christian nation advocates do not advocate anything like this. They repudiate all religiously based coercion or civil disadvantage for minorities. Yet they hold that these commitments are not at all incompatible with a nation that would offer public deference to, even official recognition of, some kind of Christian confession.[17]

According to one strand of Christian nation thinking, England only came into existence as an identifiable national community because of the arrival of Christianity. Whatever its present shortcomings, England has been and continues to be underpinned predominantly by Christian faith. As Nichols puts it, 'the Judaeo-Christian tradition [is] what is most fundamentally form-giving in English society and culture.'[18] Indeed it was the sanctifying impact of Christianity that actually unified the nation in the first place: 'the emergence [of England] as a nation coincides with its conversion.'[19] Michael Nazir-Ali echoes the point:

[T]he very idea of a unified people under God living in a 'golden chain' of social harmony has everything to do with the arrival and flourishing of Christianity in these parts. It is impossible to imagine how else a rabble of mutually hostile tribes, fiefdoms and kingdoms could have become a nation conscious of its identity and able to make an impact on the world.[20]

For him, the established status of the Church of England, daily prayers in Parliament or the national anthem are the ceremonial public expression of this Christian legacy. Such practices 'have the purpose of weaving the awareness of God into the body politic of the nation'.[21] Christian nation advocates may come up with different empirical assessments of how far that remains visible today. Nichols, for example, recognizes that 'England remains a Christian state, albeit a decayed example of the genre.'[22] But they share a common judgement that the core of the nation's historical identity is substantively Christian.

Christian faith has also formed the nation from the bottom up. As Nazir-Ali puts it:

The assumptions and values by which we live have been formed in the crucible of the Christian faith and its aftermath, the Enlightenment. This is the result of a quite specific history, and it is not at all necessary that such beliefs and values should arise in or survive in quite different contexts.[23]

For example, if the influence of non-Christian faiths, notably Islam, continues to grow, then, 'Instead of the Christian virtues of humility, service and sacrifice, there may be honour, [public] piety and the importance of "saving face".'[24] England, then, is not simply an aggregation of individual Christians, the majority of whom happen to be Christian and who happen to cohabit on the same piece of soil. The very identity of the nation as a corporate entity through time depends on its continuing to be, in some meaningful and discernible sense, grounded in the Christian faith, even if most individual citizens no longer believe in or practise that faith.[25] Thus, for public institutions to neglect or repudiate the legacy of Christian faith is to undermine the unique character of the nation and to place in jeopardy its main public achievements – freedom under law, accountable government, religious liberty, representative democracy, strong families, caring neighbourhoods, education committed to truth, perhaps the welfare state and so forth. The task of the English Christian community today, then, is to defend that legacy as far as possible where it is under threat and extend it where circumstances permit, both through evangelization among individuals and by public and political action.

Underlying such claims by Christian nation advocates, however, is a strong assumption that is not typically made explicit. The assumption is that *the nation can legitimately function as a religious agent* – a corporate entity that can adhere to a unified religious vision and be called to account for departing from it. This is the idea of a 'faithful nation', a single national-religious community capable of rendering corporate political obedience to God. Nichols grounds this duty of obedience specifically in a historical covenant, maintained in Anglican Establishment. He holds that:

> [T]he retention by the Church of England of its established status is an essential requirement if the nation as a whole is to retain narrative continuity with its own origins, which are found in the baptismal covenant reflected in the laws of the Anglo-Saxon kings.[26]

So much for the Christian nation stance. The specific implications of the Christian *state* position can now be further clarified. Consider the stance of an Evangelical campaigning organization, The Christian Institute. Its general account of the purpose of government and the political role of Christians is unobjectionable,[27] but its statement on 'Christianity and the state' is problematic:

> When a state has a majority who claim allegiance to one religion, it may not enforce that one religious belief. There will, however, inevitably be a privileging of that religion at certain public ceremonies ... [and in] education, while ensuring opt-outs for those of other faiths and none ... To fail to privilege one religion would be for the State positively to endorse either a secular humanistic philosophy ... or a 'multi-faith philosophy' ... Currently Christianity is privileged in the United Kingdom where the majority claim a Christian allegiance ... The Christian Institute sees this as entirely appropriate.[28]

Constitutional privilege, then, can properly be afforded to a faith where it forms a majority in the nation in question, on the condition that it equally respects the freedom of others.[29]

The way this is framed suggests it is an argument of general application, implying that *any* state may favour a particular religion. It is not framed as a purely local argument that the *British* state may favour *Christianity* because it is the majority faith there. But if it is a general argument, it also implies that it is legitimate, for example, for the Malaysian constitution to declare Islam 'the religion of the federation'. That constitutional provision has, however, had the effect of substantially weakening the public standing of Christian and Hindu minorities in Malaysia. Such minorities confront successive encroachments on their rights by aggressive Islamist groups who appeal to such a provision to assert their own primacy. Developments in India confirm the point. The aggressively Hindu nationalist government of Narendra Modi is increasingly, and coercively, privileging (a politicized strand of) Hinduism as the true faith of India and marginalizing Muslim and Christian minorities, in spite of the Indian constitution's formal commitment to 'secularism'. If Hinduism were to be overtly privileged in the constitution it would land such minorities in an even more precarious position. It is surely preferable to support a consistent stance of state religious impartiality, so as to empower embattled and often persecuted religious minorities (of any faith and none, not least atheists) against such hegemonic ambitions.

It is important to acknowledge that the specific idea that *the state* should officially privilege the Christian faith is not strictly essential to the broader claim that *a nation* could display a Christian character, for such a character could be defended by other means, such as education or evangelization. Nazir-Ali himself acknowledges the possibility. Confessing his growing sense that English Establishment is less and less theologically meaningful, he cites the USA as an example, thereby recognizing that significant Christian democratic influence is fully possible in a situation of state religious impartiality (whatever one makes of the particular goals advanced by it). Yet his formulation still implies that, even in the absence of a constitutional preference for Christian faith, it is still possible to issue a public appeal to the nation as a corporate religious entity.

We can further distinguish, within the Christian state position, two possible ways in which the state might express its preference for the Christian faith. It might do so by sustaining an established church, as in England or Greece, or more than one, as in Finland (Lutheran, Catholic and Orthodox). Or it might include an explicit confession of faith in its constitution, as was the case in several historically Roman Catholic European and Latin American states until the nineteenth or early twentieth centuries.[30] Remarkably, this was done in heavily secularized Canada as recently as 1982 (but wholly ineffectually).[31] Or it might do both.

A Christian nation stance, then, holds that the nation is a corporate entity that can be called to account for departing from Christian moral standards and that a direct appeal by citizens can be made to the state to uphold such standards. A Christian state stance goes beyond this and argues that the state's upholding of such standards should include an official recognition of the Christian faith, either by establishing a church or by confessing Christian faith in a constitution, or both.

The sources I have so far engaged with are hardly presented as systematic treatises. A case for disestablishment ought, however, to engage with its strongest opponents. The most sophisticated defences of a form of Establishment among British theologians I have encountered are those offered by Oliver O'Donovan and Joan Lockwood O'Donovan. They present erudite and carefully qualified arguments for the historical *possibility* of a Christian nation and Christian state (not for their theological necessity). Since Lockwood O'Donovan's account engages directly with the Tudor origins of English Establishment, it is particularly apposite at this point in the argument.[32]

Lockwood O'Donovan commends the 'legacy of English Reformation public theology as … an historical stream of Christian liberalism with continuing critical and constructive relevance for contemporary society'.[33] The goal is not to shore up Anglican exclusivism but to offer a foundation for toleration: the relevance of the Reformation legacy lies in its 'theological illumination of the wisdom of the traditional English legal approach to accommodating religious pluralism'.[34] Lockwood O'Donovan argues that the English Reformers' rich Augustinian theologies of freedom, law, community and moral formation, rooted in doctrines of creation, providence, redemption and eschatology, laid the basis for a compelling account of the distinct authorities of spiritual and temporal government. These it construed as mutually interpenetrating and supportive:

> Human government or coercive jurisdiction … belongs to the *saeculum*, the passing age of humanity's enslavement to the law of sin and condemnation, whereas the church belongs to the *eschaton*, the age of God's fulfilment of his covenantal promises to his people. Nevertheless, as the old humanity is overtaken by the new, the practices of ecclesial and civil communities remain interdependent, even interpenetrating. In that the church's proclamation is reflected in a legal framework established and enforced by human government, the church is part of the body politic, yet not of its essence. Conversely, in that the work of human government which gives concrete definition to the body politic is circumscribed and

empowered by the church's proclamation, human jurisdiction is within the church, but not of its essence.[35]

Even when the work of human government is thus 'circumscribed and empowered', however, it remains necessarily coercive and thus limited in remit. It cannot 'save', nor bring about a renewal of people's 'moral agency'; only the church's proclamation of salvation can accomplish that.[36] Legal space is thereby opened up for dissenters from the nation's official faith. But civil government still needs the resources of the church to fulfil its limited remit. If it refuses to subordinate itself to the church's saving ('eschatological') proclamation, it becomes legalistic and oppressive. Where it 'does not acknowledge its determination by the eschatological renewal of human freedom through the church's proclamation, it inevitably becomes … an instrument of humanity's enslavement to the law of sin and condemnation rather than an instrument of Gods preserving judgment'.[37]

In Lockwood O'Donovan's account of this Tudor theology, it becomes clear that, whatever the virtues of this Reformed model over its medieval predecessors, it continues to assume the legitimacy of a unified religio-political nation, one able to exercise corporate religious agency. The Reformers 'regard the essential unity of the nation as residing, not in common ethnic, linguistic or cultural bonds … but in common subjection to unified rule, an historical deposit of communal law, and, to a lesser extent, in common administrative and representative institutions'.[38] This unified rule may indeed be distributed across complementary spiritual jurisdiction ('proclamation') and civil jurisdiction ('judgement'), but they remain two modes of unified public governance. Indeed, the Reformers 'looked to the Israelite monarchy … for the authoritative model of the supreme governor's unitary jurisdiction over both the clerical and lay estates of the commonwealth'.[39]

It is important to note that nothing in my argument rules out Lockwood O'Donovan's claim that civil government and church can today be seen theologically as performing complementary 'secular' and 'eschatological' roles. Nor does it exclude that the church should seek to urge upon civil government, as best it can, all the insights emerging from the rich suite of theological themes she identifies in Tudor theology.[40] Such urgings might indeed have the effect of 'circumscribing' the pretences of civil government (insofar as it heeded them), or even of 'empowering' civil government (insofar as the church supplied moral energies conducive to the discharge of government's duties). They might result in the 'the church's proclamation' being 'reflected' in the legal framework that comes to be 'enforced by human government'; that is, theology might have shaped the discourse and justifications grounding that legal framework. That in itself implies no necessary breach of the religious impartiality of the state (which need not officially endorse the arguments leading up to its decisions). Nor does my argument deny that the church is 'part of the body politic', in the sense of acting as a constructive contributor to the common good.

I argue, however, that none of these commitments permit or require any public privileging or public legal regulation of the church as implied in the Tudor model of establishment. For the Tudors, Lockwood O'Donovan reports, included in the scope of civil jurisdiction are the church's external organization, doctrine and worship.[41] These are included because, in this age, 'the church's ministries of proclamation, constituting the highest goods of the common life, cannot be arbitrarily deprived of public legal protection'. Now if that implied only the protection of the corporate autonomy of the church, it would be unproblematic. But civil authority, the Tudors held, is also mandated to define 'those gross derelictions of ecclesiastical duty or violations of ecclesiastical order that threaten' the 'free participation of persons in the church's faith and practice'.[42] That is, political authority may intervene to protect what it recognizes as the church's true 'faith and practice' and presume to protect the 'highest goods of common life'. Both, I will argue, are beyond its proper remit. Lockwood O'Donovan adds that civil authority is tasked with 'preserving the "quietness and tranquillity" of outward conformity', which then might 'provide space for the Holy Spirit's proper action of harmonizing contending wills in a truly common judgment'.[43] I will argue that the latter could never be legitimately intended by a religiously impartial state, although it might be an indirect effect of its general protection of religion.

Can nations decide religious truth?

I now want to address the central problem underlying the Christian nation position. This is the assumption that a nation can legitimately function as a unified corporate religious agent. Typically, this assumption is justified on the basis of a particular reading of the relationship between the two 'testaments' of the Bible and the complementary redemptive 'dispensations' to which they bear witness. Christian nation advocates do acknowledge important discontinuities between these dispensations. They do not, for example, think that the principle of compulsory religious uniformity in the Hebrew polity any longer applies. They acknowledge that the New Testament assumes the desirability of civil religious liberty insofar as it attributes to government the role of establishing conditions in which the gospel may freely be preached. They reject the idea that the state may disadvantage unbelievers politically (none seek another Act of Uniformity). Finally, nor do they think that the specific content of the criminal or civil law in the Hebrew Scriptures remains valid as positive law for states in the New Testament era.[44]

While Christian nation advocates accept all these inter-testamental discontinuities, they nevertheless assume that the ancient Israelite polity – the corporate framework of the cov-enanted people of God – remains valid in one crucial respect, even in the Christian era. They hold that nation-states today can and should in some way echo – even distantly – the unified religious character of the Hebrew polity, so that we can attri-bute to contemporary nation-states the capacity, corporately and explicitly, to acknowledge God.[45]

There is a compelling theological rejoinder to this assumption. It is that this specific, covenantal character was only ever explicitly ordained by God for one people, biblical Israel. God has nowhere disclosed that he has entered into a covenantal relationship with any nation other than biblical Israel, or that other nations are obliged to or even able to seek or mirror the unique covenantal relationship existing between God and that 'chosen' nation. Without such a disclosure we could not know this. From a Christian point of view, upon the inauguration of the New Covenant, God no longer mediates his redemptive activity in the world via any special relationship with particular territorial nations. Or, if he does, this activity belongs in the realm of providence, which remains inscrutable to us unless God specifically reveals it. It is far from clear how God might do so. Not even popes, when they engage in 'reading the signs of the times' in social encyclicals, claim to have authoritative insight into the historical workings of providence. Thus, for example, John Paul II in *Centesimus Annus* makes clear that the 'analysis of some events of recent history' offered therein (the collapse of communism) 'is not meant to pass definitive judgments since this does not fall *per se* within the Magisterium's specific domain'.[46]

Scripture certainly offers the general assertion that God orders all nations providentially according to his will. It also makes occasional specific assertions that at certain junctures God chose to work through Gentile nations (Babylon) or rulers (Cyrus) as his appointed agents.[47] But there is no way we could reliably claim to know this unless it had been revealed in Scripture, since history – contrary to some nineteenth-century Romantic thinkers – does not come labelled with neon signs alerting us to providential purpose. It is one thing to confess that God continues to rule over the nations and call them to submit to his will; such a declaration was typically intended in the New Testament to provide succour to believers undergoing persecution (Acts 4.23–31). It is quite another to claim that God calls particular nations into a covenantal relationship with him akin to the one he entered into with biblical Israel.

Nichols, however, implies that 'the nation' itself has some privileged place in God's providential ordering of human societies: 'the national community [as distinct from sub-communities] ... is the form humanity has taken under Providence in this piece of earth.'[48] It is true that much of the narrative of the Hebrew Scriptures is concerned with the fate of 'the nations', principally meaning the nations surrounding Israel in the ancient Near East but extending, especially in prophetic texts, to all nations. Entirely in line with this Jewish line of thought, the apostle Paul also asserts that God 'made all nations to inhabit the whole earth, and he allotted the times of their existence and the boundaries of the places where they would live' (Acts 17.26). But no specific injunctions follow regarding the religious agency of contemporary nations. Paul adds as a reason for God's supervision of the nations, 'so that they would search for God' (v. 27). I take this to mean simply that, in sovereignly supervising nations, God is at work calling people to himself. It does not imply that nations may exercise corporate religious agency, or that they are accorded some kind of priority in God's engagement with humanity. Nations are simply one part of the human social landscape to which God relates, as creator, sustainer, judge and redeemer. Biblical Israel performed a dispensationally unique, unrepeatable role as a divinely created political community. The Hebrew and Christian Scriptures propose that this was the way God chose to reveal Godself first to fallen humanity. But there are no exegetical or theological grounds to suggest that Israel was an exemplar of some general plan to go on working covenantally through such nations in the future.

Nations under the New Covenant

This negative conclusion is reinforced by a positive strand of New Testament political theology regarding the nature of the church.[49] A useful entry point to this theology is Romans 13, a passage that has been frequently invoked to *oppose* state religious impartiality and to justify the state's favouring or even coercively imposing Christianity. Often misunderstood as a charter for virtually unquestioning obedience to any extant government, I argue that this passage in fact lays the basis for a critical, conditional theory of political authority and a theology of the religiously limited state.[50]

In Romans 13, the apostle Paul is addressing a church that found itself a marginalized, politically powerless, and at times persecuted, minority within an oppressive first-century Roman Empire. This empire was prepared to tolerate religious minorities so long as they did not challenge the officially recognized pantheon of pagan deities or question the authority of the emperor. As a former Pharisee, we can be sure that Paul's political thinking was deeply formed by Hebrew texts such as Deuteronomy 17 (a 'charter' for faithful kingship) and Psalm 72 (a prayer for a just king), as well as the larger corpus of *torah*. These texts assume that government is a servant of the one God Yahweh who holds lordship over the entire world.[51] Paul would have shared this assumption, believing that all governments, not only the ones formerly existing in biblical Israel, stood under a divine mandate to promote justice and peace, protect the weak and punish unjust behaviour. Some Jews of the period regarded Roman rule as fundamentally illegitimate, albeit necessary to submit to for prudential reasons. But Paul reaffirms to his embattled Christian readership – some of whom were tempted to think they were now beyond governmental authority – the same universal mandate of government. Government, he says, exists to promote the public good and punish wrong. Such rule is legitimate as one of many human 'authorities ... instituted by God' (v. 1); Paul says this even though he knew the Roman Empire was vainglorious, idolatrous and periodically brutal. He holds that government is appointed, negatively, as the minister of God's 'wrath' (v. 4) – it is God's agent of judgement on injustice; and positively, to promote good public conduct. Paul is appealing to the notion that the office of government (not every individual holder of it) has been divinely established.[52] The authority of the office of government derives ultimately from God, and believers, like everyone else, stand under a prima facie obligation to obey it.

We know from the preceding chapter (Romans 12) that, within the community of faith, Christians were not to 'avenge' themselves (v. 19). They must not take it upon themselves to exercise coercive justice when they are the victims of public wrongdoing. Rather, they must 'leave room for the wrath of God' (v. 19) – that is, for the state to fulfil *its* unique mandate. This mandate is, however, hedged around with conditions. For, as Paul says in Romans 13.4, in fulfilling its mandate government acts as 'God's servant for your good'. This is a coded reminder that even the Roman Empire is a *mere servant*, to whom suitable respect and honour may be due but certainly not worship, and that it has been appointed not for its own self-aggrandizement but to serve public ends. This normative vocation remains, even if only as a standing indictment of its actual practice. The passage, then, does not teach an authoritarian theory of political authority but a conditional one: government is theologically legitimate insofar as it fulfils the mandate of its office to promote justice in the public realm. There are compelling contextual reasons why Paul does not say as much here. But it follows from such a conditional theory that if government egregiously violates that mandate, then by implication it loses its legitimacy as a divine servant. It may become a potentially dangerous, autonomous hegemon of the sort graphically depicted in the book of Revelation, devouring and destroying its subjects.[53]

Paul's view of the mandate of government in this passage is essentially in keeping with the ancient Jewish theology of government as expressed in passages like Deuteronomy 17 and Psalm 72. But there is one crucial sense in which Paul's larger political theology is a momentous departure from that ancient theology. If we were to consider only the purely practical point of view, it is obvious that a religious minority under oppressive pagan rule could not possibly look to government to do what governments in Israel did, namely to enforce true religion in the public realm and eliminate false ones. Rulers in biblical Israel could do this because they were instructed in what true religion was by *torah*, in which they were to be catechized by priests and Levites and against which they were to be held to account by prophets. Paul offers not the remotest hint of such an expectation towards Roman governors. But Paul's approach is not merely a prudential accommodation to circumstance, as if he were playing a long game so that if Christians became a majority they might seek to restore something like the confessional polity of ancient Israel. Rather, the refusal to look to government to define or protect true faith has a fundamental theological grounding, spelt out in Paul's other writings and in much of the rest of the New Testament. This theological shift decisively removes the task of identifying and protecting true religion from the broader mandate of the state to promote justice.[54]

For Paul, since the arrival of Jesus on the scene of divine redemption, the very nature of the community of faith has undergone a radical and irrevocable change. God's redemptive purposes are no longer concentrated exclusively in a single territorial community but now embrace every nation. The covenant is now extended to 'the Gentiles': this was the 'scandalous' proposition that proved so bewildering to the first disciples and to the Jewish communities from which they emerged. The people of God are no longer envisaged as a single, unified religio-political entity embracing the totality of the life of a territorial community under divine positive law, and will never be so again (in this age). There are no more 'covenanted nations' in *that* sense. Such a dispensation has been superseded for ever.[55] The people of God have become a transnational, non-territorial, global fellowship of believers united in primary allegiance to Jesus Christ and in the mission to proclaim the gospel to 'all the nations'.

A key implication of this notion of the church is that, where it exists, *nations can never be religiously unified*, because the mere arrival of the church in any society immediately introduces a religious distinction into it. The church confesses the lordship of Christ over all human authorities, adheres to a loyalty higher than any human affiliation and seeks to embody a distinctive form of life reflective of that loyalty. As Nicholas Wolterstorff puts it, in New Testament theology the church 'cannot express the shared religious identity of [a whole] people, since there is no such identity'. The reason is that '[w]henever the church enters a society, it destroys whatever religio-ethical unity that society may have possessed. Now there is only religious pluralism.'[56] This is the deepest reason for suspicion towards any notion of a 'national Church' (as distinct from a church with a national vision). As Rowan Williams puts the point: 'a church which does not at least possess certain features of a "sect" cannot act as an agent of transformation.'[57]

The implication is not that the church's mission is now *non-political* but that it is *non-territorial*, no longer bound to any geographically bounded political communities and no longer able to utilize the coercive power of such communities behind the mission of the gospel. The 'kingdom of God' at the centre of the teaching of Jesus is the restored rule of God over every area of human life, so that the church must indeed witness to this total reach of God's claimed rule, including its claims upon the political order. But such a witness must be pursued by means that are radically different from the coercive political power invoked by rulers in the ancient Hebrew polity (or any other polity).Whatever political opportunities the church may come to enjoy when circumstances permit must be pursued without the advantage of such coercive power; or, rather, as New Testament writers present it, with the huge advantage of an entirely different mode of power – that of a self-giving love that is willing to suffer for the sake of the gospel. This mandate for witness is depicted as being delegated directly from the authority of the risen Jesus Christ (Matt. 28.18–20). It entails proclaiming, and enacting, the gospel of the kingdom but it is, exclusively, the *authority to testify* to the ways in which God is redeeming the totality of creation. Thus, Paul speaks of members of the faithful community as bearing the 'ministry of reconciliation' (2 Cor. 5.18). This mission of the church is not itself to rule over those outside the community of faith, but rather to witness, in word and deed, to God's ways of ruling, including the ways God intends governments to continue to rule the world (outside the church) within its own allotted sphere of public justice.

We know that this did not imply a posture of passive acquiescence in whatever the empire or its local allies threw at Christians. Paul was quite ready to invoke his own rights as a Roman citizen when treated unjustly by Roman authorities (Acts 16.35–40) – in this case for the sake of the advancement of the gospel.[58] Nor did it mean that Christians should renounce active participation in political office, where circumstances permitted. Among the early Christians were a handful of Roman officials and soldiers, who were not instructed to leave their roles but rather catechized to ensure that their public roles should be informed by their faith, within the inevitable constraints of a polytheistic, non-Christian society and imperial pagan polity. Indeed, the church in time became aware that it should, where opportunities exist, seek to steer the use of government power closer to God's abiding calling for the office of government. Where possible, government might even be indirectly shaped by an eschatological vision of the future transformation of all rule. Christians should, for example, seek from government not *mere* judgement but, as Oliver O'Donovan puts it, 'merciful judgement'[59] – an injunction already urged on rulers by Augustine. Christians thus eventually came to see Jesus' command that 'you shall not lord it over each other as Gentile rulers do'[60] as applying not only to the internal life of the church but also as informing their participation in government when that became a historical possibility. What that would mean in practice often turned out to be highly complex. But what Christians until the fourth century certainly knew it meant was that they would in no circumstances turn to the institutions of government to enforce or privilege a gospel that could only ever be authentically communicated by peaceful persuasion, as empowered by the Holy Spirit. They knew that the New Testament nowhere even hints that government could ever be entitled to exercise such power to advance true faith.[61]

My argument, then, is both that there are no chosen nations today and also that the New Testament people of God are constituted from their very inception as a *trans-national, non-territorial community*.[62] In Jesus Christ the 'Gentiles' are brought fully into a covenant relationship with God. This theological truth was enacted visibly in the trans-ethnic character of the early church in Acts, which confessed, dramatically and subversively, that in Jesus Christ 'There is no longer Jew or Greek' (Gal. 3.28). While it was always God's plan that the people of God were to be a witness to all the nations, now that plan is publicly announced to the whole world and tangibly realized in the Messiah who inaugurates a kingdom and community of global reach. Hence Jesus' departing commission to 'make disciples of all nations' (Matt. 28.19). Given this, the New Testament church can never literally assume to itself the title of 'New Israel' in the sense of a covenanted, territorial political community. Nor can Christians attribute 'New Israel' status to any nation or state, including their own – however many Christians it has within it.

This still allows, however, that the ancient Israelite polity can speak powerfully to Christians and indeed to contemporary society. It is possible to identify certain generic features of nationhood, of which biblical Israel is a unique instance, such that lessons can be learned from Israel about the proper conduct of nations generally.[63] The Israelite polity is portrayed in the Bible not as an idiosyncratic local model designed for Israel alone but as a uniquely authoritative (contextual) instantiation of God's political will for the whole of humanity. Accordingly it must remain for Christians of paradigmatic significance and continue to inform its own public engagement today.[64] One concrete application of this was the Jubilee Debt Campaign of the late 1990s in which Christian supporters invoked the provisions of Leviticus 25 behind the campaign's radical call for debt cancellation for majority world nations.[65] All dimensions of Israel's social and political life were to be expressive of a divinely given *torah*, 'instruction' in the ways of universal wisdom and justice. Such ways are of perennial validity, from which all human beings, and all polities, can learn.[66] Yet while *all* law in the Hebrew Scriptures is in some way *revelatory* of God's will, none of it is *immediately authoritative* as binding positive law either for the New Testament people of God today or for the diverse states in which they now happen to reside. Most especially, the command to rulers in ancient Israel to subject themselves explicitly to the faith of Yahweh and enforce such a confession across the whole nation cannot be applied to rulers in the New Testament era.

Neither the Bible nor theology, then, support the claim that political nations today are addressed by God as covenant partners (as the Christian nation view holds), or the attribution to them of the explicit duty to confess faith in God that was imposed on biblical Israel (as the Christian state position also claims). While Israel legitimately exercised corporate religious agency, permitting it to enforce a single confession across its territory, God no longer looks to territorial nations to exercise such agency. Of course, they can, and do, presumptuously *attempt* to do so, but such hubristic adventures usually end in hypocrisy, futility, resentment or disaster. Paul's account of government in Romans 13 and his wider theology of the church yield no support for the idea of national religious agency but point compellingly in the opposite direction. The very idea of a 'Christian nation' in this normative theological sense, then, is excluded by the most fundamental themes of New Testament theology.

Northern lights

An important contemporary implication of the New Testament political theology I have set out now beckons, though it is often resisted by Christian nation advocates. It is that, for the state today to assume the authority to declare an official public view of the truth of any faith (religious or secular) exceeds its divinely assigned mandate. Equally, the church must not seek any privileged access to, or use of, the authority of the state in furthering its spiritual purposes. It may look to the state to protect its religious freedom, but only on the same terms as other communities of faith. This follows from the principle of state religious impartiality. Seeking anything beyond that, whether in the form of exclusive recognition or formal establishment – however apparently benign – is to hanker after the now superseded model of the ancient Hebrew polity and to risk falling victim to the seductive myth of a 'national church'. To the extent that Establishment upholds the constitutional privileges of the Church of England, it rests on a theologically indefensible breach of the principle of state religious impartiality.

The religious impartiality of the state is decisive for securing the religious freedom of citizens. But, importantly, this is not only individual but also institutional. This is crucial in order to safeguard the capacity for free self-governance by the church, and other religious bodies. As noted, state religious impartiality itself does not guarantee a favourable view of religion but must go together with a robust affirmation by the state of the legitimate public presence of religious bodies and their prima facie right to autonomous self-governance. It must issue in constructive and respectful even-handed engagement with such bodies. The church does indeed possess 'corporate religious agency' and must protect it jealously against unwarranted intrusions from the state or any other body. This capacity is essential if it is to allow its loyalty to Christ to shape its entire life, unimpeded by possibly confining alliances or affiliations. Where necessary, this will involve the church's dissenting from the state's demands, or the nation's expectations, where these intrude upon that corporate religious freedom or compromise the church's spiritual integrity. State impartiality towards religion and robust ecclesial self-governance go hand in hand. Defining the proper spheres of authority of each institution is thus a vitally important task.

I propose that a cogent account of these complementary spheres of authority appears in the Articles Declaratory of the Constitution of the Church of Scotland in Matters Spiritual.[67] Articles IV–VI are the critical ones for my argument:

IV. This Church, as part of the Universal Church wherein the Lord Jesus Christ has appointed a government in the hands of Church office-bearers, receives from Him, its Divine King and Head, and from Him alone, the right and power subject to no civil authority to legislate, and to adjudicate finally, in all matters of doctrine, worship, government, and discipline in the Church, including the right to determine all questions concerning membership and office in the Church, the constitution and membership of its Courts, and the mode of election of its office-bearers, and to define the boundaries of the spheres of labour of its ministers and other office-bearers. Recognition by civil authority of the separate and independent government and jurisdiction of this Church in matters spiritual, in whatever manner such recognition be expressed, does not in any way affect the character of this government and jurisdiction as derived from the Divine Head of the Church alone, or give to the civil authority any right of interference with the proceedings or judgments of the Church within the sphere of its spiritual government and jurisdiction. V. This Church has the inherent right, free from interference by civil authority, but under the safeguards for deliberate action and legislation provided by the Church itself, to frame or adopt its subordinate standards, to declare the sense in which it understands its Confession of Faith,[68] to modify the forms of expression therein, or to formulate other doctrinal statements, and to define the relation thereto of its office-bearers and members, but always in agreement with the Word of God and the fundamental doctrines of the Christian Faith contained in the said Confession, of which agreement the Church shall be sole judge, and with due regard to liberty of opinion in points which do not enter into the substance of the Faith. VI. This Church acknowledges the divine appointment and authority of the civil magistrate within his own sphere and maintains its historic testimony to the duty of the nation acting in its corporate capacity to render homage to God, to acknowledge the Lord Jesus Christ to be King over the nations, to obey His laws, to reverence His ordinances, to honour His Church, and to promote in all appropriate ways the Kingdom of God. The Church and the State owe mutual duties to each other and, acting within their respective spheres, may signally promote each other's welfare. The Church and the State have the right to determine each for itself all questions concerning the extent and the continuance of their mutual relations in the discharge of these duties and the obligations arising therefrom.

This is a bold declaration of full independence of the church over against the state in all matters pertaining to its theological identity and purpose.[69] It may come as a surprise to English readers that these Articles are appended to the Church of Scotland Act 1921.[70] How is it that the Kirk's own principles of internal order came to be affirmed in an Act of the British state? The short answer is that, given the Church of Scotland's unique constitutional standing prior to 1921, state legislation was required in order to clarify the civil law consequences of its reunion with the United Free Church, which took place in 1929.[71] The Articles were, however, drawn up by the Kirk, not the state. The preamble acknowledges that 'they have been prepared with the authority of the General Assembly of the Church'.[72] As one commentator puts it, the 1921 Act 'may be regarded as a *recognition* by Parliament of the Church's constitution, rather than a *conferment* of a constitution'. It expresses the 'underlying notion of a co-ordinate jurisdiction of church and state, each supreme within its own sphere'.[73] It has been described as 'in effect a treaty between Church and State'.[74]

The Articles do not explicitly affirm the principle of state religious impartiality. But by virtue of their assertion of the spiritual autonomy of the Kirk, and of the state's deference to them, they implicitly bolster it. With only two minor rewordings they could satisfy it. First, Article VI asserts the right of the Church of Scotland to give 'testimony' to the Lordship of Christ over the state, not that *the state* must explicitly and officially 'render homage to God'. It could render such homage simply by acting justly, but the Article could make that explicit. Second, Article III, while avoiding the language of 'establishment', does still speak of the Church of Scotland as a 'national church representative of the Christian Faith of the Scottish people'. That phrase should be dispensed with. But the Articles are entirely free of the adverse jurisdictional features I will identify in English Establishment. The recognition of the Kirk as 'national church' imposes no constitutional burdens such as those afflicting the Church of England.[75] The Kirk can thus be described as 'national and free'.[76] I propose that the jurisdictional theology of Articles IV–VI is more faithful to a New Testament theology of church and state than any Anglican establishmentarian rendition. In the next two chapters, using these Articles as a benchmark, I show how English Establishment falls short of that theology.

In turning to these 'northern lights', I follow many others who have looked with interest and at times envy to Scottish arrangements.[77] I differ from many Church of England observers, however, in proposing that the Church turn wistful appreciation into practical emulation, although I do not suggest that Scottish arrangements be exactly replicated in England. I propose that the Articles can usefully clarify and inspire the Church of England's own necessary resetting of its future relations with the British state.

Conclusion

In this chapter I have outlined a 'theology of disestablishment' – a biblical and theological defence of the principles of the religious impartiality of the state and the autonomy of the church. Taken together, those principles are my fundamental argument against Establishment. If that theology is compelling, Establishment is theologically illegitimate, whatever empirical advantages it may bring. I have argued that the New Testament's vision of the church as a voluntary, transnational and non-territorial fellowship is a radical departure from the model of the covenanted, religio-political, territorial nation witnessed, uniquely and unrepeatably, in biblical Israel. The assumption of corporate religious agency grounding this model is invalid when applied to any other polity, even ones deeply impacted by Christianity. This model, however, dominated much of the church's political thinking from the era of Constantine until well after the Reformation (although it began to be repudiated by sixteenth-century Anabaptists and seventeenth-century Protestant Dissenters). Such a model continued to shape the church–state theologies of many denominations, not only the Church of England, even into the twentieth century. It is a tacit assumption behind most defences of the Christian nation position. In turn, that position, even in attenuated form, sustains the problematic vision of a 'national church' which still today underpins many arguments for establishment. Against it, we need to recover a robust theology of the church's overriding loyalty to Christ and of the freedom of the church over against both state and nation, and of the state as lacking the authority to identify religious truth and thus to favour any religion. The Articles Declaratory of the Church of Scotland offer a powerful starting point in recovering such a theology, even though they too stand in need of correction. The Church of England should learn from them as it seeks to forge a better theology of the distinct, complementary and at times contending authorities of church and state, beyond Establishment. The next two chapters delve into the innards of Establishment and show why they blur these distinct authorities in troubling ways.

Notes

1 Michael Nazir-Ali, 'Breaking Faith with Britain', *Standpoint* 1 (June 2008), p. 47. For a fuller statement, see *Triple Jeopardy for the West: Aggressive Secularism, Radical Islamism and Multiculturalism* (London: Bloomsbury, 2012). In 2021, Nazir-Ali became a Roman Catholic.

2 'Law, Morality and Religion in the Family Courts', Keynote address given by Sir James Munby at the Law Society's Family Law

Annual Conference, 'The Sacred and the Secular: Religion, Culture and the Family Courts', London, 29 October 2013.

3 See Andrew Copson, *Secularism: Politics, Religion, and Freedom* (Oxford: Oxford University Press, 2017); Craig Calhoun, Mark Juergensmeyer and Jonathan VanAntwerpen, *Rethinking Secularism* (New York: Oxford University Press, 2011).

4 *Refah Partisi (Welfare Party) v Turkey* (2003) 37 EHRR I, para. 91.

5 See, for example, *Khaira v Shergill* (2014) UKSC 33.

6 Notwithstanding *laïcité*, the French state subsidizes some church buildings for just this reason.

7 *Lautsi v Italy* (2012) 54 EHRR 3.

8 See Dominic McGoldrick, 'Religion in the European Public Square and in European Public Life – Crucifixes in the Classroom?', *Human Rights Law Review* 11.3 (2011), pp. 451–502.

9 Rowan Williams, *Faith in the Public Square* (London: Bloomsbury, 2012), p. 26.

10 Since all four nations of the UK today have been overwhelmingly Christian since the Middle Ages, the distinction between 'Britain' and 'England' does not much affect an assessment of the Christian nation stance at this point. But England is unique among these nations in having a church with intimate legal ties to the state, but also lacking its own devolved government. Defenders (or opponents) of *English* Establishment must continue to look to the *British* state to uphold it (or dismantle it).

11 Aidan Nichols, 'Christianity, Secularisation and Islam', *Standpoint* 2 (July 2008), p. 46. See also *Christendom Awake: On Re-Energising the Church in Culture* (Edinburgh: T&T Clark, 1999). His call for a reimagining of the 'Christendom state', however, seems not to depend on establishment at all (ch. 6).

12 For scholarly efforts providing grist to that mill, see Tom Holland, *Dominion: The Making of the Western Mind* (London: Little Brown, 2019); Larry Siedentop, *Inventing the Individual: The Origins of Western Liberalism* (London: Allen Lane, 2014). See also Nick Spencer, *Freedom and Order: History, Politics and the English Bible* (London: Hodder & Stoughton, 2011); Nick Spencer, *The Evolution of the West: How Christianity has Shaped our Values* (London: SPCK, 2016).

13 Opponents of the Christian nation view sometimes suggest that it is merely a reactionary posture advanced by those unable to come to terms with their own loss of power and status in the 'post-Christendom' era. This impulse is definitely at work, most egregiously in the catastrophic complicity of 'Evangelicals' in the ascendancy of Donald Trump (see Ronald J. Sider, ed., *The Spiritual Danger of Donald Trump:*

30 *Evangelical Christians on Justice, Truth, and Morality* (Eugene, OR: Cascade, 2020)). But it is important to assess the theological arguments for the position on their own merits.

14 The Methodist Church's *A Report on Church, State and Establishment* (Peterborough: Methodist Church, 2004) critically discusses this second view (paras 53–82).

15 The point is confirmed in Rex Adhar and Ian Leigh, *Religious Freedom in the Liberal State*, 2nd edn (Oxford: Oxford University Press, 2013).

16 For example, Mary Warnock, *Dishonest to God: On Keeping Religion out of Politics* (London: Continuum, 2010).

17 Some Christian nation advocates imply that a recognized ecclesial body (the Church of England, perhaps) needs to instruct the state on what true religion is, since it cannot judge this itself. But this is not intended to imply the conferring of political or legislative power on an ecclesial body. The Lords Spiritual, often defended by Christian nation advocates, are not a valid counter-example, since the 'legislative power' they wield is minimal and depends entirely on persuasion.

18 Nichols, 'Christianity', p. 44.

19 Nichols, 'Christianity', p. 44, 46.

20 Nazir-Ali, 'Breaking Faith', p. 45. There is something in this historical claim. For an account of the emergence of sacral monarchy in Britain and its central role in the nation's emerging identity, see Ian Bradley, *God Save the Queen: The Spiritual Dimension of Monarchy* (London: Darton, Longman and Todd, 2002), ch. 3. Bradley depicts sacral monarchy as a Christianization of earlier pagan models.

21 Nazir-Ali, 'Breaking Faith', p. 45.

22 'Christianity', p. 47.

23 Nazir-Ali, 'Breaking Faith', p. 47.

24 Nazir-Ali, 'Breaking Faith', p. 47. Writing in the *Sunday Telegraph* in 2008, he lamented the fact that public life was increasingly dominated by a deceptive 'multi-faithism' which, far from heralding a tolerant pluralism, was merely a cover for a coercive form of secularism ('Extremism flourished as UK lost Christianity', *Sunday Telegraph*, 7 January 2008). Nichols echoes the point: 'A Judaeo-Christian society is by definition not a multicultural one' ('Christianity', p. 47). He nonetheless contemplates a role for 'the Islamic imamate' in the House of Lords.

25 Advocates often cite polls reporting that, in spite of neither 'believing nor belonging', a majority of the population still self-identify as 'Christian'. The 2021 Census, however, may disclose that this number has dropped to a plurality (Harriet Sherwood, 'Less than half of Britons expected to tick "Christian" in UK census', *Observer*, 20 March 2021,

www.theguardian.com/uk-news/2021/mar/20/less-that-half-of-britons-expected-to-tick-christian-in-uk-census, accessed 25.10.2021).

26 'Christianity', p. 47.

27 The Christian Institute, 'Governments Exist to Restrain Evil', *The Christian Institute*, www.christian.org.uk/who-we-are/what-we-believe/governments-exist-restrain-evil/, accessed 25.10.2021.

28 The Christian Institute, 'Christianity and the State', *The Christian Institute*, www.christian.org.uk/who-we-are/what-we-believe/christianity-and-the-state/, accessed 25.10.2021.

29 Nichols echoes the point: '[W]hat is never an open question – *pace* the secularists – is that the state has the duty to guard the spiritual civilization of its own society. For the legislature and judiciary, that means being guided in the formulation and interpretation of laws by the moral ethos that forms a society's spiritual patrimony' ('Christianity', p. 46). I explore a fuller statement of this anti-neutrality argument by Nigel Biggar in Chapter 5.

30 For a British defence of this view, see David Field, 'Samuel Rutherford and the Confessionally Christian State', in Chris Green, ed., *A Higher Throne: Evangelicals and Public Theology* (Nottingham: IVP, 2008), pp. 85–120.

31 This may surprise some readers, since Canadian public institutions are more secularized than British ones – which is one piece of evidence that a constitutional recognition of God or Christianity does little to stem the tide of secularization. In 1999 the British Columbia Court of Appeal declared the provision 'a dead letter'. Charles Lewis, 'God's place in Charter challenged', *National Post*, https://nationalpost.com/holy-post/gods-place-in-charter-challenged/, accessed 25.10.2021.

32 I engage with Oliver O'Donovan's thoughts on Establishment in Chapter 4. I respond to his broader political theology in 'Political Eschatology and Responsible Government: Oliver O'Donovan's Defence of Christian Liberalism', in *A Royal Priesthood? The Use of the Bible Ethically and Politically. A Dialogue with Oliver O'Donovan*, ed. Craig Bartholomew et al. (Grand Rapids, MI: Zondervan, 2002), pp. 265–308.

33 Joan Lockwood O'Donovan, 'The Liberal Legal Legacy of English Church Establishment: A Theological Contribution to the Legal Accommodation of Religious Plurality in Europe', *Journal of Law, Philosophy and Culture* 6.1 (2011), pp. 17–45, p. 28. See also Lockwood O'Donovan, *Theology of Law and Authority in the English Reformation* (Atlanta, GA: Scholars Press, 1991).

34 'Liberal Legacy', p. 28.

35 'Liberal Legacy', p. 30.

36 'Liberal Legacy', pp. 32–8.

37 'Liberal Legacy', p. 31. Lockwood O'Donovan notes that this was a recurring deficiency in Tudor political theology, including Hooker's: 'No more than his [Puritan] adversaries did Hooker appreciate the full institutional implications of the supersession of the Mosaic by the gospel law, the effect of this supersession on the authority and content of communal legislation, whether civil or ecclesiastical ... In both cases a rival, limiting authority and law to that of Jesus Christ has been erected' (*Theology of Law and Authority*, p. 160).

38 'Liberal Legacy', pp. 30–1.

39 'Liberal Legacy', p. 38.

40 Or, for example, those of William Tyndale, as described by Rowan Williams in 'William Tyndale (c. 1494–1536): The Christian Society', in Rowan Williams, *Anglican Identities* (London: Darton, Longman and Todd, 2004), pp. 9–23.

41 'Liberal Legacy', p. 43.

42 'Liberal Legacy', p. 43.

43 'Liberal Legacy', p. 43.

44 For example, Reformed Protestants invoke the Calvinist principle stated in the *Westminster Confession* (19.4) that it is not the precise individual injunctions of Mosaic law which are binding on Christians today but only 'the general equity thereof' – the principles of justice underlying it. See Harold G. Cunningham, 'God's Law, "General Equity" and the Westminster Confession', *Tyndale Bulletin* 58.2 (2007), pp. 289–312.

45 For an overview of sacral monarchy in the Old Testament, see Bradley, *God Save the Queen*, ch. 2.

46 *Centesimus Annus* (1991), §3. www.vatican.va/content/john-paul-ii/en/encyclicals/documents/hf_jp-ii_enc_01051991_centesimus-annus.html, accessed 25.10.2021.

47 These occasional references are being abused today. See Judd Birdsall and Matthew Rowley, 'Stop weaponizing the Bible for Trump: No politician is a Cyrus, David or Caesar', *Washington Post*, 19 June 2019, www.washingtonpost.com/religion/2019/06/19/stop-weaponizing-bible-trump-no-politician-is-cyrus-david-or-caesar/, accessed 25.10.2021.

48 'Christianity', p. 44. On a theology of nationhood, see Joan Lockwood O'Donovan, 'Nation, State, and Civil Society in the Western Biblical Tradition', in Oliver O'Donovan and Joan Lockwood O'Donovan, *Bonds of Imperfection: Christian Politics, Past and Present* (Grand Rapids, MI: Eerdmans, 2004), pp. 276–95; Nigel Biggar, *Between Kin and Cosmopolis: An Ethic of the Nation* (Cambridge: James Clarke & Co, 2014), ch. 1; Doug Gay, *Honey from the Lion: Christianity and the Ethics of Nationalism* (London: SCM Press, 2013), ch. 4. Gay offers an appealing 'Augustinian civic nationalism' that renounces imperialism, essentialism and absolutism (p. 81).

49 Such a strand shapes Nigel G. Wright's view of Establishment in 'A View from One of the Free Churches', in R. M. Morris, ed., *Church and State: Some Reflections on Church Establishment in England* (London: UCL Constitution Unit, 2008), pp. 15–22.

50 For a fuller statement of this position, see Nicholas Wolterstorff, *The Mighty and the Almighty: An Essay in Political Theology* (Cambridge: Cambridge University Press, 2012), ch. 8. There are specific contextual features shaping Paul's reflections in this passage (such as the reference to paying taxes), but I agree with Wolterstorff that its underlying theology has broad theological application.

51 Deuteronomy 17 evokes the wider teaching of *torah* regarding the twin mandate to pursue righteousness (*tsedekah*) – the complex fabric of right relationships marking a human community under God – and justice (*mishpat*) – the actual delivery of justice, which was to be both speedy and impartial. In Psalm 72, one of the 'royal' psalms portraying an ideally just king, the content of the justice prayed for is in keeping with the detailed depiction of justice throughout *torah*, with the special focus here on the king's role of actively securing justice for the poor since they are least able to defend themselves.

52 Or, we might at least say that he is implying that wherever some kind of stable order of government exists that does not systematically tyrannize its people and offers some measure of public justice, it must be construed as legitimate, as a gift of providence for the good of society.

53 What to do in the face of such a government turned out to be a complex question in subsequent Christian thought and practice. There are, for example, long histories both of passive submission and of calls for resistance against 'tyranny' as a usurpation of legitimate authority.

54 This view, admittedly, was mostly rejected in mainstream political theology for much for the 1,500 years of what we know as 'Christendom'. See, for example, Oliver O'Donovan and Joan Lockwood O'Donovan, eds, *From Irenaeus to Grotius: A Sourcebook in Christian Political Thought* (Grand Rapids, MI: Eerdmans, 1999).

55 This is not to suggest that, from a Christian theological point of view, the Jewish people have now disappeared from divine history, that their status as a 'chosen', 'covenanted' people has been abolished – a problematic view known as 'supersessionism'. Paul seems clearly to reject such a view in Romans 9—11. My argument is only committed to the view that God no longer works salvifically through covenanted, religio-political, territorial nations; the Jewish people could be seen as retaining a salvific role quite apart from such a territorial form, and thus irrespective of the existence, or ethical performance, of the modern state of Israel.

56 Wolterstorff, *The Mighty and the Almighty*, p. 123. Empirically,

however, that has not invariably been true. For instance, Ian Bradley points out how the first Christian missionaries to what was to become 'Britain' deliberately targeted rulers first, on the (often correct) assumption that the whole nation would then convert (*God Save the Queen*, ch. 3). But insofar as that strategy has indeed been used (as it has also in Africa), it must surely be called into question theologically, since the New Testament knows nothing of corporate conversions by entire tribes or nations. That is true even if, as Bradley argues, the effect was the substantive Christianizing of Anglo-Saxon societies (pp. 57–9).

57 He goes on: 'If there is a case for the Church's establishment it must be cast in terms of the Church's witness to a community without boundaries other than Christ – not the Church's guardianship of the Christian character of a nation (which so easily becomes the Church's endorsement of the *de facto* structures and constraints of the life of a sovereign state) ... The legal establishment of a church *might* be a state's witness to the reality of goals beyond its own, even of a state's acknowledgement of being answerable to the community of human beings as such; though it must be said both that legal establishment in a sovereign state such as ours (having no concept of limited sovereignty) begs a good many questions, and that it is doubtful whether such a situation could speak of unrestricted human community when it will inevitably be seen as privileging of one of a number of religious groupings within the state' (*On Christian Theology* (Oxford: Blackwell, 2000), p. 234).

58 It is thus not that the church eschewed all forms of power. The church could avail itself of legal rights, or own property, both legitimate exercises of public legal power. It could also organize itself and discipline its own members, requiring forms of power internal to the church, albeit always subject to gospel norms.

59 *The Desire of the Nations* (Cambridge: Cambridge University Press, 1996), pp. 256–61.

60 This is my paraphrase of Matthew 20.25–28.

61 See Timothy Samuel Shah and Allen D. Hertzke, eds, *Christianity and Freedom: Volume I: Historical Perspectives* (New York: Cambridge University Press, 2016).

62 In *God Save the Queen* (ch. 3), Ian Bradley overlooks this vital New Testament emphasis. He concentrates on the motif of Jesus' 'kingship' in the Gospels. He rightly recognizes that Jesus redefines kingship but does not acknowledge the New Testament's fundamental detachment of this idea from territorial, national political kingship. It is certainly right to say that 'Christian monarchy is to be patterned on [Jesus'] own royal attributes of righteousness, justice, mercy, wisdom, peace and humility' (p. 45). But this does not imply that monarchy is

explicitly to confess faith in Jesus Christ or to have any formal relationship to a church.

63 An instructive attempt to do this is offered by Oliver O'Donovan, who proposes that we understand the nation, or, as he terms it, 'the people', as a community rooted in a shared moral tradition and unified by a common political defence of the common good. See *The Ways of Judgment* (Grand Rapids, MI: Eerdmans, 2005), ch. 9. I respond to his view in 'Representing a People: Oliver O'Donovan on Democracy and Tradition', *Political Theology* 9.3 (2008), pp. 295–307.

64 On Israel as a 'paradigm' for the life of the church, see Christopher J. H. Wright, *Old Testament Ethics for the People of God* (Leicester: IVP, 2004), pp. 65–73.

65 See *Jubilee Debt Campaign*, https://jubileedebt.org.uk/, accessed 25.10.2021.

66 *Torah* is not a law code in anything like the modern sense. For an excellent overview, see Jonathan Burnside, *God, Justice, and Society: Law and Legality in the Bible* (New York: Oxford University Press, 2011). See also O'Donovan, *Desire of the Nations*, ch. 2.

67 'Church of Scotland Act 1921', *Legislation*, www.legislation.gov.uk/ukpga/Geo5/11-12/29, accessed 25.10.2021. The Articles are printed in R. M. Morris, ed., *Church and State in 21st Century Britain: The Future of Church Establishment* (Basingstoke: Palgrave Macmillan, 2009), pp. 88–90.

68 This refers to the Westminster Confession, the Church of Scotland's official doctrinal basis. The Church of England's nearest equivalents would be the Thirty-Nine Articles and the Book of Common Prayer.

69 It is echoed in the United Reformed Church's *Basis of Union* (1972), which asserts: 'We believe that Christ gives his Church a government distinct from the government of the state. In things that affect obedience to God the Church is not subordinate to the state, but must serve the Lord Jesus Christ, its only Ruler and Head. Civil authorities are called to serve God's will of justice and peace for all humankind, and to respect the rights of conscience and belief: while we ourselves are servants in the world as citizens of God's eternal kingdom.' Quoted in Geoffrey Roper, 'View of A Critical Friend – From the United Reformed Church', in R. M. Morris, ed., *Church and State: Some Reflections on Church Establishment in England* (London: UCL Constitution Unit, 2008), p. 24.

70 See Gay, *Honey from the Lion*, pp. 176–82. Gay points out that the goal of the drafters of the Articles was to resist both 'Erastianism' and 'Voluntarism' (p. 178).

71 This was required in response to a previous House of Lords decision about the assets of the Free Church, and to give reassurance to the

United Free Church about the relationship between the UK state and the united church, were union to go ahead. Thanks to Doug Gay for clarification of this point.

72 The Act could not come into effect unless the Assembly first affirmed the Articles. This maintains the principle laid down in 1592 when the Scottish Parliament guaranteed the liberties and presbyterian form of government of the Church of Scotland.

73 Colin Munro, quoted in Morris, *Church and State in 21st Century Britain*, p. 84. This echoes the language of 'sphere sovereignty' used by the Dutch neo-Calvinist Abraham Kuyper, *Lectures on Calvinism* (Grand Rapids, MI: Eerdmans, 1931), pp. 105–6. On my definition of 'establishment', mere legal 'recognition' does not suffice to make a church 'established', as the Church in Wales Act 1914 and the Methodist Church Act of 1976 show (notwithstanding the vestigial privileges retained by the former). It is therefore potentially misleading for the Methodist Church to describe itself as 'established' by law (Methodist Church, *Report on Church, State and Establishment*, para. 33).

74 Morris, *Church and State in 21st Century Britain*, p. 81 (quoting Vernon Bogdanor).

75 There have been ongoing debates about whether the Kirk is in fact 'established' at all. See David Fergusson, *Church, State and Civil Society* (Cambridge: Cambridge University Press, 2004), pp. 183–4. The Kirk's few residual privileges include the royal oath (to protect Presbyterianism in Scotland), a royal appointed High Commissioner to the General Assembly and a right of the Kirk's ministers to solemnize marriage (Morris, *Church and State in 21st Century Britain*, pp. 83–7).

76 Morris, *Church and State in 21st Century Britain*, p. 84.

77 As do Iain McLean and Scot Peterson in 'A Uniform British Establishment', in Mark Chapman, Judith Maltby and William Whyte, eds, *The Established Church: Past, Present and Future* (London: T&T Clark, 2011), pp. 141–57. They argue that adopting the Scottish model 'would make the Church of England more credible as part of the liberal, democratic British constitution' (p. 141). That may be so, but my claim is that it would bring it into line with the New Testament theology of church and state set out above. See also Iain McLean and B. Lindsey, *The Church of England and the State: Reforming Establishment for a Multifaith Britain* (London: New Politics Network, 2004).

3

Deconstructing Establishment: Church, Crown and Government

It is four hundred years since the Tudor 'Settlement of Religion', a thoroughly political arrangement if ever there was one, but fantasised by generations of prelates and propagandists into a hallowed myth about the Crown, our Nation and the Church. It will help our discussions to be rid of it. (Valerie Pitt)[1]

Introduction

In this and the next chapter, I 'deconstruct' Establishment. I explore the unique constitutional relationships existing between the British state and the Church of England and show why they are problematic. Wesley Carr calls these 'high establishment'. They are ancient, labyrinthine and idiosyncratic.[2] They do not all proceed from a single source and they could not be swept away in a single act. The most important components of high establishment can, however, be conveniently grouped into three categories reflecting the constitutional structure of the modern British state.[3] They correspond to the three central organs of state: the executive (Crown and government),[4] the legislature (Parliament) and the judiciary (on which I say little). A fourth component of Establishment – part of what Carr calls 'earthed establishment' – consists of legal obligations on local parishes, which I address in Chapter 5. The present chapter addresses the relationship between Church, Crown and government and considers four linked elements:

Royal Supremacy; Protestant succession; the coronation and accession oaths; and crown appointments.[5] To make sense of what remains of them today we cannot avoid briefly delving back into an unappealing history.

Legacies of supremacy

The 'Royal Supremacy' establishes the monarch as 'Supreme Governor' of the Church of England. This remains a principal constitutional fountainhead of Establishment. It was most evocatively expressed in Henry VIII's Act of Supremacy (1534), by which he replaced papal authority over the Catholic Church in England with the authority of the English monarch.[6] England in the sixteenth century still reflected the organic social vision dominating European Christendom since the early Middle Ages. This was itself partly the legacy of pagan traditions of sacral monarchy and partly that of the coercive imposition of Nicene Christianity by the emperor Theodosius as the official religion of the Roman Empire, and the criminalization of alternatives.[7] In this organic vision the nation was seen as a single Christian society (*corpus Christianum*). Such a unified Christian commonwealth was understood to be governed by two distinct but intimately coordinated authorities, the 'spiritual' authority of the Church and the 'temporal' authority of civil government. Across Europe the magisterial Reformation certainly brought about significant shifts in the balance of power between the two authorities – mostly in favour of civil government – but it did not initially challenge the model of a unified Christian commonwealth. It did, however, as Edward Norman points out, demand new clarity about the Church's legal status:

> It was assumed that the relationship of Christianity and public life in medieval England presupposed an exclusive protection of the Catholic Faith; only at the time of the Reformation, when the jurisdiction of Rome was abandoned, and the State in consequence needed to re-define its religious responsibil-

ities, was it necessary for a legislative structure to spell out the exact form of Church and State relations.[8]

This was the precise origin of what we today refer to as 'Establishment', or the Church 'by law Established'.[9] But it did not amount to a rejection of the model of an organic society in which a single religion was lawful. As Peter Cornwell puts it, 'if, in its insistence on unqualified national autonomy, the English Reformation was radical, it was profoundly conservative in its identification of Church and nation.'[10] The English Reformation did not break with the principle that a state was entitled to require a single public confession across its entire territory – the 'territorial principle'; that had to wait until the Toleration Act of 1689, which still left the Church of England in an overwhelmingly superior and territorially privileged position.[11] Calvin was a jealous defender of the jurisdiction of the church, a critic of the encroachment of temporal power on it and an opponent of the exercise of papal authority over temporal power. Yet even he asserted that among the purposes of civil government was 'to cherish and support the external worship of God, to preserve the pure doctrine of religion, to defend the Constitution of the church'.[12]

The idea that a temporal ruler should play a leading role in the affairs of the church was wholly familiar to Henry VIII. Medieval and early modern rulers routinely did so – by, for instance, appointing bishops or creating new episcopal sees – with or without the support of the church hierarchy. In pre-Reformation England this was seen as compatible with an acceptance, however grudging at times, of the supremacy of the papacy over the Catholic Church everywhere. Since the fourteenth century, however, the tussle between the pope and English kings had again intensified. The latter were striving to curtail what were widely perceived to be serious abuses of ecclesiastical power by the Catholic Church.[13] There was much elite and popular support for William Tyndale's claim that it was time for 'princes to resume authority over ecclesiastics, and to humble the usurping hierarchy'.[14] But Henry VIII's declaration that the English monarch be supreme, not only over 'civil' but also *'ecclesiastical* causes', was still a radical innovation, implying a formal and complete casting off of papal jurisdiction over the Catholic Church in England.[15] It was the nationalization of English Catholicism, powered by a resurgent 'Erastianism' in which the Church was henceforth to be extensively governed by temporal political power, the 'monarch in Parliament'.[16] As Rivers puts it: 'Establishment meant the assertion of new forms of centralized Governmental control over the church and an elevation of the church to a bearer of national identity in an ideologically splintered international context.'[17]

Yet what exactly were the 'ecclesiastical causes' now falling under political jurisdiction? The Act of Supremacy, and the series of preceding and following statutes and instruments by which Henry VIII, and later monarchs including Elizabeth I, consolidated or extended their authority over the English Church, did not impose comprehensive political control over it.[18] In spite of their wide-ranging scope, these statutes did not entirely abolish the long-standing medieval distinction between matters falling under the unique spiritual authority of the Church and those falling under the temporal authority of the state. This duality was to be reaffirmed in Article 37 of the Thirty-Nine Articles, which distinguishes between two kinds of power: that reserved exclusively to clergy, of 'ministering either of God's Word, or of the Sacraments'; and that given only to civil magistrates, to 'rule all estates and degrees committed to their charge by God, whether they be Ecclesiastical or Temporal'. The Henrician statutes did not transfer the former kind to temporal rulers.[19]

What, then, did 'ecclesiastical estates and degrees' include? 'Ruling all ecclesiastical estates' was thought to confer on the monarch extensive powers to *enforce the rulings of the Church* in matters of doctrine, liturgy and internal order. It affirmed the sovereign's full authority to implement reforms that the Church itself was empowered to introduce – that is, 'which … by spiritual authority … may lawfully be reformed'.[20] That latter clause was an important qualification: the Act of Supremacy was not supposed to license Henry VIII to concoct novel doctrines or liturgies out of his own head. Yet Henry and his wily and ruthless lieutenant Thomas Cromwell in fact turned out to play highly assertive and controversial roles in shaping the content of the reforms that 'spiritual authority' was then to propose for legal enforcement by the state. As A. G. Dickens puts it, Henry VIII saw himself as 'the functioning head of his Church and chief physician to the souls of his subjects'.[21] This activist role was not resisted by most of the parties vying for influence over the sixteenth- and seventeenth-century English Church. On the contrary, each side was all too pleased to have royal (or parliamentary) power deployed on their side and equally appalled to see it utilized on the other.

This model of jurisdictional interaction was not radically changed in the Elizabethan Settlement of 1559. Elizabeth did retreat from her father's more presumptuous Erastianism: she did not seek to intervene personally in Church affairs to the degree or in the manner that her father had. She also had to contend with a Parliament that now exercised 'co-ordinate' status in such affairs.[22] Parliament was to continue to do so until 1919, when the Enabling Act restored a considerable measure of Church self-governance. Yet even today, the monarch formally retains 'supreme authority over all ecclesiastical causes'. Canon A7 of the Church's canon law continues to assert that the monarch 'has supreme authority over all persons in all causes, *as well ecclesiastical as civil*'.[23] The great theorist of this settlement, Richard Hooker, firmly upheld the principle, and no influential Anglican theologians challenged it until the nineteenth century.[24] The tainted legacy of the Church's subordination to the state has not yet been formally and completely cast off.

In apparent defence of the monarch's role as Supreme Governor (if not the sixteenth-century practice of it), Paul Avis invokes the traditional argument that it is a valid expression of the involvement of a 'lay person' in the governance of the Church. He sees this as in keeping with the Reformation principle of the 'universal priesthood of the baptized' (also suggesting that a church committed to this principle 'is likely to be a broad and tolerant church').[25] But below the surface of this claim is, again, the problematic assumption that in a Christian nation, spiritual and temporal authorities are simply two modes of a unified system of governance and that what we today call 'church membership' and 'citizenship' are, indeed, essentially co-terminous.[26] The implication of my argument in the previous chapter, however, is that the very concept of a 'lay' person is an ecclesial, not a political, status. Certainly there should be a role for lay governance within the Church, but that is entirely different from claiming that those who hold office in the state are entitled by virtue of *that* office to share in Church governance. The very concept of 'laity' is an ecclesiological term having no valid application in the state.[27]

Today, of course, the state's control over the Church's doctrine and liturgy and over much else has been drastically reduced and those areas transferred to General Synod. Yet the legacy of the Act of Supremacy remains the fundamental basis on which the state still exercises a residual (but non-trivial) degree of legal control over the Church. The sixteenth-century Acts of Supremacy conferred upon the state the right to deploy its legal powers to give coercive effect to decisions on doctrine, liturgy, church order and clerical appointment that fall squarely within the 'spiritual' life of the Church. Such matters concern the way in which the Church fulfils its definitive task of defining and proclaiming the central tenets of the Christian faith and ordering its life in accordance with them. The Church of England was thus legally born from an intrusive assertion of state power over 'ecclesiastical causes' that fall within the Church's unique 'spiritual jurisdiction'.[28] In stark contrast, Article IV of the Scottish Articles rightly asserts that the church has 'right and power *subject to no civil authority* to legislate, and to adjudicate finally, in all matters of doctrine, worship, government, and discipline in the Church', and denies to civil authority 'any right of interference with the proceedings or judgments of the Church within the sphere of its spiritual government and jurisdiction'.[29]

In the light of this history, the first step towards disestablishment should be for the Church finally to renounce all traces – even symbolic ones – of the Erastianism underlying the Act of Supremacy and its associated statutes and embrace the thrust of the jurisdictional theology captured in the Scottish Article IV. The Church should acknowledge, if only to itself, that the Tudor settlement involved a grotesque intrusion by the state into the Church's spiritual jurisdiction – that its legal foundation was birthed from what without exaggeration can be called a jurisdictional heresy. The point is not to issue retrospective historical blame but to make unambiguously clear where the Church stands today. Having attained such theological clarity in its own mind, it must then take the necessary steps to neutralize any legal implications following from Royal Supremacy that remain in force. The most immediate would be the ending of the monarch's role as Supreme Governor.[30]

She doth protest too much

Royal Supremacy is inseparably linked to the obligation that the monarch be 'in communion with' the Church of England, as stipulated in the Act of Settlement of 1701.[31] This does not require the monarch to be a member of the Church of England but does require that he or she be Protestant. Historically, the reason for insisting on Protestant succession in 1701 was to prevent the accession of another Roman Catholic monarch, an occurrence that had precipitated serious political conflict in the period leading up to the Glorious Revolution of 1688.[32] That rationale, obviously, no longer has any traction today, but the principle of Protestant succession remains straightforwardly discriminatory. The requirement that the monarch be 'in communion' with the Church of England continues to exclude Roman Catholics because the Roman Catholic Church does not regard itself as 'in communion with' the Church of England. In response to the complaint of discrimination, defenders of Establishment place the onus on the Roman Catholic Church to change its own stance towards communion with the Church of England. But they must know that, for conscientiously held doctrinal reasons (notably, the view that Anglican orders are 'invalid'), there is no prospect of the Catholic Church doing so any time soon. Senior Roman Catholics understandably continue to express discontent with this case of 'symbolic exclusion'.[33] In 1999, the Scottish Parliament backed a resolution calling for an end to the discrimination involved in Protestant succession.[34]

An element of religious inequality is, then, entrenched at the peak of the British constitution. How important this is, in a state which in every other important respect is committed to upholding religious equality, is a matter of judgement. Some might argue that this is a small price to pay for the benefits of a continuing bond between Crown and Church. Whether or not that is the case, I do not argue against Protestant succession on the grounds that it might depart from principles of legal equality governing the rights of individual citizens.[35] For the institution of hereditary monarchy is itself in tension with those principles (an issue that would require a discussion beyond the scope of this book).[36] Instead, I argue against it because it exceeds the proper jurisdiction of the state. If it is in principle illegitimate for the state to express an official preference for a particular faith or denomination, then Protestant succession is, and always was, inherently unjustifiable (however historically explicable in its time).

In 2013, the requirement that heirs to the throne could not *marry* a Roman Catholic was abolished.[37] But Protestant succession itself should be terminated.[38] The effect of this, combined with that of ending Royal Supremacy, would indeed be momentous. The Crown would no longer enjoy any special constitutional relationship with England's historically dominant Church.[39] Any continuing relationship between it and the Church of England would henceforth be a *voluntary* one – which is not the same as a *private* one.

Some would lament these moves as a 'secularization' of the monarchy. But they would be so only in the specific sense of being a step closer to the principle of state religious impartiality, not in the sense that the occupants of the institution would have to suppress their faith in public or take distance from the Church of England or the Christian faith. There is no reason why a monarch would be prevented from maintaining a close relationship to the Church. The Church could continue to welcome the monarch and other royals as members, if they wished, offering them whatever spiritual support and ministry they sought. The Church could also still preside at functions such as royal weddings, baptisms and funerals – *if requested*. It might do so on an ecumenical basis. But a disestablished Church could then, if it wished (and if it could muster the courage), *set the terms of such occasions itself* rather than being obliged to fulfil a suite of possibly confining and burdensome expectations set by the state.[40]

Others would lament such steps as threatening the very foundation of the monarchy. Breaking the historic link between state and (a Protestant) Church would, they might warn, put the monarchy itself in jeopardy.[41] Avis, for example, worries that detaching monarchy from Church would pose the question of what the constitutional rationale of monarchy would be.[42] In the same vein, Ian Leigh claims that, 'In Britain, a hereditary monarch without an Established Church is inexplicable: the two stand or fall together in terms of historical rationale.' His specific concern is that the 'Windsor family enjoy their current position solely because their ancestors provided a guarantee of a Protestant succession to the throne.'[43] Severed from the Church they are pledged to protect, the Windsor's right of succession is placed in doubt.

Such anxieties betray an English insularity that besets many defenders of Establishment. As we know from many other well-functioning constitutional monarchies, there are perfectly adequate and straightforward answers to the question of what the rationale of a monarchy might be. For example, a monarch can serve as ceremonial head of state in a political community formally committed to upholding law, justice, liberty and the common good, but without exercising any authority over the

Church or standing in any special relationship to a church. An ancient rationale meaningless to the great majority of citizens can and should be replaced by a contemporary one that stands a chance of eliciting public legitimacy. Among other things, it would serve as an excellent topic for citizenship education in schools, creating an opportunity for students to reflect on the purposes of the political order they were to live under and the diverse philosophical or religious groundings that different citizens might propose for it. Disestablishment would leave the British monarchy in England in essentially the same position it currently occupies in Wales, which seems quite content to enjoy its own prince exercising no formal role in the Church in Wales. There is no evidence that the rationale for the monarchy is in doubt in that nation.

Interestingly, notwithstanding his staunch defence of monarchy, Ian Bradley is open to abandoning both Protestant succession and the Supreme Governorship, and to an ecumenical and multi-faith coronation (along the lines of the service marking the opening of the Welsh Assembly in Llandaff Cathedral in 1999).[44] Yet he urges that the sacred character of monarchy be preserved:

> monarchy has a key role to play in the recovery of the metaphysical imagination and the revaluing of religion in contemporary Britain. As an essentially spiritual and sacred institution, it is particularly well placed to lead the resacralisation of our secular society, to heal the land and to promote spiritual values, quite apart from its other perhaps more widely acknowledged roles in promoting integration, stability, order and community at a time of fragmentation and dislocation.[45]

I am sceptical of monarchy's empirical capacity to contribute to the spiritual goals named here, irrespective of the personal virtues of the officeholders. But, again, my central argument is that it is in principle illegitimate for any organ of state to aspire to exercise such a national spiritual leadership role, even if only by means of symbolic power. And, as noted, constitutional monarchies without close ties to a church seem just as able to contribute to political goals, such as national integration and stability, as Britain's.

Crowning success?

The Church plays a central role in the coronation of a new monarch, which traditionally takes place in Westminster Abbey in a service at which the new monarch receives communion and takes a religious oath.[46] Malcolm Brown defends the practice as 'not just a bit of invented pomp' but 'a solemn religious rite in which the Church of England, in its priestly role representing God who was incarnate on earth in Christ, confers upon the monarch her temporal and spiritual authority'.[47] Bradley soars even higher:

> The monarch is offered to the people, and to God, and dedicated to a life of selfless service and duty. [Coronations] also involve a hallowing and consecration, a dedication to God of an individual and a nation, a setting apart and an invocation of divine blessing. They express particularly vividly the difficult and unfashionable Christian themes of vocation, discipleship and obedience. In the absence of a written constitution in the United Kingdom, coronations have also proclaimed the basis on which our government rests and our laws are cast ... If we lose them, or if we strip away too much of their symbolism and mystery, we take away much of the sacred significance of the Crown and we also lose a key moment of consecration and rededication in the religious life of the nation.[48]

The practice of sacral coronation was established in the Middle Ages and continued after the Reformation.[49] Under the Coronation Oath Act of 1688, the Archbishop of Canterbury (or another bishop) is required to administer the Coronation Oath. This was revised in 1953 to include three pledges: to govern according to the law of the land(s);[50] to 'cause Law and

Justice, in Mercy, to be executed in all your judgements'; and to 'maintain the Laws of God and the true profession of the Gospel'. The third pledge secures Protestant succession. It is elaborated as the obligation to 'maintain in the United Kingdom the Protestant Reformed Religion established by law ... and to maintain ... the settlement of the Church of England, and the doctrine, worship, discipline, and government thereof, as by law established in England'. In addition, the monarch takes the Accession Oath, either at the Coronation or at the first State Opening of Parliament after coronation. The oath is determined by the Accession Declaration Act of 1910 and also consists of a pledge to maintain Protestant succession.[51]

The same objection arises here as against other features of Establishment. For a head of state to pledge either to maintain a particular church denomination, or to defend the 'true profession of the Gospel', or even to uphold 'the law of God', breaches the principle of state religious impartiality. For any state organ to endorse one such religion as the nation's officially preferred faith (or religion generally) exceeds the boundaries of its authority.

The pledge to uphold Reformed Protestantism in England (and Scotland) and to maintain the 'doctrine, worship, discipline and government' of the Church of England would, unamended, generate deep unease ahead of the next coronation. The 1953 wording will not survive scrutiny, but any proposal as to what should replace it would not be disclosed while the Queen is still alive. We can only assume that serious conversations are already taking place in private about what it might be.[52] It will surely be advantageous if, when the time comes, these are opened up to public consultation. Prince Charles himself has entertained the idea that, given the religiously plural nature of British society today, he would wish to be a 'defender of faith' rather than 'Defender of the Faith'.[53] Although the latter title is not linked to the Coronation Oath,[54] the same sentiment will surely influence discussions about how the oath he will take should be revised.[55]

A spirited defence of a Christian, indeed predominantly

Anglican, coronation service has been offered by Nick Spencer and Nicholas Dixon. On the basis of compelling survey evidence, they argue that such a service still commands majority public support and that it could be amended in order to make it more modern, more meaningful and more inclusive.[56] However, they ignore the fundamental question of the theological and constitutional justification of such an event, appearing to assume its legitimacy on the basis of its longevity. But my argument that the coronation breaches the principle of state impartiality would still hold irrespective of what public opinion thinks (although, admittedly, it would not gain much political headway in the face of strong public opposition).

Some defenders of current arrangements would lament the loss of any reference to a 'transcendent' source of political authority if the ceremony were 'secularized'. They would claim that it would remove a sense of accountability to a higher power or source of meaning, eliminating a vital limit on state hubris. The claim is sometimes made of Establishment generally, although the coronation is thought to be the moment at which its potency is most poignantly revealed. Adrian Hastings, for example, asserts that Establishment has the effect of 'symbolically limiting the sovereign of the secular state by publicly recognising the principle of "God's servant first"'. Establishment 'functions [today] ... as the servant of a healthy dualism, a system in which religion is accepted as not being finally subject to state authority but bearer of a kind of independent sovereignty which merits public recognition'.[57] Brown goes further in claiming that 'the source of ultimate authority will remain problematic unless we build in some concept of God. If power is conferred by a human authority, it can become manipulated or taken away by human authority.'[58] We therefore need an Established Church 'bound into the structures of the State – not subservient to them, but cognizant of its role at the apex of the symbolism of authority, but at the base of the pyramid of power'.[59]

The 'transcendent source' claim in fact turns out to be one of a larger class of arguments often mounted in defence of Establishment in general. The argument is that where a monarchy is linked to a church, the political order is able to sustain higher, deeper and perhaps more fragile values, which are not adequately represented in other parts of the system.[60] Thus Martyn Percy writes: 'monarchy may be said to "represent" metaphysical values in society that partly guarantee the rights and freedoms of individuals and communities' and can 'embody civic virtues such as voluntarism and charity'.[61] He asserts that 'the presence of an established religion within a reticulate and complex ecology of establishment ensures that questions of value, ethics and justice can be raised within the midst of the governance of Parliament, and in the very heart of a consumerist society.'[62] Thus, 'The role of a national, established Church may therefore be primarily sacrificial and sacramental in character.'[63] In the same vein, William Fittall claims:

> On the basis of the experience of recent decades, there is a good case for claiming that a reformed, constitutional monarchy, together with a tolerant and hospitable Establishment of the Church of England, has helped to make this country a more tolerant and inclusive society than many where more secular principles have long been entrenched at the heart of the State.[64]

There are two responses to this cluster of claims. First, on my argument, ending a sacral coronation is a mandate of a proper theology of the limits of the state; it is itself a Christian demand. Fittall worries that if the monarch no longer symbolically receives authority at the hands of an Archbishop, 'we would have become a different sort of society'.[65] Probably most of *society* would not notice the difference at all. But we would indeed have acquired a different sort of *constitution*, one that more consistently upheld the principle of the religious impartiality of the state. From my perspective, this would make it *more Christian*. As David Fergusson puts it:

[T]he notion that the office and person of the monarch in some special way mediate the presence of God is more akin to the panegyric of Eusebius than to the desacralised concept of kingship that one finds in the Old Testament and in Jesus' encounter with Pilate ... Although the Queen displays publicly a strong sense of Christian vocation, the future of the monarchy is not well served by inflating its metaphysical significance.[66]

Second, as far as I can tell, neither a sacral coronation nor any other element of Establishment have in fact contributed to respect for the transcendent values or virtuous practices celebrated by the voices quoted above, either in the state or in wider society. If the claim is to amount to more than a piece of self-congratulatory poetry or a self-deluding myth, some evidence for it surely needs to be adduced. That evidence would need to show that societies like ours with established churches (or other ways of officially recognizing a faith) have, other things being equal, performed better than those without them (those against whom Fittall compares us favourably). Possible comparators might be historically Christian, and now liberal democratic, countries such as Germany or the Netherlands. Would anyone be bold enough to suggest that England would come out ahead of countries like these in any such comparison? Yet we need not even leave the borders of the UK to make the point. As Peter Cornwell puts it, supporters of Establishment:

point to somewhat elusive streams of healing which are alleged to pass into the life of the nation through the ties between church and state. A mysterious 'X' is added to the quality of the national life, of which countries labouring under the disability of disestablishment are deprived. It is all very difficult to grasp. Are the moral standards of the English manifestly better than those of the Welsh?[67]

It is true that one occasionally hears periodic echoes of deference to such higher values and virtues from the British political
classes. They often surface, reassuringly, in the Queen's Christ-
mas messages or other public speeches. But it is deeds not
words by which such claims must be assessed.

So is credible evidence to be found of any aspect of high
establishment having actually served, for example, to curtail
successive British *government's* readiness to introduce unjust
policies, practice intolerance, promote consumerism, despoil
the environment or circumvent the rule of law? To the extent
that governments have refrained from doing so, surely it is
overwhelmingly because of the combined power of public
values working their way through the system, courageous
political leadership, democratic mobilization and constitutional restraints. On that claim quite a lot of possible evidence
could be adduced.

Nor is there any credible evidence that the values or virtues
that are supposedly promoted by Establishment have shaped
society's behaviour in any tangible way. Let me take one possible example from many: the pervasive racism that continued
to be experienced by many immigrants from the Caribbean,
and then the Indian subcontinent, *in the period following the
Christian coronation of 1953.* That event was no doubt a
moment of considerable national significance.[68] But whatever
uplifting and unifying impact it may have had for many, it
seems not to have done much to ensure that racial tolerance
governed either state or popular attitudes towards such immigrants (though the Queen herself has set a fine example, not
least as Head of the Commonwealth, as have other members
of the royal family).[69] Indeed the Church of England was itself
culpable in its failure to welcome many Anglican immigrants
of that generation into its churches, and to speak out against
racism in society and government.[70] It took widespread cultural change – to which the Church did eventually contribute
– backed by legislation such as the Race Relations Act 1965, to
begin to counter such racism. We do well to recall Cornwell's
warning about the dangers of clinging to myths about the

moral efficacy of Establishment when they have lost all contact with the real world: 'we are left, not simply with harmless and amusing ornaments but mischievous purveyors of nostalgia which inhibit us from coming to terms with reality ... [Such] symbols frankly encourage delusion, and delusion is always a barrier to spiritual advance.'[71]

I have been scrutinizing the claims of those who defend a sacral coronation, or Establishment generally, in virtue of their supposed capacity to remind state and society of the import-ance of 'transcendent' values and wholesome virtues. I have found their claims implausible. Let me return now to the specific issue of coronation.

What form might a post-Establishment installation of a monarch take? My own proposal would be for a ceremony of civil investiture to take place in a venue such as Westminster Hall, presided over, perhaps, by the President of the Supreme Court.[72] This would send the signal that the head of state's authority should be construed as deriving from the constitu-tion and exercised alongside, and balanced by, other organs of state.[73] The content of the ceremony could be shaped by a suit-ably august body of advisors – constitutional lawyers, political philosophers and religious leaders, informed by the (perhaps less predictable) findings of a 'People's Assembly'. It should be endorsed by Parliament.[74] In such a civil ceremony, monarchs would pledge allegiance to the constitution and laws of the land, commit themselves to advise governments in the ways of justice and the common good, displaying special concern for the poor and marginalized and respecting the plural cultural, ethnic and religious traditions of the people.

It could, perhaps, take inspiration from the following hypo-thetical Article I of a new Scottish constitution, proposed by the Church of Scotland theologian Doug Gay:

• This constitution, without compromise to equality under the law or to the rightful jurisdiction of the law, recognizes that Scotland's people acknowledge different sources of law, right, truth and goodness, to which they believe our positive laws, including the constitution, are both accountable and subordinate, even when enacted by due democratic process.

- This constitution recognizes the value and wisdom of the Christian tradition and its long influence upon Scotland. In particular, it acknowledges the belief of many of Scotland's people that the state is accountable to God, from whom its power and authority derives.[75]
- It recognizes also the value and wisdom of other religious traditions and of secular, humanistic worldviews and the differing accounts they may give of the ultimate sources of law and the good.
- This constitution establishes neither religion nor secularism, but acknowledges their varied traditions of thought and belief, welcoming the insights and wisdom they may bring to democratic deliberation and to the civic and ceremonial life of the nation.
- This constitution expresses the democratic consensus of the people of Scotland on basic laws and fundamental rights.[76]

I would also invite those inclined to lament the ending of a sacral coronation to contemplate a radical new possibility opened up by it. The Church could invite a new monarch (Anglican or not, indeed Christian or not) to a 'service of blessing and exhortation' in, say, St Paul's Cathedral, before or after a civil investiture.[77] Such a service could, if the monarch were Christian, include sentiments from the current Accession Oath cited above, such as to 'cause Law and Justice, in Mercy, to be executed in all your judgements'; and to 'witness to [rather than 'maintain'] the Laws of God and the true profession of the Gospel'.

Under such an arrangement, the Church would be able to shape the terms of the event itself, instead of offering ceremonial embellishment for a service the content of which is heavily determined by the expectations of a secular-minded state.[78] A Roman Catholic monarch might, of course, turn for such personal succour to Westminster Cathedral; a Methodist to Methodist Central Hall; a Welsh Anglican to St David's Cathedral; a Scottish Presbyterian to St Giles' Cathedral;

or (follow the logic) a Pentecostal to Kensington Temple. Whatever the location, prayers would be offered for the new monarch for the faithful discharge of their duties and exhortations made to him or her to work for the justice, peace and flourishing of the nation. Government ministers might also be invited, although they should not count on having all the front seats reserved for them. Seating them further back (with appropriate security) would send the right signal that they, too, need to learn humility in their political roles. A stirring sermon on what biblical prophets thought about unjust rulers might be given by a prominent preacher. Participants might even pledge allegiance to the monarch, conditional on him or her fulfilling the commitments they had just made. Even more radically, the Christian churches might jointly offer such a service on an ecumenical basis. Imagine the powerful reconciling symbolism of a Roman Catholic cardinal, the President of the Baptist Union, and others, offering prayers for divine wisdom and courage over a kneeling British monarch in St Paul's Cathedral or Westminster Central Hall. All of this could be 'public' but none of it would be 'official'.

Some might worry that a voluntary, non-official event would attract less national attention than an official ceremony. I think the BBC would remain keen to cover such an occasion. It might even show up at Kensington Temple – indeed such a location might even boost its ratings (even if initially discomfiting its royal correspondents). Whatever the option chosen, the sheer novelty of a voluntary request by a new monarch for the prayers of the English (or British) church(es) would offer a marvellous opportunity to the Church to engage in just the kind of 'public explanation' of its social mission I am calling for in this book.

Two further matters need brief mention. First, I suggested St Paul's Cathedral as a possible location for a voluntary service of post-investiture blessing (for an Anglican monarch), in case access to Westminster Abbey had become complicated. This could depend on the outcome of negotiations on the jurisdiction of the Abbey as a 'royal peculiar'. Given that the Abbey has for centuries functioned as a kind of national religious site, it is not inconceivable that the government of the day might advise the Crown to insist on retaining immediate jurisdiction over it following disestablishment.[79] Unfortunately, I fear there would be an ample supply of clergy willing to staff it, if their bishops would give them permission (under such circumstances, I hope they would not). In the event of the loss of control over the Abbey, however, St Paul's Cathedral would be a tolerable fall-back.

Second, I have been assuming so far that the royal family would continue to adhere to Christianity. But if a new monarch had converted to another faith, there is no reason on my argument why they should not voluntarily seek spiritual succour at a different place of worship – say, London Central Mosque, or Shri Swaminarayan Hindu Temple in Neasden. Traditionalists might wince at the prospect, but they might reflect on whether they have a principled argument against such a possibility, as distinct from a visceral aversion. The same principle would also apply if, in some distant future, the monarchy was replaced by a republic with an appointed head of state who was an adherent to another faith – perhaps a figure of the stature of a Jonathan Sacks, a Sayeeda Warsi or an Umesh Chander Sharma (Co-Chair of the Hindu Council UK)?[80]

Hiring and firing

Formally, the Crown retains the authority to appoint the two archbishops, 43 diocesan bishops and 68 suffragans, 28 cathedral deans, 30 residentiary canons and the 6 Church Estates Commissioners. It also has a role (shared with the Lord Chancellor and the Duchy of Lancaster) in the appointment of nearly 700 parish incumbents. This is formally done on the advice of the government, chiefly the Prime Minister. I consider only the case of diocesan bishops, since whatever jurisdictional principles apply to them would also apply lower down the hierarchy.[81] The Crown's authority to appoint bishops predates the Act of Supremacy 1534, originating in the Appointment of Bishops Act of 1533 and the Suffragan Bishops Act of 1534, but it expresses the same principle.

Deference to Royal Supremacy is symbolized by the fact that appointed bishops are still required to make an act of homage to the sovereign at a ceremony attended by a cabinet minister. That symbolic remnant of ecclesial obsequiousness should, of course, end. But it is the Crown's role, via the Prime Minister's office, in the process of appointment that is more serious. After centuries in which the Prime Minister led the process of selection, important changes were introduced in 1976, shifting the balance of power decisively in favour of the Church. Today the selection process for diocesan bishops starts in the diocesan Vacancy in See Committee which reports to the Church's Crown Nominations Commission (formerly Crown Appointments Commission [CAC]), which until recently submitted two names to the Prime Minister, ranked in order of preference.[82] The Church always hoped that the first name would be chosen, but there was no requirement on the Prime Minister to do so, and it is widely assumed that in a few cases that did not happen. For example, it is reliably reported that in 1998 Tony Blair rejected both names proposed for the see of Liverpool by the CAC, after which James Jones was appointed.[83]

A recurring official justification of why the state should play a role in the appointment of bishops has been that, since diocesan bishops might later find their way into the House of Lords, without a prime ministerial role appointments would be made to the House of Lords by a body outside the state.[84] Another, endorsed by the Church itself, is that since bishops perform an important civic and not only a religious function in their dioceses, it is important they have the trust of civic authorities. This, so the argument goes, is enhanced by a governmental role in the appointment. Note, however, that this amounts to an admission that the Church cannot trust itself to make its most senior appointments without a constitutional obligation to seek outside advice. Perhaps the most surprising argument from the side of the Church was voiced by the Archdeacon of Pontefract during a General Synod debate against Colin Buchanan's proposal to abolish the state's role: 'what makes us think that the Prime Minister, Downing Street or the monarch are any less open to the Spirit of God than this Synod or our Church?'[85] One certainly cannot rule out that such bodies might be vehicles of the Spirit, but it might be thought preferable generally to rely on the body specifically instituted by God for the purpose, namely the Church. Or, as Buchanan put the point more brutally during the debate over a successor to Archbishop George Carey in 2003:

> it is screamingly inappropriate for the political leader who emerges by vote from the governing party in the House of Commons to have thereby the power to make or to block the candidates for leadership in the Church of England ... The manoeuvrings in the current archiepiscopal vacancy have highlighted the sorry state of our episcopal appointments procedures.[86]

The Church's Van Straubenzee Working Party had issued a proposal in 1992 to eliminate the Prime Minister's role in Church appointments, while retaining the Crown's, but this was not acted upon.[87] However in 2007, Gordon Brown surprised the Church by unilaterally relinquishing any active personal role for the Prime Minister in all senior Church appointments.[88] Whether Brown no longer considered the concern about the House of Lords valid or had simply overlooked it is not clear. Perhaps, as a Presbyterian, he had imbibed the spirit of the Articles Declaratory. In June 2021, some claimed that even the remaining 'messenger boy' role left to Number 10 may need to be temporarily transferred (to, for example, the Lord Chancellor) if Boris Johnson's marriage in a Roman Catholic church counted as him 'professing the Catholic religion', rendering him formally ineligible to advise the monarch on such a matter.[89] The point is disputed (previous Prime Ministers have included a dissenter, David Lloyd-George, and a Unitarian, Neville Chamberlain, without generating concern on the matter).

The 2007 change and the flurry of concern over Boris Johnson's eligibility only serve to press more acutely the long-standing question whether the existing machinery of Crown involvement in appointing bishops now has any real point. Robert Morris predicts that the position of the Crown Appointments Advisor will atrophy anyway: 'the active link with the executive will disappear ... [I]n reality it is difficult to see how such an officer could play anything other than an increasingly redundant walk-on part as a paper shifter for a post-box Prime Minister.'[90] But it appears that *the Church* seemed more anxious that a state-appointed official be retained in the process than did the government. In 2007, the Church reaffirmed that someone appointed by the Crown should continue to play an advisory role in the appointment process, in order that 'the wider "public voice" was heard'.[91] As Morris notes, the person was 'billed as bringing some consciousness of and experience from the world outside the Church of England'.[92] But why did the Church feel the need to turn to the state for such advice? Did it not already know enough people with experience outside the Church – in touch with the 'wider public voice' – on whom it could call? Might it perhaps have found such streetwise people even among its very own national and diocesan *houses of laity*? Equally, since nothing would prevent a disestablished Church from continuing to seek advice from any quarter it wished, why cling on to a legally imposed formality of doing so?

The material effect of the state's power of appointment over senior Anglican clergy has been steadily diminishing since 1976, and the 2007 change further confirmed that trend. The shift brings the Church of England a step closer to the jurisdictional model of Article IV of the Scottish Articles, which asserts the Church's inherent 'right to determine all questions concerning membership and office in the Church'. But the fact that the ceremonial and procedural veneer lingers on in England, however, is a standing reminder of the Church's historic deference to the state in appointing its most senior pastors. Oliver O'Donovan rightly points out that the Crown's power of *making appointments* to such posts does not include the power to *determine the criteria of appointment* or to *select qualified candidates* for them.[93] He registers no objection to the Crown's role in the former. But a church's choice of its highest leadership is one of the most influential decisions it can make in setting its own spiritual course, and the state should not play even a residual formal role in such decisions. Looking back, it is astonishing how long the Church has been prepared meekly to tolerate – even to covet – a role for the state in these momentous decisions. Even though it has now secured decisive influence over the process, it would nevertheless send an important signal to the state if it took the initiative in finally terminating the latter's remaining role and bringing the matter formally and completely under its own roof.

Conclusion

This chapter has argued that the 'higher architecture' governing the constitutional links between Church, Crown and government must be radically reset. The Crown must be formally divorced from the Church, involving an end to the role of the monarch as Supreme Governor of the Church and thus any role for state officials in the Church's senior (or junior) appointments, and the abolition of a sacral coronation and its replacement by a ceremony of civil investiture. Changes to the accession ceremony would also be required. The myth of 'lay governance' of the Church by representatives of bodies outside it must be finally put to rest. In addition, Protestant succession should be brought to an end. In the Conclusion to the book, I suggest some of the principal legal or other changes these reforms might require. They would be complex and time-consuming. It is crucially important, then, that if the Church is to go down that route it must first get clear in its own mind what its theology of church and state is. The Articles Declaratory can guide it in that process, even if the final shape of its new settlement with the British state is other than that of the

Church of Scotland. To create the psychological and spiritual space for new thinking, the Church must, as Valerie Pitt puts it, finally be 'rid of the hallowed myth about the Crown, our Nation and the Church' that still cramps its imagination.

Notes

1 Valerie Pitt, 'The Protection of Faith?', in Tariq Modood, ed., *Church, State and Religious Minorities* (London: Policy Studies Institute, 1997), p. 36.

2 For an overview of the historical transitions from 'confessional uniformity' to 'establishment' to 'secularism', see Julian Rivers, *The Law of Organized Religions: Between Establishment and Secularism* (Oxford: Oxford University Press, 2010), chs 1, 11.

3 The categories overlap because the British state is not modelled on a strict 'separation of powers' like the USA. For example, the government is drawn from Parliament; the monarchy is understood as the 'Crown in Parliament'; and until 2009 the nation's highest court was located in the legislature.

4 Constitutional writers sometimes distinguish 'state' from 'Crown' but nothing hinges on this for my argument. I will treat the Crown as an organ of state, even though it only wields 'executive' power via the government.

5 For an overview and defence of current links between Crown and Church, see Ian Leigh, 'By Law Established? The Crown, Constitutional Reform and the Church of England', *Public Law* (Summer 2004), pp. 266–73.

6 The Act declared him 'Supreme Head' of the Church. Repealed by Catholic Queen Mary I, the Act was replaced under Elizabeth I by the second Act of Supremacy 1559, which designated the monarch 'Supreme Governor'. Extinguished under Cromwell, it was again restored in 1660.

7 In the Edict of Thessalonica of 380, issued by Theodosius I, Valentinus II and Gratian. Constantine had only introduced a policy of general religious toleration within the empire, declared in the Edict of Milan of 313 (enacted with his eastern counterpart Licinius).

8 'Notes on Church and State: A Mapping Exercise', in R. M. Morris, ed., *Church and State: Some Reflections on Church Establishment in England* (London: UCL Constitution Unit, 2008), p. 9.

9 Rivers, *Law of Organized Religions*, p. 323.

10 'The Church of England and the State: Changing Constitutional

Links in Historical Perspective', in George Moyser, ed., *Church and Politics Today: The Role of the Church of England in Contemporary Politics* (Edinburgh: T&T Clark, 1985), p. 42.

11 That status steadily declined from the seventeenth to the twentieth centuries as religious toleration widened and religious pluralism expanded. As Rivers puts it, what occurred was 'a slow transition from the maintenance of one true religion to the principle that there is, in law, no false religion ... [Around] the middle decades of the nineteenth century, English law underwent a fundamental reversal of orientation. Rather than assuming that all religion was unlawful except for that of the established church and other "sects" expressly tolerated by Act of Parliament, the underlying assumption became that all religion was lawful unless it breached some specific prohibition' (*Law of Organized Religions*, p. 24).

12 He goes on: and 'that idolatry, sacrileges against the name of God, blasphemies against his truth, and other offenses against religion may not openly appear and be disseminated among the people ... in short, that there may be a public form of religion among Christians, and that humanity may be maintained among them' (Calvin, *On God and Political Duty*, ed. John T. McNeill (Indianapolis, NY: The Bobbs-Merrill Company, 1956), p. 47).

13 A. G. Dickens, *The English Reformation* (London: Fontana, 1967), chs 5, 6. The parallel French struggle against papal authority went under the name of 'Gallicanism'. See Emile Perreau-Saussine, *Catholicism and Democracy: An Essay in the History of Political Thought* (Princeton, NJ: Princeton University Press, 2012).

14 *Practice of Prelates* (1530), quoted in Joan Lockwood O'Donovan, *Theology of Law and Authority in the English Reformation* (Atlanta, GA: Scholars Press, 1991), p. 58.

15 Paul Avis notes, without criticism, that Royal Supremacy was constructed 'for national self-defence', against the papacy (*Church, State and Establishment* (London: SPCK, 2001), p. 23).

16 On the intellectual background to English Erastianism, see Lockwood O'Donovan, *Theology of Law and Authority*. She identifies Marsilius as its chief inspiration and Thomas Cromwell as its leading practitioner, observing that Henry VIII's efforts to dominate the church were part of a wider ambition of legal centralization, 'in which the legislative organ of the King in Parliament was absorbing the medieval liberties (e.g. of church, town corporation, and guild) and subordinating all other law to itself' (pp. 70–1).

17 *Law of Organized Religions*, p. 323.

18 The Henrician ones included: Supplication of the Commons Against the Ordinaries 1529, 1532; Act in Restraint of Appeals 1533;

Appointment of Bishops Act 1533; Suffragan Bishops Act 1534; Act for the Submission of the Clergy 1534; Act in Restraint of Annates 1534; Dispensations Act 1534. See Dickens, *English Reformation*, ch. 6. The Appointment of Bishops Act 1533 in fact largely codified the existing practice, which had been in place even before Magna Carta.

19 As Avis notes, the distinction was later expressed by the Anglican theologian William Van Mildert (1765–1836) as that between the 'power of order' (*potestas ordinis*) – 'that power which confers the capability of exercising spiritual functions' and which derives exclusively from Christ as mediated via the officers of the church – and 'the power of jurisdiction' (*potestas jurisdictionis*) – the power to 'appoint particular persons to exercise spiritual functions throughout the state' and which is possessed by civil government (*Church, State and Establishment*, p. 28). This is broadly in line with the Tudor jurisdictional distinction commended by Lockwood O'Donovan, discussed in Chapter 2.

20 The Act speaks of 'full power and authority from time to time to visit, repress, redress, record, order, correct, restrain, and amend all such errors, heresies, abuses, offenses, contempts and enormities, whatsoever they be, which by any manner of spiritual authority or jurisdiction ought or may lawfully be reformed, repressed, ordered, redressed, corrected, restrained, or amended, most to the pleasure of Almighty God, the increase of virtue in Christ's religion, and for the conservation of the peace, unity, and tranquillity of this realm'.

21 *English Reformation*, p. 412.

22 Dickens, *English Reformation*, pp. 412–13. He writes: 'No longer was the throne occupied by a crowned theologian, confounding Parliaments and bishops with God's learning; its occupant was an adroit and devious politician, operating through the interstices of Statute Law' (p. 413). See also Lockwood O'Donovan, *Theology of Law and Authority*, p. 112.

23 'Canons of the Church of England, Section A' (emphasis added), *The Church of England*, www.churchofengland.org/about/leadership-and-governance/legal-services/canons-church-england/section#b7, accessed 25.10.2021. Article 37 of the Thirty-Nine Articles of 1571 ('Of the Civil Magistrates') also affirms Royal Supremacy in declaring that 'The Queen's Majesty hath the chief power in this Realm of England, and other her Dominions, unto whom the chief Government of all Estates of this Realm, whether they be Ecclesiastical or Civil, in all causes doth appertain, and is not, nor ought to be, subject to any foreign Jurisdiction.'

24 See Avis's survey of Anglican theorists of church and state from the seventeenth to the twentieth centuries (*Church, State and Establish-*

ment, ch. 6). On Hooker, see Lockwood O'Donovan, *Theology of Law and Authority*, pp. 151–3.

25 Avis, *Church, State and Establishment*, p. 29. Avis does not mention that the evolving 'settlement' included a series of Acts of Uniformity (1549, 1552, 1559, 1662) imposing Anglican liturgy and doctrine throughout England and discriminating against Catholics and Puritans. These Acts undermine the view that the settlement was the fount of Anglican 'comprehensiveness'. Malcolm Brown, for example, rather implausibly claims that the Church of England performed the vocation of unifying the nation after the Reformation and again after the Civil War and that the ecclesiology created by the settlement 'embodied important Christian virtues of tolerance and remedies against hubris which have been a significant export to the whole Communion' ('Establishment: Some Theological Considerations', *Ecclesiastical Law Journal* 21 (2019), pp. 336–7).

26 This is explicit in Richard Hooker, *Of the Laws of Ecclesiastical Polity*, ed. Arthur Stephen McGrade (Cambridge: Cambridge University Press, 1989), p. 130. Luke Bretherton classes Hooker as an example of Anglican 'integralism', a position assuming a fusion of church and nation. He contrasts this with the 'comprehensive' view according to which the church, while not co-terminous with the nation, assumes a nationwide duty of care. He terms his own position 'consociational', a pluralist model influenced by J. N. Figgis (*Christ and the Common Life: Political Theology and the Renewal of Democracy* (Grand Rapids, MI: Eerdmans, 2019), pp. 181–6). My argument shares this commitment to pluralism while also affirming a national vocation for the Church.

27 In the New Testament, *laos* refers to the whole people of God, not only the non-ordained.

28 I do not suggest it was *theologically* born from state power. The work of English Reformation theologians such as Tyndale, Cranmer and Ridley was a substantial and independent source of Church reform and would likely have brought about some reforms of the Catholic Church even without Henrician Erastianism. On the political implications of English Reformed theology, see Lockwood O'Donovan, *Theology of Law and Authority*. She judges that the principal challenge facing such theologians during Henry's reign was 'to place the church's authority and discipline solidly on an evangelical footing' (p. 4); that is, to ensure that they were responsive not only to law but also to gospel. None fully succeeded. Cranmer, for example, fell far short. For him, 'neither God's law nor man's law provides an institutional restraint on the sovereign's legislating: his political will carries absolute authority, even when it contravenes the teaching of Scripture and the tradition of the realm. It is Cranmer's lamentable judgment that the divine author

of truth and righteousness continues to entrust their presence in the civil community to a single supreme arbitrator ... [This is] the Henrician face of Marsilius, which simply substitutes the plenary power of the Crown for that of the pope' (p. 90).

29 Emphasis added. The strictly limited role of the monarch in the proceedings of the Church of Scotland is summarized thus: 'The Sovereign is represented each year at the General Assembly by a Lord High Commissioner, who sits in a throne gallery overlooking the Assembly, but does not enter the Assembly itself. While the Sovereign has no role in the government of the Church, the Queen has personally attended General Assemblies in 1960, 1969 and 2002 and, when in residence at Balmoral Castle, she traditionally worships at Crathie Kirk' ('History', *The Church of Scotland*, https://churchofscotland.org.uk/about-us/our-structure/history, accessed 25.10.2021).

30 This would require, inter alia, consultation with some members of the Commonwealth, as provided for in the Statute of Westminster 1931. It is hard to imagine them mounting much resistance.

31 This confirmed the provision contained in the Coronation Oath Act 1688 and the 1689 Bill of Rights, and later reaffirmed in the Act of Union 1707. See Lucinda Maer, 'The Act of Settlement and the Protestant Succession' (London: House of Commons Library, 2011).

32 For an account of the history of Protestant succession, see Ian Bradley, *God Save the Queen: The Spiritual Dimension of Monarchy* (London: Darton, Longman and Todd, 2002), ch. 5.

33 Robert Morris, 'Half-Opening Cans of Worms: The Present State of "High" Establishment', *Law and Justice* 172 (2014), p. 13.

34 R. M. Morris, ed., *Church and State in 21st Century Britain: The Future of Church Establishment* (Basingstoke: Palgrave Macmillan, 2009), p. 38.

35 Arguably, it breaches the Human Rights Act 1998 by denying to anyone in line to the throne a basic religious freedom enjoyed by every British citizen.

36 My argument for disestablishment is neutral on hereditary monarchy. I would be content to live under an elected or appointed head of state in a British republic, even while acknowledging the emotional loss for some that an ending of the monarchy would entail. The German model appeals, in which the President is elected by the Bundestag and electors chosen by the regional parliaments. The Dutch or Spanish constitutional monarchies might also be worth emulating. But my opinion on this question is irrelevant to the argument at hand.

37 The Act also replaced male primogeniture with 'gender blind' primogeniture (Morris, 'Half-Opening').

38 Somewhat muting the force of this demand, Morris suggests

that the Supreme Governor role, given its complete dependence on ministerial advice, no longer threatens the Church of England and could be carried out without difficulty by a non-Anglican (*Church and State in 21st Century Britain*, pp. 201–2). But the 'symbolic exclusion' would still offend.

39 Ending Protestant succession would also belatedly send the signal that Britain has formally and finally repudiated the deep strain of anti-Catholicism that was profoundly formative of its modern national consciousness from the eighteenth until the twentieth centuries. See Bradley, *God Save the Queen*, pp. 111–15.

40 See, for example, Jonathan Chaplin, 'Religion, Royalty and the Media', *Guardian Cif Belief* (1 May 2011), www.theguardian. com/commentisfree/belief/2011/may/01/christianity-royal-wedding, accessed 25.10.2021.

41 Morris, *Church and State in 21st Century Britain*, pp. 197–202.

42 See also Wesley Carr, 'Crown and People: Reflections on the Spiritual Dimensions of Establishment', 16 September 2001, Jubilee Reflections at Westminster Abbey: A Series of Lectures on God, Church, Crown and State.

43 'By Law Established?', pp. 269–70.

44 *God Save the Queen*, pp. 194–8.

45 *God Save the Queen*, p. xix.

46 The Abbey is a 'royal peculiar', meaning a church exempt from the 'visitational jurisdiction' of the diocese in which it lies (normally that of the bishop, the 'Ordinary') and subject instead to the immediate jurisdiction of the monarch as 'Supreme Ordinary'. Others include St George's Chapel, Windsor and the Chapels Royal.

47 Brown, 'Establishment', p. 338. For an account of the complex choreography of coronations, see Wesley Carr, 'This Intimate Ritual: The Coronation Service', *Political Theology* 4.1 (2002), pp. 11–24.

48 Bradley, *God Save the Queen*, p. 93.

49 On the history of sacral coronations in Britain (and a detailed account of the 1953 coronation), see Bradley, *God Save the Queen*, ch. 4. Bradley alludes to the pagan origin of sacral coronations, arguing, however, that they have been substantively Christianized.

50 The plural reference here is to British Dominions and Colonies existing in 1953.

51 'I do solemnly and sincerely in the presence of God profess, testify and declare that I am a faithful Protestant, and that I will, according to the true intent of the enactments which secure the Protestant succession to the throne of my Realm, uphold and maintain the said enactments to the best of my powers according to law.' After accession, the monarch also takes an oath before the Privy Council to uphold Protestantism

in Scotland as prescribed in the Treaty of Union 1707. This is distinct from the Protestant Religion and Presbyterian Church Act 1707, securing the Reformed and Presbyterian polity of the Church of Scotland. The Act speaks of the Church of Scotland as 'by law established' (Doug Gay, *Honey from the Lion: Christianity and the Ethics of Nationalism* (London: SCM Press, 2013), pp. 170–3).

52 See Robert Hazell and Bob Morris, 'Swearing in the New King: Accession Declaration and Coronation Oaths' (London: UCL Constitution Unit, 2018), www.ucl.ac.uk/constitution-unit/sites/constitution_unit/files/180_swearing_in_the_new_king.pdf; Bob Morris, 'Inaugurating a New Reign: Planning for Accession and Coronation' (London: UCL Constitution Unit, 2018), www.ucl.ac.uk/constitution-unit/sites/constitution-unit/files/181_-_Inaugurating_a_New_Reign.pdf, accessed 25.10.2021.

53 He later clarified that he would retain the latter title while also protecting other faiths: www.princeofwales.gov.uk/will-prince-wales-be-defender-faith-or-defender-faith, accessed 25.10.2021. John Duddington has noted that the Latin term could equally be translated as 'defender of faith', but not 'defender of faiths' ('The Legal Basis of the Title "Defender of the Faith"', *Law and Justice* 156 (2006), p. 71). Thanks to Paul Barber for this reference.

54 It was conferred by the pope on Henry VIII prior to 1534 in gratitude for Henry's attack on Luther's doctrine. Thus, originally it meant defender of the Catholic faith.

55 Morris has suggested that the monarchy is instrumentalizing 'Anglican multifaithism' in order to shore up its own legitimacy ('Half-Opening', p. 22).

56 Nick Spencer and Nicholas Dixon, *Who Wants a Christian Coronation?* (London: Theos, 2015). They respond in part to the National Secular Society's legal challenge to the coronation rite on the grounds that it discriminates against the consciences of non-Christians, breaches their human rights and thus alienates them from a major, identity-forming national ceremony. Their survey evidence does seem to refute the claim that a Christian coronation would be experienced by most as alienating, but they seem untroubled by the fact that a minority would find it quite seriously so.

57 'The Case for Retaining the Establishment', in Modood, *Church, State and Religious Minorities*, p. 45.

58 'Establishment', p. 339. Similarly, Lockwood O'Donovan asserts that 'when public law dissociates itself from God's law in its Trinitarian fullness, it loses sight of its derivative, dependent and subordinate status in relation to the divinely ordained goods and rights of human moral community' ('The Liberal Legacy of English Church Establish-

ment: A Theological Contribution to the Legal Accommodation of Religious Plurality in Europe', *Journal of Law, Philosophy and Culture* 6.1 (2011), p. 44).

59 'Establishment', p. 339.

60 See, for example, Avis, *Church, State and Establishment*, pp. 30–2.

61 'Opportunity Knocks: Church, Nationhood and Establishment', in Mark Chapman, Judith Maltby and William Whyte, eds, *The Established Church: Past, Present and Future* (London: T&T Clark, 2011), p. 30.

62 'Opportunity Knocks', pp. 31–2.

63 'Opportunity Knocks', p. 32.

64 'Perspectives from within the Church of England', in Morris, *Church and State: Some Reflections*, p. 78. Tom Wright poses the question whether 'we want leaders and rulers who will pledge themselves, not to ideals of justice and mercy which come ultimately from God, but simply to whatever the people may want?' ('God and Caesar, Then and Now', Jubilee Reflections at Westminster Abbey: A Series of Lectures on God, Church, Crown and State, 22 April 2002, p. 10). But this is a tendentious way to pose such a question, as if the choice were either an explicitly religious state or one driven by mere populism.

65 'Perspectives from within the Church of England', p. 78.

66 *Church, State and Civil Society* (Cambridge: Cambridge University Press, 2004), p. 178.

67 *Church and Nation* (Oxford: Blackwell, 1983), p. 56.

68 Bradley alludes to a claim made in 1953 by two (left-wing) social scientists (Edward Shils and Michael Young) that the coronation 'was the ceremonial occasion for the affirmation of the moral values by which the society lives. It was an act of national communion' (quoted in *God Save the Queen*, p. 85). Evidence of reconciliation among estranged neighbours in the aftermath of the coronation was cited, and the claim made that the event had enabled people to endorse values such as generosity, charity, loyalty, justice, respect for authority and individual dignity (p. 86). Those claims strike me as speculative and based on at best selective evidence.

69 See Shridath Ramphal, 'The Queen and her Stand against Racism in the Commonwealth', *The Round Table: The Commonwealth Journal of International Affairs* 11.2 (2021), pp. 290–2.

70 See Kenneth Leech, 'The Church and Immigration and Race Relations Policy', in Moyser, *Church and Politics Today*, pp. 201–20.

71 *Church and Nation*, pp. 56–7.

72 Morris also calls for 'a more modest [ceremony] of public investiture or enthronement without sacramental ceremony' (*Church and State in 21st Century Britain*, p. 210). The Fabian Society pamphlet,

The Future of the Monarchy (London: Fabian Society, 2003), proposes a similar model.

73 This would indeed signal a significant shift in the traditional meaning of the 'Crown' within the larger constitutional order, but only such as to bring it into closer conformity with several other constitutional monarchies.

74 Doug Gay has described how another momentous civic event, the opening of the reconvened Scottish Parliament in May 1999, could still be profoundly meaningful even without being overtly religious. Gay, *Honey from the Lion*, pp. 110–14. It happened to take place in the Kirk's Assembly Hall because Holyrood had not yet been completed.

75 Note that this clause does not amount to the state itself confessing such a belief, only that it recognizes the importance of such a belief to some of its own people.

76 *Honey from the Lion*, pp. 185–6.

77 This possibility is also supported by the National Secular Society (*Rethinking Religion and Belief in Public Life: A Manifesto for Change* (London: NSS, 2016), p. 61).

78 Relatedly, Theo Hobson has some withering observations on the compromising position the Church found itself in arising from the wedding and subsequent divorce of Charles and Diana, and from Diana's funeral (*Against Establishment: An Anglican Polemic* (London: Darton, Longman and Todd, 2003), pp. 37–43).

79 Wesley Carr as cathedral Dean observed without apology that it is 'a shrine to national achievement and endeavour, with its monuments and tombs, its flags and windows' ('A Developing Establishment', *Theology* 102 (1999), p. 2). But by allowing it to become such a shrine, the Church has made it more vulnerable to a predatory state. The Dutch neo-Calvinist thinker Herman Dooyeweerd rightly claimed that the Abbey 'partly functions as a national museum', in which 'objects of an explicit political [nature] are placed in the church building where they do not belong, e.g. coats of arms, flags, standards, etc.' (*A New Critique of Theoretical Thought*, vol. 3 (Amsterdam: H. J. Paris/Philadelphia: Presbyterian and Reformed Publishing Company, 1953–58), p. 558).

80 In 2021, Sharma received the 'The Hubert Walter Award for Reconciliation and Inter-Faith Cooperation' from the Archbishop of Canterbury. I assume that if a new head of state had no religious faith they would find the official civic ceremony in Westminster Hall adequate.

81 I say 'lower down', but cathedral deans are often seen as peers of bishops. There is also the issue of the propriety of the patronage system, whereby extra-ecclesial bodies (such as confessional societies like Church Pastoral Aid Society, Oxbridge colleges, the Crown etc.)

have rights to nominate incumbents. I agree with the proposal in The Ecclesiastical Law Society's 'Working Party on "Disestablishment" Report' that patronage should be abolished entirely (George Spafford, Roger L. Brown and Ben Nichols, *Ecclesiastical Law Journal* 6 (2002), pp. 267–8). But whatever the Church decides on the future of patronage, there should be no role for any state agency.

82 For many years, the Prime Minister's Appointments Secretary (PMAS), a senior civil servant based in 10 Downing Street, advised the PM on such matters but now this role has been transferred to the Crown Appointments Adviser (CAA) based in the Cabinet Office.

83 Andrew Atherstone, 'Gospel Opportunity or Unbiblical Relic? The Established Church through Anglican Evangelical Eyes', in Chapman, Maltby and Whyte, *The Established Church*, p. 80 (citing Kenneth Medhurst, 'The Church of England: A Progress Report', *Parliamentary Affairs* 52 (April 1999), p. 285). Blair apparently preferred someone who would maintain former Bishop David Sheppard's social justice commitments in the city – a commendable instinct in itself. On this, see also Jason Loch, 'Tony Blair and the Bishopric of Liverpool', *A Venerable Puzzle* blog, https://venerablepuzzle.wordpress.com/2020/07/16/tony-blair-and-the-bishopric-of-liverpool/?fbclid=IwAR3FxlUJs32e-hTCVUdedCWtAhNZXnStPj6b65aGv_6hifHNPjoE2kK_gbs8, accessed 25.10.2021. On the likely politics behind Sheppard himself being passed over for both London and Canterbury, see Andrew Bradstock, *David Sheppard: Batting for the Poor. The Authorized Biography of the Celebrated Cricketer and Bishop* (London: SPCK, 2019), pp. 252–6.

84 Morris, *Church and State in 21st Century Britain*, p. 51.

85 Quoted in Atherstone, 'Gospel Opportunity', p. 89.

86 Quoted in Hobson, *Against Establishment*, p. 49.

87 Morris, *Church and State in 21st Century Britain*, p. 60.

88 *The Governance of Britain* (Government Paper Cm 7170), paras 57–66.

89 Section 18 of the Roman Catholic Relief Act 1829, as amended, says: 'It shall not be lawful for any person professing the Roman Catholic religion directly or indirectly to advise his Majesty, or any person or persons holding or exercising the office of guardians of the United Kingdom, or of regent of the United Kingdom, under whatever name, style, or title such office may be constituted, or the lord lieutenant of Ireland, touching or concerning the appointment to or disposal of any office or preferment in the Church of England, or in the Church of Scotland; and if any such person shall offend in the premises he shall, being thereof convicted by due course of law, be deemed guilty of a high

misdemeanour, and disabled for ever from holding any office, civil or military, under the Crown.'

90 *Church and State in 21st Century Britain*, p. 57.

91 Church of England, *Crown Appointments in the Church of England: A Consultation Paper from the Archbishops* (October 2007), para. 13. Oliver O'Donovan also defends the role of the Crown in terms of the value of 'sympathetic advice from outside the ecclesiastical structures' ('Establishment', submission to the Commission of Inquiry on Faith and Nation of the Evangelical Alliance (London: Evangelical Alliance, 2006), p. 20).

92 *Church and State in 21st Century Britain*, p. 57.

93 O'Donovan, 'Establishment', p. 17.

4

Deconstructing Establishment: Church and Parliament

It is not well known enough that the General Synod is a delegated body of Parliament. In respect of the law, it has similar
powers to a government department, and, when it wants to
change the law, it lays those changes ... before the Commons
... [W]hile the hierarchy of the Church grandstand their
political views to journalists, rather than speak about their
genuine concerns with elected politicians, MPs are now looking at the Church of England to make sure that it serves its
purpose to support communities across the country.
(Chris Loder MP)[1]

Introduction

Sentiments like those expressed by Chris Loder were often
made in Parliament a century ago at the time of the 'Prayer
Book Crisis', when Parliament twice vetoed the Church's
considered proposals for liturgical reform. MPs again briefly
flexed their muscles around the time of the transfer of substantial legislative power to General Synod in 1970. They did
so even as late as the 1990s and 2000s, when Parliament was
invited to approve the ordination of women as priests, and
then bishops. Many in the Church's leadership have probably
been quietly hoping that such attempts by Parliament to shape
the Church's internal decisions would die a natural death, as
parliamentarians, following declining public interest, lose the
will to involve themselves in the Church's affairs.

The statement above, however, is from September 2021. It appears in an article in *Church Times* titled 'Parliament is watching closely', in which Mr Loder reports on a marked increase of interest among Conservative MPs in the Church of England. He sees among them 'growing appreciation of the Established Church and the part it plays in society'. Parliament is 'the most Christian' it has been for some time: the 2019 election changed not only its political complexion but also its 'faith make-up'. A Church of England WhatsApp group apparently has 'dozens' of Conservative MPs; there are now theology graduates on the back benches, some going on pilgrimage together; and the Second Church Estates Commissioner now faces more 'Church Questions' than there is time to answer.

But Mr Loder also reports several mounting concerns among these MPs: the Church's overly restrictive lockdown policies; its lack of political neutrality; its loss of commitment to the parish as a focus of community and tradition; and the 'bloated woke bureaucracy' ruling it.[2] From the standpoint of the argument of this book, such opinions are legitimate for any member of the Church of England to hold (although I do not share them). And there is no reason why, when such members become MPs, they should relinquish them. As Church members, they remain free to voice such concerns via the normal channels of Church governance, such as General Synod or diocesan synods. Or they could, for example, join the 'Save the Parish' campaign. But Mr Loder is announcing that he and his parliamentary colleagues are poised to deploy their privileged constitutional platform in Parliament to try to influence the Church's internal affairs. He himself sponsored a Commons Early Day Motion seeking to annul General Synod's own legislation reforming the governance of the Church Commissioners.

In warning of MPs' willingness to deploy Parliament's authority over the Church in order to amend or overturn the Church's own plans or decisions, Mr Loder is doing nothing whatsoever constitutionally improper. General Synod is indeed a 'delegated body of Parliament', since it derives its authority from the Enabling Act 1919 (though it is a mistake to suggest that its powers are akin to those of a government department). The remote foundation of that Act is the Erastianism of the sixteenth-century English Reformation. The fact that since 1970, across the vast majority of its internal affairs, the Church now initiates its own decisions in General Synod is often cited as the reason why disestablishment is an unnecessary and pointless diversion. It is often suggested that, even without disestablishment, the Church is, like the Church of Scotland, already effectively 'national and free'. But the fact that Mr Loder and his colleagues retain the constitutional authority to issue thinly veiled threats to the Church in this way reminds us that the legacy of parliamentary control, although residual, is a burden that the Church's leadership – even those among them who might share Mr Loder's views – should no longer meekly tolerate.

Alongside the burden of parliamentary supervision, the Church also enjoys an important parliamentary privilege that is problematic in a different way: the presence of the 'Lords Spiritual'. This chapter shows how these two features of Establishment remain troublesome breaches of the principles of state religious impartiality and church autonomy.

Taking the Measure

The principal regulations governing the Church of England come in two forms: 'canons', that is, items of canon law, which still require formal Crown approval;[3] and 'Measures', which also require Royal Assent. Measures are a form of subordinate parliamentary legislation which, within their scope, 'have the force and effect of an Act of Parliament'.[4] Both are part of the 'law of England' – a fact that may startle newcomers to the subject. This is not so for any other religious body in the UK (or any other liberal democracy). The laws of the Methodist Church or the canon law of the Church in Wales are not part of the law of the land, since from the standpoint of the state these churches are essentially voluntary associations.

This does not mean that they must *see themselves theologically* as voluntary associations,[5] only that they are governed by their own internal 'rules', which are treated *by the state* as matters of private contract. The peculiar intertwinement of the law-making powers of Parliament and the Church of England has two jurisdictionally unique – and, I argue, perverse – results that still survive. One is that Parliament can make law for the Church of England (even though there is a convention that Parliament will now let the Church take the initiative in legislation). The other is that the Church of England can initiate changes to the law of England; uniquely in the UK, a body formally outside the state has the right to initiate legislation in Parliament.[6]

For much of the eighteenth and nineteenth centuries, the Church lacked any effective instruments of self-government and was mostly ruled directly by Parliament.[7] The traditional defence of parliamentary control, formulated classically by Richard Hooker, was that it was necessary for the 'voice of the laity' to be heard in Church governance. As Colin Buchanan puts it, 'by this means the layman was governed by his elected (lay) representatives in his religious life as well as in the rest of his personal and civic life.'[8] A long-standing concern was, as the Chadwick Report expressed it, that to leave Church affairs entirely to the Church's own organs of governance (Convocations, the Church Assembly, General Synod) would risk a 'narrowing of viewpoint': 'The House of Commons is the lay representative of the Church of England' and would fulfil that role better than lay representatives in these Church organs.[9] I know of no serious Anglican theologian who would explicitly defend that formulation today. It was, however, alluded to by some traditionalist Anglican MPs during the passage of the women's ordination Measure in 1993. Frank Field, for example, asserted that it was MPs' role 'to protect the interests of constituents who may be adversely affected by a Measure'.[10]

Parliamentary governance of the Church began to evolve in the late nineteenth century, but the most dramatic change occurred in 1919 with the passage of the Enabling Act, giving the right of legislative initiative to a newly created Church Assembly.[11] In 1969, this was reconstituted as General Synod. All pieces of ecclesiastical legislation, called 'Measures', now originate from Synod. One of the first was the Worship and Doctrine Measure 1974, which finally brought major swathes of the Church's internal life under the authority of General Synod.[12] But things are not quite so simple.

A Measure initiated by General Synod and which has also passed through its own Legislative Committee is then forwarded to Parliament's Ecclesiastical Committee, composed of members of both Houses nominated by the Lord Chancellor. The Ecclesiastical Committee prepares a report for Parliament advising on the 'expediency' of the Measure, but cannot amend it. Constitutionally, Parliament could in principle veto a Measure, although it now abides by a convention not to do so (one that, however, Chris Loder's intervention suggests may not be entirely firm). A resolution of both Houses is then required, following which the Measure is presented for Royal Assent, at which point it becomes the law of the land. Church officials may complain about how cumbersome this process is. But the principled objection to it remains the jurisdictional offence occurring where the Church is required to submit important aspects of its internal governance for (even formal) approval by an organ of state. Even if the Church always got its way promptly and without interference from Parliament or government, by continuing to subject itself to this constraint it objectively sends a signal to the state (whatever it *thinks* it is doing) that it cannot yet trust itself with full autonomy and still craves the legislative oversight of political authority. As Buchanan pugnaciously puts it:

> the issue is *not* whether Parliament rarely or ever restricts our freedom, or blocks our policies. It is whether the powers should reside there at all ... [T]he issue is *not* whether we can get a Measure through Parliament without arousing opposition or causing fluttering in dovecots; it is simply whether Parliament is God's ordained instrument of ecclesiastical

policy-making, to which, as a matter of *theology*, we *must* be subject, or whether it is a secular court inappropriately giving judgement in spiritual things.[13]

In fact, however, the requirement of parliamentary approval of Measures *does* leave the Church exposed to material interference in its internal affairs. Such interference is no longer on the scale of the 'Prayer Book Crisis' of the late 1920s (which the Enabling Act 1919 had proved powerless to prevent), but it is not negligible. In 1984 the House of Commons declined to approve the Appointment of Bishops Measure even though it had been deemed expedient, if narrowly, by the Ecclesiastical Committee. In 1989 it rejected by 51 to 45 the Clergy (Ordination) Measure, a proposal designed to permit the ordination of remarried divorcees with previous spouses still alive and those married to them. This had also only narrowly passed the Ecclesiastical Committee. Amended by General Synod, it was finally approved in 1990.[14] In 2002 the Ecclesiastical Committee itself declined to approve as expedient the Church of England (Pensions) Measure, requiring the Church to submit a new Measure later that year.

Even when Parliament does not block or delay a Measure, it can still exercise substantive influence over it. Judith Maltby relates how this occurred during Ecclesiastical Committee deliberations on both women's ordination in the 1990s and women bishops in the 2000s. In 1993 the Committee succeeded in extracting greater concessions for opponents to women priests than the Church had initially sought in a 1992 Measure proposing women's ordination. The Committee in effect manoeuvred the Church into introducing new provisions beefing up episcopal oversight for opponents, later boasting about their achievement to Parliament.[15] Maltby judges that 'the Ecclesiastical Committee played a major role in constructing the final package of provisions for opponents of the ordination of women'.[16] On one occasion, she observes, Church representatives at the Committee were 'interrogated with remarkable aggression'.[17]

By 2010, however, parliamentary opinion on gender equality had shifted. Maltby details how, during the 2000s, the Church came under sustained parliamentary pressure to expedite moves towards the ordination of women bishops (in the form of Early Day Motions, parliamentary debates and questions, even a Ten Minute Bill to allow women bishops, proposed by Andy Reed MP).[18] Thus, in 2010, Tony Baldry MP, Second Church Estates Commissioner, felt the need to warn General Synod in his maiden speech that the Church should be 'under no illusion ... that a difficult task could become impossible if I had to steer through the House of Commons any Measure which left a scintilla of a suggestion that women bishops were in some way to be second-class bishops'.[19] In other words, if the Church proposed anything that appeared to clash with the now politically dominant equality agenda, it might not get its way. This was the issue on which the Prime Minister, David Cameron, (in)famously urged in Parliament, 'The Church needs to get on with it, as it were, and get with the programme.'[20] As Maltby expresses the implied warning in Baldry's speech: 'The same Erastian relationship which had helped to launch Flying Bishops in the early 1990s, might very well be brought to bear to ground them for good in the 2010s.'[21] Maltby rightly notes that Baldry was not threatening a new parliamentary assertiveness in Church affairs but simply reminding Synod of the normal process by which the Church's legislation is approved.[22] These episodes make clear that, whatever one's stance on women's ordination (I am in favour), for Parliament to possess a right to shape the Church's own decisions on such a matter is a clear breach of the spiritual autonomy of the Church.[23]

Could such an arrangement nevertheless be defended as a price worth paying for other advantages? Writing in 2006, Oliver O'Donovan entertained four considerations to that end. First, the Church's right to initiate legislation (by Measure) provides a 'critical bulwark against hostile legislation [from Parliament] ... and against unintended interference in the Church'.[24] But the story of the Ecclesiastical Committee's role in the processes of approving women priests and bishops suggests that this supposed restraint is ineffective. While current arrangements did indeed prevent Andy Reed's 'hostile' bill from proceeding, they did not prevent Parliament from effectively forcing on the Church a provision (justified or not) it had not sought.

Second, O'Donovan holds that, 'because it is legally impossible to legislate for the Church of England other than by way of synodical consultation, it is politically impossible to treat other churches in a high-handed way.'[25] This, however, is challenged by the state's treatment of Catholic adoption agencies. The 2007 Sexual Orientation Regulations were deployed (by a government led by the then Anglican Tony Blair) to deprive the right of such agencies to set adoption policy according to their church's own moral doctrine.

Third, a disestablished Church, he warns, might find itself coerced by court judgements into reaching a decision on, for example, women bishops without any possibility of theological deliberation on the matter.[26] This seems not to have been borne out in relation to women bishops. But it was evident in a 2007 case, akin to *Percy* in Scotland, where a Church of England decision to dismiss staff it judged to have deviated from its theological or behavioural expectations was overridden. The diocese of Hereford was found to have breached anti-discrimination employment law in turning down a gay youth worker for a post on the grounds that his commitments were judged incompatible with the Church's teaching.[27] This occurred without the Church being able to complete a process of 'theological deliberation' on the matter (indeed, it has still not completed it). The Church's right to legislate has proved unable to prevent such a development.[28]

Fourth, the Church's right to initiate legislation, O'Donovan holds, affords the 'possibility of influence of the church on the legal culture as a whole', the latter being part of its 'service' to the state.[29] This, however, seems powerfully rebutted by Parliament's comprehensive and contemptuous rejection of the Church's stance on same-sex marriage in 2013, in which it was not merely defending its own liberty but making a case about the good of heterosexual marriage in general.[30]

Note that these rejoinders to O'Donovan stand irrespective of one's views of the substance of the Church's preference on those matters. My argument here is not a veiled defence of 'conservative' positions on them but a claim about proper jurisdiction. In the light of all this, Jeremy Morris's larger judgement seems correct:

> Establishment does not preserve significant influence for the Church at the very heart of government. On the contrary, the very development of the British State over the last century and a half has almost taken for granted the Church's *irrelevance* in most areas of policy. Establishment does not preserve Christian truth as an operative principle in government because the vast majority of our fellow citizens choose for it not to be so.[31]

I would stress that, irritating and distracting though the pressures of Parliament's role in Church legislation may be, my critique of it would apply *even if no such pressures were ever applied*. The same argument applies here as with earlier instances of Establishment, namely that Parliament's supervising role breaches the principle, expressed in the Scottish Article IV, that the Church receives from Jesus Christ the 'right and power subject to no civil authority to legislate, and to adjudicate finally, in all matters of doctrine, worship, government, and discipline in the Church'. And if, beyond governing its own affairs, the Church wishes to continue to shape the 'legal culture' of the UK – as I certainly hope it does – let it do so via the normal democratic channels of influence available to everyone else.[32]

Benching the bishops

Forty-two diocesan bishops are eligible to sit in the House of Lords, although the number sitting at any one time is 26. This includes the two archbishops, the Bishops of London, Durham and Winchester, and the 21 other longest-serving diocesan bishops. The Lord's Spiritual (Women) Act 2015 now provides that, whenever a vacancy arises during the ten years following the Act, the position must be filled by a female bishop, if one is eligible.

As noted, the presence of the bishops in the House of Lords long predates the Reformation and their right to sit is not dependent on Tudor statutes. Bishops have held seats as 'the Lords Spiritual' since medieval times. This has led some to suggest they are not part of Establishment proper. However, because they are a case of a 'special privilege and responsibility' of the Church of England, I count them as such. As recently as 2008, the government itself clearly regarded them similarly.[33] The Lords Spiritual are not mandated to speak for the Church collectively but hold their positions as individual bishops. Today, they are one of very few examples in Europe of guaranteed religious representation in a national legislature.[34] This is not in itself an argument against them, but it might be expected to have evoked a stronger public defence from the Church than has been forthcoming.

The most important objections to this arrangement again derive from the principle of state religious impartiality.[35] One is that for representatives of one religious denomination to enjoy an automatic right of membership of the legislature denied to other faith communities assumes that the state has the authority to judge between faiths as to which is deserving of such a public privilege. I have argued that the state cannot claim such authority. The other is a corollary: singling out one religious body for such a privilege sends the signal that other faith communities (religious or secular) are not deserving of such a standing, thus treating them as symbolically second class and, moreover, denying Parliament an adequate share of their wisdom.[36] To mitigate that inequality, the Wakeham Commission on reforming the House of Lords recommended in 2000 a reduction in the number of Lords Spiritual to 16 and the appointment of members from other Christian churches and non-Christian faiths. However, in 2002 the House of

Commons Public Administration Select Committee recommended terminating the automatic right of bishops to sit in the Lords after the next election but one, while accepting that they could be considered for appointment in a reformed chamber.[37] The 2007 White Paper on Lords reform also recommended a reduction, although the House of Commons at the time indicated its preference for a wholly elected second chamber.[38] The Joint Committee on the Draft House of Lords Reform Bill also took up the issue in 2012. A majority of the committee proposed reducing the number of bishops in the Lords from 26 to 12, but the bill did not proceed.[39] Currently, House of Lords reform – long overdue for many other reasons – seems indefinitely stalled.

Defenders of the Lords Spiritual typically claim that their presence brings two benefits. One is that, as with other elements of Establishment, having bishops in the Lords serves to defend the interests not only of the Church of England but also of other churches and other faiths. As Adrian Hastings puts it, 'The bishops in the House of Lords cannot really be there as Anglican but rather as representatives of spirituality, a voice of Christianity and indeed of religion wider than Christianity.'[40] Rowan Williams, giving oral evidence to the Joint Committee in 2011, accepted that other faiths also had a right to be represented in the Lords and that it would be 'insulting' for Anglican bishops to assume they were entitled to speak for them, but that until a better system was established they would need to continue to do so.[41]

The other supposed benefit is that the presence of bishops helps elevate the level of debate about vital matters of national concern, at times allowing the airing of broader or deeper concerns that might not surface adequately in the contributions of the Lords Temporal.[42] Joan Lockwood O'Donovan claims that, while the bishops amount to only 3 per cent of the House's members, they 'make a disproportionately weighty contribution to debates about legislation of a morally significant and/or controversial nature, or affecting religious institutions'.[43]

Doubts have been expressed on both counts. On the first – the question of inclusion – the Methodist Church's *A Report on Church, State and Establishment* called on the Church of England to realize that 'we do not always feel represented or included when it is claimed that ... the bishops speak for all Christians, or for all people of faith.'[44] I already noted in Chapter 1 that, while some leaders of other faith groups have defended the Lords Spiritual as promoting inclusion, others – including churches in Scotland, Wales and Northern Ireland – have voiced the same concern as the Methodists.

On the second – the question of competence – concern has been voiced about the quality of the overall performance of the Lords Spiritual in view of their infrequent attendance, their lack of technical expertise and the absence of distinctiveness in what they say.[45] Since my argument concerns the *right* of bishops to sit in the Lords, not their *competence* to do so, I do not need to take a firm position on that question. I recognize, however, that it is difficult to see how bishops with already onerous diocesan responsibilities can adequately fulfil the demanding role of active membership of a legislative chamber, however well briefed.

Of course, I do not literally want to 'bench' the bishops (to take them off the field entirely). I appreciate many of their contributions in the Lords. But there is, again, low-hanging fruit available to address the concern about time and competence: in a reformed Lords, the Church could nominate its own *laypeople* with appropriate experience as its representatives (assuming it, alongside other faith groups, had a right to nominate). If the Church were reluctant to see such a role transferred to its lay members, that would surely send the signal that it did not trust them to speak on its behalf, perhaps because they lacked sufficient theological expertise or were not close enough to the local communities represented by diocesan bishops. And if these were real problems, the appropriate responses would surely be not to send already overburdened bishops into a political role for which they cannot be assumed to have had any preparation, but to ensure that laypeople are better equipped for such a role. That laypeople can acquire such skill is already amply evident from the many existing Christian members of the House of Lords who already speak with seasoned, and locally grounded, faith-motivated voices (perhaps some of them are members of Chris Loder's WhatsApp group). The people they need might, in fact, already be *in situ*.

John Habgood, however, raises the further objection that to rely on laity alone would be to lose an important symbolic message conveyed by the Lords Spiritual. In response to the question, 'Why not be satisfied with lay Christians doing a lay job' in Parliament, he argues that bishops in the Lords 'constitute a permanent and visible reminder of the relationship between Church and State'. It is their presence *as bishops* that counts: 'in a field of activity which is rich in symbolism of many kinds, it is the symbolism rather than individual success [of the bishops] or corporate power, which is important and which still manages to represent a residual national commitment to the Christian faith.'[46] I have already argued that such a 'national commitment' at the level of state institutions is problematic on principle. I would add that, given that such symbolism is now, in any case, extremely threadbare, the balance of judgement now tilts decisively toward competence as the desirable quality in Christian parliamentarians. As Peter Cornwell succinctly puts it: 'If the removal of bishops from the House of Lords were to be read as the church opting out of the life the nation, that would only show what a wrong and muddled idea of the church's involvement we have projected through such symbols.'[47]

Even if there were merit in the Church's defences of its bishops' presence in the Lords, they are, again, strictly irrelevant to the constitutional principle at stake. The key objection is the breaching of jurisdictional boundaries involved.[48] The point is not that faith-inspired voices (religious and secular) have no place in a representative legislature. There is nothing in my jurisdictional theology that excludes clergy from being eligible for membership of an appointed second chamber. In a suitably reformed House of Lords there should certainly remain the option of nominating a wide array of voices from any location in civil society, as is already partially the case now. This is an expression of 'vocational representation', a notion defended by several Anglican theologians.[49] Such a process might be presided over by a new, suitably representative appointments commission (from which sitting politicians would be excluded), making recommendations according to agreed criteria of eligibility (expertise, societal sector, representativeness, ethnic or geographical or gender diversity and so forth). The Church of England might well want to nominate candidates for consideration – clerical or lay. So might the Roman Catholic Church, the Muslim Council of Britain or Humanists UK.[50]

The idea of religiously based (indeed any form of) vocational representation faces the standard objection that it is difficult to come up with a suitable method by which eligible nominees might be identified. Certainly, religious representatives could not be allocated seats according to the latest census results or estimates of national attendance at places of worship. Where no authoritative national religious institution exists (as, for example, in Sunni Islam), identifying representatives could be contentious. Suffice it to say that I do not think this hurdle is insurmountable. Vocational representation is already implicitly operative in other appointments to the House of Lords, the nominating committee of which has to consider, for example, which business or trades union leaders to nominate. So long as no strict arithmetical proportionality is expected and the nomination process is open to as wide a range of suggestions as possible, the difficulties can surely be managed for most practical purposes. This assumes, of course, that a reformed second chamber would (as I hope) retain at least some appointed members and not become a mere replica of a party-dominated elected House of Commons.

Here a larger consideration beckons regarding the place of the Lords Spiritual. I suggest that the contribution made by them to bringing Christian influence to bear on law and public policy (as distinct from making thoughtful speeches), however valuable, is much less substantial than that from either Christians in the House of Commons or lay members in the Lords. Many such Christians are members of the cross-party fellowship Christians in Parliament, now recognized as an All-Party Parliamentary Group. But even more important is the work of Christian citizens across the nation in numerous political and other public settings outside Parliament. Supporting Colin Buchanan's 1994 General Synod motion, Elaine Storkey pointed out that much of the Church's opportunities for service in no way depend on Establishment. She noted, first, that many non-established denominations 'have many links with Members of Parliament, with House of Lords people, Euro-MPs, and so on'. Beyond formal politics, she also reports:

> I myself am not a bishop ... Yet I too have spoken to veterinary surgeons, the BMA, single-parent families, endless media consultations, educational institutions, universities, incest survivors, multi-faith conventions, retirement homes, hospices and so on in the past year. Why? Because of my links with the State? No, because I love Jesus Christ and the people of this country.[51]

If the Church wishes to continue to 'speak to the nation', it should surely devote by far the greatest proportion of its energies to supporting those much more effective sources of influence. 'Losing the Lords' would not put too much of a dent in that larger influence and could help concentrate minds and resources on how to make it more effective.

I briefly note another role played by the Lords Spiritual, the leading of daily prayers in the House of Lords at the start of each day. Such prayers are an item of the official business of Parliament. On my argument they too amount to a breach of the principle of state religious impartiality. This practice has understandably come under renewed attack in a report of the All-Party Parliamentary Humanist Group.[52] After disestablishment, prayers would not be part of the official business of either Lords or Commons but would be a voluntary act taking place in some other location in the Palace of Westminster, led, perhaps, by the Speaker's Chaplain or some qualified lay person.[53] Parliamentarians of other faiths might wish to hold their own prayers or religious devotions on the same basis.[54]

On the money

The statutory body called the Church Commissioners (CC) was created in 1948, charged with managing the Church's assets responsibly and ensuring that the Church fulfils its obligations under charity law. Six of the 33 commissioners hold their position ex-officio as officers of state, and others are appointed by the Crown. While the CC's predecessor bodies were created by Acts of Parliament, the CC itself was established by the then National Assembly of the Church of England – by Measure, followed by parliamentary approval. The CC is accountable to Parliament via the Second Church Estates Commissioner, who must be an MP and is expected to be a member of the Church of England. This is not a mere formality. In 2009, the Commissioners had to seek parliamentary consent to a decision to spend £187 million capital as income.[55] Irrespective of whether we judge that decision to be prudent, it amounts to more intrusive state control of the Church of England's finances than that experienced by any other religious body. My proposal is simply that, after disestablishment, the CC would be governed only by, and answerable only to, the Church of England, without any role for Parliament or Crown appointees. The role of Second Estates Commissioner would cease. The CC is already a charity and thus, like other churches or religious bodies, accountable to the Charity Commission; this would continue, again as an example of the general regulatory role of the state over non-state bodies. While the logistics of such a reform could be legally complex, it is hard to see on what principled grounds either the Church or the state could object to it. Again, however, this effect of disestablishment would need to be accompanied by a call to the Charity Commission not to impose on the CC (or any other religious body) too narrow a definition of what counts as a legitimate charitable purpose, an issue on which there is cause for concern.[56]

Conclusion

This chapter has argued that the Church needs to reset its constitutional relationships with Parliament. First, it must dispense with the remaining legacy of parliamentary involvement in its own legislative processes.[57] The Church's entitlement to initiate parliamentary legislation (and thus make the law of the land) should cease. The Ecclesiastical Committee, and all traces of parliamentary supervision, should end. The Church of England's law should become legally equivalent to the internal rules of any other religious body in the UK, such as the Methodist Church. Bishops should not enjoy an automatic right to sit in the House of Lords, but a reformed Lords could allow nominations of clergy or lay representatives of the Church of England on the same terms as those of other religious (and secular) bodies. In the Conclusion, I indicate some of the possible constitutional or other steps needed to reach these objectives. The first challenge, however, is for the Church to come to the point of acknowledging that these 'special' legal ties to Parliament are theologically problematic. It is time for the Church finally to cast off the remaining traces of parliamentary control of its spiritual jurisdiction and send the signal that it trusts itself to manage its own internal affairs without external supervision. And it is time for it relinquish the privileged access of its senior leadership to the legislative process and signal clearly that it is content to enjoy complete parity in this regard with other faith groups, thereby sending the signal that it fully embraces the principle of democratic equality.

Notes

1 'Parliament is watching closely', *Church Times*, 17 September 2021.

2 For a forceful statement of similar views, see Jim McConalogue, Rachel Neal and Jack Harris, *Rotting from the Head: Radical Progressive Activism and the Church of England* (London: Civitas, 2021).

3 The Church's 'canons' are, since 1969, devised only by General Synod. Unlike Measures, they do not require parliamentary approval. Crown endorsement of canons is now purely ceremonial.

4 Church of England Assembly (Powers) Act 1919, ss. 4 and 3(6). Thanks to Paul Barber for this reference.

5 The point is noted in the Methodist Church's *A Report on Church, State and Establishment* (Peterborough: Methodist Church, 2004), para. 105.

6 As Julian Rivers puts it: 'Parliament is still the legislature for the church, although the church has received a measure of autonomy – not by granting it independence in spiritual matters, but by giving it privileged access to the legislative process' (*The Law of Organized Religions: Between Establishment and Secularism* (Oxford: Oxford University Press, 2010), pp. 324–5).

7 Convocations met only rarely between 1717 and 1855, at which point they were restored, albeit with limited powers and still relying on Parliament to enact Church legislation. Elements of Erastianism lingered on, however. The Judicial Committee of the Privy Council was still deciding a controversial doctrinal dispute over baptismal regeneration as late as 1850 (the *Gorham* judgment). Even in 1874, Parliament was legislating on liturgical matters in the Public Worship Regulation Act – the last such example (R. M. Morris, ed., *Church and State in 21st Century Britain: The Future of Church Establishment* (Basingstoke: Palgrave Macmillan, 2009), pp. 28–30).

8 Colin Buchanan, *Cut the Connection: Disestablishment and the Church of England* (London: Darton, Longman and Todd, 1994), p. 118.

9 *Church and State: Report of the Archbishops' Commission* (London: Church Information Office, 1970), p. 18.

10 Quote in Morris, *Church and State in 21st Century Britain*, p. 107. For a fuller defence of parliamentary control, see Frank Field, 'The Church of England and Parliament: A Tense Partnership', in George Moyser, ed., *Church and Politics Today: The Role of the Church of England in Contemporary Politics* (Edinburgh: T&T Clark, 1985), pp. 55–74.

11 For a summary of the procedure, see Morris, *Church and State in 21st Century Britain*, pp. 42–3.

12 The Church is, however, still bound by the statutory duty to make available the forms of service in the Book of Common Prayer.

13 *Cut the Connection*, pp. 68–9. Emphasis original. The Chadwick Report almost stumbled upon this insight at one point. Reporting that MPs, especially non-Anglicans, felt increasingly uncomfortable adjudicating matters internal to the Church, it concludes: 'We do not see how Parliament could recognise an "aberration", i.e. could properly decide whether a change in liturgy or in the formulation of doctrine amounted to a fundamental change in the character of the Church ... Members of Parliament themselves believe that they are ill-fitted to perform the task of an impartial tribunal in this sphere' (*Church and State: Report of the Archbishops' Commission*, p. 23).

14 Colin Podmore, 'Self-Government Without Disestablishment: From the Enabling Act to the General Synod', *Ecclesiastical Law Journal* 21 (2019), p. 327.

15 Judith Maltby, 'Gender and Establishment: Parliament, "Erastianism", and the Ordination of Women', in Mark Chapman, Judith Maltby and William Whyte, eds, *The Established Church: Past, Present and Future* (London: T&T Clark, 2011), pp. 102–13. This was the 'Provincial Episcopal Visitor' (PEV or 'Flying Bishops') scheme.

16 Maltby, 'Gender', p. 104.

17 Maltby, 'Gender', p. 106.

18 Maltby, 'Gender', p. 113–21.

19 Maltby, 'Gender', p. 99.

20 House of Commons Debates, 21 Nov. 2012, vol. 553, col. 579.

21 Maltby, 'Gender', p. 99.

22 One Anglican peer, Baroness Berridge, warned the Church in 2013 that parliamentary patience with the Church's delay to ordaining women bishops was wearing thin, hinting darkly that, 'as the hereditary peers can testify, eviction is not without precedent' (www.baronessberridge.com/women-bishops-in-the-house-of-lords/, accessed 15.10.2021).

23 Maltby herself does not explicitly draw this conclusion but merely observes that different protagonists variously endorse or attack parliamentary control depending on whether or not they approve of its preferences.

24 'Establishment', submission to the Commission of Inquiry on Faith and Nation of the Evangelical Alliance (2006), p. 14.

25 'Establishment', p. 16.

26 'Establishment', p. 15. O'Donovan supported women bishops.

27 The diocese was later ordered to pay £47,000 compensation

to the candidate. 'Bishop loses gay employment case', *BBC News*, 18 July 2007, http://news.bbc.co.uk/1/hi/wales/6904057.stm, accessed 15.10.2021; '£47,000 fine for Bishop sued by homosexual youth worker', *Christian Institute*, 12 February 2008, www.christian.org.uk/news/47000-fine-for-bishop-sued-by-homosexual-youth-worker/, accessed 15.10.2021.

28 The diocese could, however, have avoided this outcome had it been clear in advance that its stance on sexual ethics constituted an 'Occupational Requirement' for the position. I owe this observation to Julian Rivers.

29 'Establishment', p. 14.

30 As noted, Parliament did grant churches an exemption from any duty to conduct same-sex marriage services in their own buildings. This, then, at least offers partial support for O'Donovan's first consideration. For details, see Introduction to the present book, note 16, p. 12.

31 He is strictly correct to add: 'The general irrelevance of the Church to government is not in itself … a reason for further disestablishment.' Jeremy Morris, 'The Future of Church and State', in Duncan Dormor, Jack McDonald and Jeremy Caddick, eds, *Anglicanism: The Answer to Modernity* (London: Continuum, 2003), pp. 167–8. But such irrelevance does undermine a key defence of Establishment. Emphasis original.

32 I defend the possibility of promoting 'faithful law' in *Faith in Democracy: Framing a Politics of Deep Diversity* (London: SCM Press, 2021), pp. 115–16. The Church's contribution to the Churches' Legislation Advisory Service (CLAS), which responds to government proposals on legislation, could also continue after disestablishment. Other religious bodies operating under its umbrella are non-established. On CLAS, see David Harte, 'The Church of England and the State: A National Church for a Plural Nation', *Law and Justice* 168 (2012), p. 36.

33 'The relationship between the Church and State is a core part of our constitutional framework that has evolved over centuries. The presence of Bishops in the House of Lords signals successive Governments' commitment to this fundamental principle and to an expression of the relationship between the Crown, Parliament and the Church that underpins the fabric of our nation' (White Paper, *An Elected Second Chamber* (Cm 7438), para. 6.45), quoted in Morris, *Church and State in 21st Century Britain*, p. 217).

34 Others include the Bishop of Sodor and Man, who holds a seat in the Tynwald.

35 *Time for Reflection: A Report of the All-Party Parliamentary Humanist Group on Religion or Belief in the UK Parliament* (2019–

2020) invokes this and other arguments (not all of which I endorse) to call for an end to the presence of the Lords Spiritual (pp. 10–17).

36 There is the additional inequity that only an English Church has such a privilege, leaving out the other three nations of the UK. The Wakeham Commission thus proposed adding seats for five Christian representatives from Scotland, Wales and Northern Ireland.

37 Responding to the earlier White Paper, *The House of Lords: Completing the Reform* (2001), the Archbishops' Council opposed a reduction to 16, claiming that the Church needed at least 20 'to maintain the parliamentary service we seek to offer' (quoted in Andrew Partington and Paul Bickley, *Coming Off the Bench* (London: Theos, 2007, p. 21)).

38 William Whyte, 'What Future for Establishment?', in Chapman, Maltby and Whyte, *The Established Church*, p. 182.

39 Robert Morris, 'Half-Opening Cans of Worms: The Present State of "High" Establishment', *Law and Justice* 172 (2014), p. 18.

40 'The Case for Retaining the Establishment', in Tariq Modood, ed., *Church, State and Religious Minorities* (London: Policy Studies Institute, 1997), p. 46.

41 Morris, 'Half-Opening', p. 19.

42 Grace Davie endorses that judgement (*Religion in Britain: A Persistent Paradox*, 2nd edn (Chichester: Wiley Blackwell, 2015), p. 96).

43 'The Liberal Legacy of English Church Establishment: A Theological Contribution to the Legal Accommodation of Religious Plurality in Europe', *Journal of Law, Philosophy and Culture* 6.1 (2011), p. 19.

44 Methodist Church, *Church, State and Establishment*, para. 95. The Methodist Church has produced critics of Establishment but has never been officially committed to disestablishment. See David Carter, 'Methodism and Establishment', in Chapman, Maltby and Whyte, *The Established Church*, pp. 158–79.

45 See Andrew Partington and Paul Bickley, *Coming Off the Bench* (London: Theos, 2007); Morris, *Church and State in 21st Century Britain*, pp. 220–3. Bishops also play little role in the legislative scrutiny and revision functions of the Lords.

46 *Church and Nation in a Secular Age* (London: Darton, Longman and Todd, 1983), pp. 100–1.

47 *Church and Nation*, p. 66.

48 This issue of principle is not mentioned in Partington and Bickley, *Coming Off the Bench*.

49 Such as John Milbank and Adrian Pabst, *The Politics of Virtue: Postliberalism and the Human Future* (London: Rowman & Littlefield International, 2015); Nigel Biggar, 'Why Christianity benefits Secular Public Discourse, and Why, Therefore, Anglican Bishops should sit in

a Reformed House of Lords', *Theology* 117.5 (2014), p. 326; Oliver O'Donovan, 'Establishment', p. 12. The idea was recognized in the Chadwick Report, *Church and State: Report of the Archbishops' Commission*, p. 46.

50 The Roman Catholic Church currently debars priests from holding political office (canon 285 §3). However, the prohibition is susceptible to a Vatican dispensation. In a response to a government consultation on reform of the House of Lords, the Bishops' Conference has suggested it would be prepared to request one if the offer of such a seat were proposed. Thanks to Paul Barber for this observation. The Catholic Church could in principle also nominate lay Catholics. O'Donovan makes the interesting suggestion that nominations from the churches might be made by the Council of Churches in Britain and Ireland ('Establishment', p. 13) (now Churches Together in Britain and Ireland). In evidence to the Wakeham Commission, the Church of Scotland opposed creating seats in the Lords for its ministers due to a long-standing theological reservation about clergy holding political office (see Iain McLean and Scot Peterson, 'A Uniform British Establishment', in Chapman, Maltby and Whyte, *The Established Church*, pp. 151–2). Perhaps nominations might be made from relevant All-Party Parliamentary Groups (APPGs), such as Christians in Parliament, the APPG on Faith and Society, the APPG on British Islam, the All-Party Parliamentary Humanist Group and others.

51 Quoted in Andrew Atherstone, 'Gospel Opportunity or Unbiblical Relic: The Established Church through Anglican Evangelical Eyes', in Chapman, Maltby and Whyte, *The Established Church*, p. 94.

52 *Time for Reflection*, pp. 18–19.

53 *Time for Reflection* also reasonably calls for a review of the role of the Speaker's Chaplain, along the lines of the devolved parliaments or London Assembly (pp. 8–9).

54 In addition to the Anglican chapel, St Mary Undercroft (a royal peculiar), there is also a multi-faith prayer room situated next to Westminster Hall.

55 McLean and Peterson, 'Uniform British Establishment', p. 156.

56 In 2010, Rivers voiced the concern that 'It is almost inevitable that public benefit will become the sole and determining test for charitable status, and the religious or other dimension will carry no weight *as such*' (*Law of Organized Religions*, p. 334). Emphasis original.

57 I concur with the proposals to that end in *Time for Reflection*, pp. 20–1.

5

Disputing Establishment: Secularism, Neutrality, Sectarianism?

Introduction

Using the church–state theology of the Scottish Articles Declaratory as a working benchmark, I have in the last two chapters argued that Establishment upholds non-trivial breaches of the jurisdictional boundaries between the Church of England and the British state. That is my central case against it. In this and the next chapter, I want to shore up that argument by critiquing four common defences of Establishment. Few articulations of these arguments address the jurisdictional question at all, but they are influential nonetheless. The first argument is that disestablishment would amount to a needless and damaging 'concession to secularism'. The second is that, given the impossibility of a 'neutral state', disestablishment would effectively allow the establishment of a non-Christian world view. The third and fourth arguments express different facets of the idea that the Church must uphold a 'national mission' to England. The third is that disestablishment would signal a retreat from the Church's *pastoral* responsibility to the whole nation. The fourth is that disestablishment would bring about a withdrawal of the Church from national *political* engagement. In this chapter I consider the 'concession to secularism' argument, the 'anti-neutrality' argument and the 'national pastorate' argument. The next chapter explores the 'national political engagement' argument.

The 'concession to secularism' argument

Defenders of Establishment frequently warn that for the Church *itself* to seek disestablishment would be to 'send the wrong signal' to a society already undergoing pervasive secularization. They claim it would suggest a retreat of faith from the public square. Jonathan Sacks even warned that it would amount to 'a significant retreat from the notion that we share any values and beliefs at all'.[1] Paul Avis asserted in 2001 that Establishment 'remains a constitutional defence against the complete secularization of the state'.[2] Tom Wright thinks that 'the main motive for disestablishment ... is the old secularist agenda.'[3] The concession to secularism argument is not a new one. It was voiced in 1936 by Bishop Cyril Garbett, who warned that 'at a moment when Europe was in a restless condition, and anti-Christian movements were rife, it would be a very grave matter if the connection between Church and State were broken, because the world at large would interpret it as a national repudiation of Christianity.'[4]

The phrase 'sending the wrong signal' is widely invoked by advocates of this argument. It appears, for example, in the Evangelical Alliance report, *Faith in the Nation*. In the course of discussing bishops in the House of Lords, it suggests that for the Church to take the initiative in their removal 'would send out quite the wrong signal to society in general because it would be understood as a diminution of Christian involvement in society'.[5] In a *New Statesman* interview in 2008, Rowan Williams, who had experienced a fully autonomous church for ten years as a bishop and then Archbishop of the Church in Wales, conceded that it would not be 'the end of the world' if the Church of England were disestablished. Yet even he hesitated to commend it, fearing that the state's motivation for it 'would be mostly to do with ... trying to push religion into the private sphere'.[6] Many seem afflicted with the worry that disestablishment would inadvertently deliver a gratuitous victory to an exclusive form of secularism. Jeremy Morris, himself open to a significant evolution of Establishment, still holds that formal disestablishment 'would not easily escape the charge of retreat and retrenchment ... [and] the perception of many that this was a consequence of failing appeal'.[7] Such a concern has, as noted in the Introduction, led other faith communities to defend Establishment because, they claim, it sustains the public presence and legitimacy of faith in general.[8]

The first task is to explore what precisely those expressing this anxiety might mean by 'secularism'. For, as Edward Norman rightly points out, 'if severance of the connexions of religion and the state is ever contemplated [in England] the precise nature of secularity would itself require definition.'[9] What would be the relationship between the religiously impartial state I am arguing for and the plurality of religious bodies in England? Rowan Williams' distinction between 'procedural' and 'programmatic' secularism can serve us here. 'Procedural secularism' is:

> the principle according to which the state as such defines its role as one of overseeing a variety of communities of religious conviction and, where necessary, assisting them to keep the peace together, without requiring any specific public confessional allegiance from its servants on guaranteeing any single community a legally favoured position against others.[10]

Its outcome is 'a crowded and argumentative public square which acknowledges the authority of a legal mediator or broker whose job it is to balance and manage real difference'.[11] This is entirely compatible with the model of 'equitable public pluralism' I defended in Chapter 2.

As I read it, procedural secularism implies a religiously impartial state. But if it does, then it is essential to recognize that disestablishment would be *a concession to the right kind of secularism*. It is a needed concession because Establishment is theologically improper. The Church ought to make such a concession. But rather than framing it as a 'concession', the Church ought boldly to declare that this is now its current theology of church–state jurisdictions and commit itself to disestablishment as a corollary of that theology. Of course, it might have to put up with a fair bit of triumphalist gloating from more militant secularist quarters ('We won!'; 'The Church has finally been dragged into the twenty-first century'; 'Christendom is over'; and so forth). But that would hardly be the Church's first experience of such gloating and if it cannot cope with a bit more now, it never will.

Procedural secularism could, then, essentially endorse the following statement from two leading secular humanists:

> [The] uncoupling of church and state [is] a commitment to the open society that recognizes the privileging of any one religious denomination ... as a real inequality ... Secularism is not atheism and it is not anti-religious – in fact it benefits both the religious and the non-religious in their aspect as members of a single society. It provides a genuinely neutral framework within which we can express ourselves as a community, and in a diverse society it is a necessity.[12]

By contrast, 'programmatic secularism' means a campaign led by the state to impose a secularist world view across as many areas of public life as possible. Such a campaign would subvert procedural secularism. It entails the setting aside of religious views of some social practice and imposing a secularized view in law and public policy instead. Thus marriage, for example, might be redefined as nothing more than a revocable legal 'contract'. Defenders of traditional Christian marriage hold that the state's redefinition of marriage in 2013 as equally open to same-sex couples is just such an example of programmatic secularism (although the Church of Scotland changed its mind on that in 2018, followed by the Methodist Church in 2021; the Church of England at large is currently divided on the matter).[13] In contrast to procedural secularism, programmatic secularism intentionally brings about the progressive 'secularization' of society and culture by downward pressure from the state. Programmatic secularism is ruled out by the principle of a religiously impartial state. Such a state cannot remain impartial among diverse faith commitments if it actively promotes a world view such as secular humanism. The imposition of any faith, religious or secular, by the state exceeds its proper jurisdiction. The most effective way to combat programmatic secularism is to champion procedural secularism. Disestablishment as I conceive it is entirely compatible with procedural secularism; indeed, it flows from its logic. It does not promote programmatic secularism. Rather, it promotes equitable public pluralism.

In assessing the causes of the 'secularization' of society, it is also important to keep in mind that upward pressures from society and culture are far more influential contributors to secularization than downward pressures from the state. The progressive transformation of marriage from its traditional meaning to its current, increasingly contractual one was caused more by social and cultural change from below than by legislation, which, many would argue, was simply 'catching up with' social reality.[14] Equally, 'consumerism' – which theologians often regard as a 'secularist' lifestyle – has not been decreed by the state but has emerged as the outcome of millions of individual and corporate choices over many decades, albeit indirectly aided and abetted by various state policies. Defending constitutional privilege for a church cannot stem such cases of corrosive cultural development (if you think they are corrosive). Equally, abolishing such privilege need not in any way promote them.

Suppose the Church had come to the point of agreeing that Establishment is theologically indefensible and resolving to move beyond it. It should not pre-emptively cower before anticipated public perceptions that disestablishment would be a 'concession to secularism', but seek to correct those perceptions. The risk that disestablishment would be misunderstood by wider society then becomes a *challenge of public explanation*, not an argument for maintaining the status quo. Indeed, it should be aware that the concession to secularism argument could, as Simon Barrow notes, become a 'self-fulfilling prophecy': 'If Christians argue that the end of establishment will be a victory for secularism ... they can hardly complain when it is interpreted as just that.'[15]

Indeed, for the Church *itself* to take the initiative in this direction could present it with a marvellous opportunity for creative public apologetics – if only it could gain sufficient theological clarity and confidence about what it was actually doing and why. The Church would need to acknowledge its historical complicity in unwarranted religious privilege; commit itself to the principle of state religious impartiality; declare its opposition to programmatic secularism; propose a robust theology of equitable public pluralism in which the autonomy of religious organizations is made legally secure; reassure people of its continuing desire to serve the whole nation; and articulate its own substantive public theology of justice and the common good. That would send *exactly the right kind of signal* to state and society.

The 'anti-neutrality' argument

The second defence of Establishment I consider is the 'anti-neutrality' argument. It holds that, if Christianity is not accorded public privilege, something else will fill the vacuum. Not only is Christian public privilege theologically warranted, but, in its absence, some other faith or world view will almost inevitably come to assume a comparable position of public pre-eminence.

The clearest statement of this argument I have found among British thinkers is from Nigel Biggar. Biggar seeks to turn the tables on secular liberalism by arguing that it is actually Anglican Christianity that can sustain the health of 'liberal society', by keeping it 'humanist'[16] – hence the title of his principal essay on the theme: 'Why the "Establishment" of the Church of England is Good for a Liberal Society'.[17] His argument is framed within a larger critique of political liberalism's claim that the state should maintain a posture of 'neutrality with regard to conceptions of the good'. He does not reject 'liberalism' as such but wants to propose a surer grounding for liberal principles. Biggar has in mind four features of Establishment: the coronation service; the requirement that the monarch be in communion with the Church of England; the right of bishops to sit in the House of Lords; and the Church's privileged position in education.[18] Establishment in these senses is worth defending, he argues, because it supplies the kind of unified, shared metaphysical and ethical vision that is necessary to undergird a liberal society. The secular liberal notion that the state can adopt a posture of 'neutrality' regarding such visions is, he claims, illusory. His goal is to show that Establishment 'serves as a public affirmation of one world view that sustains a liberal humanist anthropology and a liberal ethos, in a world where humanist liberalism is under threat and in need of defence and promotion'.[19]

Biggar constructs his argument as a critical response to John Rawls's conception of 'public reason', which Rawls thought would supply a fund of generally accessible political principles enabling society to unite around common political loyalties and to draw on a shared framework of discourse. Biggar appreciates Rawls's acknowledgement that liberal public reason is not wholly neutral but depends at least upon definite moral commitments found only in certain 'comprehensive doctrines'. Yet:

> Rawls believes that public discourse – the discourse of parliament and the law courts, and perhaps also of public rituals – should not involve religious references, but should be conducted in terms of 'public reason'. Public reason comprises the set of liberal moral values and such anthropological tenets as are necessary to make sense of it, upon which various 'reasonable' comprehensive doctrines converge … [that is] the 'overlapping … consensus', which he believes can be made to float free of the various larger theological and metaphysical views that sustain it.[20]

Biggar shares Rawls's aspiration to seek such a consensus but denies that its contents could be detached from the particular comprehensive doctrines that support them. Public reason cannot remain neutral towards comprehensive doctrines, a feature revealed by the fact that such doctrines 'give rise to significant disagreements within the common terms of public reason'.[21]

> [L]iberal humanist space is not indefinite. Nor should it be taken for granted; it is under threat from a variety of anti-humanisms. Liberal public institutions that would survive, then, cannot afford to take a neutral position on ethics and anthropology. Nor can they afford to be neutral with regard to which larger views of the world dominate public culture, since some of these are positively subversive of liberal ethics and anthropology. Liberal public institutions therefore need to foster worldviews that commend the virtues necessary for liberal public discourse to flourish.[22]

Biggar's next move is to argue that not just any world view can serve this purpose. A liberal society must identify one among the plurality of available humanistic world views and affirm it as its favoured doctrine: 'a single set of public institutions and rituals cannot simultaneously affirm a variety of worldviews without sounding impossibly dissonant and incoherent.'[23] Given that such institutions cannot endorse merely a common ethic without the deeper moral and anthropological presuppositions on which it rests, 'they must choose one supportive humanistic worldview to represent'. For 'a single national set of public institutions and rituals cannot simultaneously affirm rival doctrines.'[24]

In England, Anglican Christianity is the best available world view for this purpose, he claims, for four reasons. First, at its best it has furnished and can still furnish exactly the sort of comprehensive foundation necessary for the liberal humanist virtues on which a liberal society rests. And there is no other strong contender waiting in the wings – 'no obvious challenger to the sitting candidate'.[25] Second, Establishment has proved itself in England and elsewhere to be wholly compatible with extensive religious freedom for non-Anglicans. Third, although Establishment does involve the public privileging of one world view, it does not breach the liberal principle of equal respect. Against the complaint that it amounts to a 'symbolic ostracism' of non-Anglican (and even more so, non-Christian) citizens, Biggar holds that such a public privileging 'need not imply lack of due respect'. This is because 'a historic religion might deserve certain privileges. Unequal treatment may have cogent reasons that do not amount to an offence against the equal human dignity of citizens. Inequality can still be equitable.'[26] Fourth, it is likely that Establishment still enjoys the tacit if not explicit support of a majority of English citizens.[27]

Biggar's first claim is a bold one that would be disputed by many historians (some of whom argue that English liberalism owes much more to the Dissenters than to Anglicans).[28] But for the purposes of this argument let me assume, at least, that Anglicanism today is '*a* strong contender' for the role of shoring up vital moral sources for key English liberal democratic principles. Let me also assume the plausibility of his claims about religious liberty and religious equality. And I have already explained that I do not regard his fourth, sociological, point as decisive for my central jurisdictional argument.

My critique of Biggar's position focuses on a significant shift of focus he makes during the course of his argument which, I suggest, hampers his case. He moves from speaking about the contents and presuppositions of liberal public *reason* to a reference to liberal humanist *space* and a liberal humanist *ethos*, and on the basis of those claims draws conclusions about liberal public *institutions* and *rituals*. His argument that public reason is not neutral but cannot be engaged in without resort (even if unwitting) to particular comprehensive doctrines is certainly plausible. I also agree that a liberal humanist ethos – which I take to be a broad cultural commitment to public values such as trust, mutual tolerance and respect, dialogue and so forth – does not arise automatically but requires active cultivation on the part of public institutions. I would only add here that such an ethos is not primarily generated by *state* institutions but much more by institutions such as the family, school, voluntary association, media, religious community and so forth. The state can indirectly encourage the generation of such an ethos by supporting these institutions so that they may nurture it in their own specific ways. I agree, however, that the state is obliged directly to cultivate at least those *political* values on which the state itself immediately relies: respect for law, non-violence, a commitment to a minimum degree of political participation, respect for democratic procedure and so forth.

Yet to accept these points is not yet to have argued conclusively that the *state* is also obliged *officially* to endorse a *world view* that generates support for either these wider public values or the narrower political values just listed. The claim that 'public reason is not neutral with regard to comprehensive doctrines' does not compel the conclusion that 'Liberal public institutions therefore need to foster worldviews that commend the virtues necessary for liberal public discourse to flourish.'

In the first place, the meaning of 'liberal public institutions' needs to be clarified. If state schools are included in this term, then it is true that they may be construed as having a duty to promote what Biggar calls a 'liberal ethos', and perhaps even to encourage world views favourable to such an ethos. But a school should not be seen as part of the state. The state is under much tighter restrictions than any non-governmental body regarding its power to officially favour a particular world view, however widely such a world view may be supported among its citizenry. The task of fostering world views conducive to what Biggar terms 'a liberal ethos' lies beyond the jurisdiction of the state itself and falls to other institutions. It is no doubt an absolutely essential task for the long-term health of a liberal society. But that does not mean it lies within the authority or the power of the state to fulfil it. The state is not empowered to try to guarantee the moral and spiritual – as distinct from the political and legal – conditions of its own continued existence.

Further, it may indeed be true that 'a single national set of public institutions and rituals cannot simultaneously affirm rival doctrines', but there is, of course, another way of avoiding that dilemma: the state should avoid *officially* affirming *any* comprehensive doctrines. This is not to lapse into the claim that the actions of the state are morally neutral, which I have already argued is implausible. Arguably every legislative, executive or judicial act of the state implies some de facto moral commitment. Yet this is not to say that the state must officially – *de jure* – endorse any comprehensive doctrine that might undergird such morality. The question of how far acts of state actually embody those moral or comprehensive commitments depends on the particularities of the act and on the weight of the public reasoning that went into bringing it about.[29]

The outcome of a contested deliberative sphere cannot be predicted in advance. Will it produce what Biggar calls 'dissonance'? Here we need to distinguish policy dissonance from intellectual dissonance. The risk of public contestation over deep moral or religious commitments leading to dissonant pieces of legislation will be partially curtailed by virtue of the inherent tendencies towards coherence within the civil service, within the parliamentary drafting process and then within any subsequent judicial interpretative process. Dissonance in the realm of executive action – as when foreign policy goals are seen to be inconsistent – is more likely. Yet degrees of dissonance in both types of policy are familiar and liberal states seem capable of surviving them, even if they make for bad policy. Such states also display quite frequent cases of intellectual dissonance. This occurs, for example, when late pregnancies are terminated on one floor of a hospital while assiduous attempts to save the lives of premature babies are made on another; or when the Treasury lowers taxes to boost economic growth, thereby increasing carbon emissions, while the Committee on Climate Change urges that such emissions be reduced. Such incoherence is regrettable and damaging but cannot be eliminated and does not threaten the state itself. In any case, it is not clear that Anglican Establishment in any way currently mitigates this incoherence.

The state can never be morally neutral and is not even spiritually neutral in a de facto sense. My argument, however, is that the state lacks the jurisdiction to explicitly offer any *de jure* endorsement of any world view or comprehensive doctrine. It should conform to the principle of impartiality among alternative faiths (religious or secular). The ensuing official silence on ultimate truth-claims need not in itself contribute to the further secularization of the state or enable anti-humanist world views to gain greater purchase on the state. Those consequences will only transpire if Christians, or other religious groups, deliberately opt to retreat from conscientious, faith-based democratic engagement. That would be their choice, not the state's. In the next chapter I offer suggestions on how the Church of England, at least, could better practise such engagement.

The 'national pastorate' argument

While the 'concession to secularism' and 'anti-neutrality' arguments could be used to defend Christianity in general, the two sides of the 'national mission' concern – the pastoral and the political – are more specifically Anglican. It is driven by the specific concern that disestablishment would send the signal that the Church of England is no longer committed to the nation as a whole – that it would amount to a renunciation of its historic national mission. A number of distinct arguments have been invoked to defend Establishment in such terms. They apply to both the pastoral and the political sides of 'national mission' but can best be addressed here. I consider two that are frequently mounted: the doctrine of the incarnation, and the idea of a 'national Church'.

It may come as a surprise to outsiders to these debates that the notion of 'incarnation' is invoked to support English Establishment. The notion is deployed to show why the Church should have a special sense of identification with its *own* nation. Advocates are indeed right to claim that the doctrine of the incarnation underwrites a commitment to 'the particular'.

It offers a powerful general affirmation of the importance of local, ethnic or national particularity (as, by the way, do the doctrines of creation and providence, but these seem to be less often invoked). Humans are created as embodied, situated, storied, social and cultural beings, and Jesus' incarnation profoundly affirms those features of the human condition. But notice that when enlisted by national mission advocates, an appeal is being made from a fundamental doctrine shared by the universal church, to the highly idiosyncratic local features of the Church of England's relation to the United Kingdom of Great Britain and Northern Ireland.

Malcolm Brown, for example, suggests that incarnation means that 'the state of the society in which the Church is embedded matters to God and ... the pursuit in that society of the common good is integral to its mission.'[30] But such a claim can, of course, be equally invoked by non-established churches to justify *their* sense of national mission. He goes on to assert that 'in the constant tension between mission and purity, establishment operates as a counterbalance to introspection.'[31] Again, however, the Church in Wales or the Methodist Church, for example, seem no more vulnerable to 'introspection' than the Church of England, even without special ties to the state. Warming to the same theme, Martyn Percy holds that the role of the Established Church is 'sacrificial and sacramental'. As 'incarnate', the Church:

> must live with its ambiguities, lack of definition, mystery, distinctiveness and power. It actively seeks intra- and interdependent social, political and constitutional relations for the sake of social flourishing, to bear witness to the incarnation, and to anticipate the Kingdom that is yet to come.[32]

Again, other churches seem quite capable of coping with ambiguities and promoting interdependent social relations.

As Bishop of Durham, Tom Wright also defended Establishment in terms of 'incarnation':

the reality of an established church, here in the north-east of England at least, is ... about partnerships in education, in ecology, in peacemaking, in climate campaigning ... about the church being alongside people when they are hurting most ... about the church being the voice of the voiceless, the loyal and courageous opposition to wrong-headed ideas and the equally loyal and courageous supporter for right-headed ideas, wherever the ideas come from. It is about the church refusing to confine its work to those who come looking for spiritual help, because we know that the God who became incarnate in Jesus went about inaugurating the kingdom, which was and is a reality whether or not people acknowledge it. And it is about a society that recognises that the church has this role and that it's a good thing that it does, and that sets up structures to make sure it goes on having and exercising it. Where we are right now, historically and culturally, *a vote for Disestablishment would be a vote against Incarnation.*[33]

That final line (the emphasis is added) might strike some as a touch hyperbolic. In mitigation, however, Wright is evidently referring here to 'earthed Establishment', which I am arguing will remain largely untouched by ending 'high Establishment'. The implausible claim that to vote for disestablishment is to vote against the incarnation needs to be translated as the entirely compelling one that 'the Church of England should remain committed to local embedded engagement for the common good'. But such a commitment does not depend on maintaining privileged constitutional ties to the state.

These arguments from 'incarnation' do not begin to furnish a justification for English Establishment. Generic fundamental doctrines like the incarnation can offer no succour to the local peculiarities of something like English Establishment. Incarnation does not endorse just anything 'particular'. A highly idiosyncratic arrangement like Establishment could only be justified (if at all) in terms of carefully contextualized historical and jurisdictional reasoning – on which the doctrine of the incarnation is, shall we say, studiedly neutral. The church can fully celebrate all the 'particular' created goods affirmed by incarnation and live a fully incarnational faith, yet without enjoying any special ties to the state. Attempts to deploy 'incarnation' for such a purpose ironically turn it into a ahistorical concept abstracted from its grounding in biblical history. The Jesus recorded in the New Testament, the Incarnate One, certainly valued the particularity of his Jewish identity, his family, his locality. Yet he often found himself at radical variance with the religious and political establishments of his day. The doctrine of incarnation can surely equally, if not more compellingly, be invoked to justify a distanced, oppositional stance towards society and state, as one of identification with them.[34] As Simon Barrow puts it:

> The idea that things such as parliamentary prayers, the supremacy of the English monarch or even the presence of bishops in the House of Lords somehow ensure that the operation of government is undergirded by the subversive memory of Jesus is more than a little fanciful.[35]

And there is no credible doctrine of the incarnation without that subversive memory.[36] This does not mean that the Church must necessarily be in perpetual and fundamental opposition to whatever happens to be its political order. But it certainly suggests deep scepticism about entering into constitutional entanglements that might blunt such opposition where it is called for.

So much for the 'incarnational' defence of 'national mission'. Can the 'national Church' defence do any better? I have already argued that this idea cannot be justified if it means a church presuming to embody or represent a whole nation. Are there better renditions? For Paul Avis, the core of the idea of a national church is national *recognition*:[37] when a church's 'national commitment' is 'met with national recognition ... we talk of the establishment of the church'.[38] Only establishment in this sense – 'the recognition on the part of the state of the contribution of Christian ministry to the health of civil society' – 'can provide a basis for the pastoral responsibility of the Church at large'.[39] The claim is imprecise: the Welsh Church Act 1914 and the Methodist Church Act 1976 are in one sense acts of 'national recognition' yet they serve to confirm the relevant churches as legally non-established. The claim is also mistaken: in the rest of this chapter I will argue that the Church can with complete success exercise pastoral responsibility to civil society, and the state, without being established. The only act of 'recognition' required in order for a church to pursue a national mission is for the state to acknowledge it as a lawful, self-governing organization, entitled, like any other, to contribute to social and political life. No special or privileged recognition by the nation is required.

As indicated, the national mission defence of Establishment turns out to consist of two distinct anxieties that require separate treatment. Both already appeared pretty much fully formed in 1939 in T. S. Eliot's argument against disestablishment in *The Idea of a Christian Society*. Addressing a nation on the verge of war, Eliot warned of 'the gravity of the abdication which the Church – whether voluntarily or under pressure – would be making' if disestablishment occurred:

> [W]e must pause to reflect that a Church, once disestablished, cannot easily be re-established, and that by that very act of disestablishment separates itself more definitely and irrevocably from the life of the nation than if it had never been established. The effect on the mind of the people of the visible and dramatic withdrawal of the Church from the affairs of the nation ... of the Church's abandonment of all those who are not by their wholehearted profession of faith within the fold – this is incalculable ... [D]isestablishment instead of being the recognition of a condition at which we have arrived, would be the creation of a condition the results of which we cannot foresee.[40]

The first anxiety voiced here is that disestablishment would amount to the Church's abandonment of its *pastoral responsibility towards the whole nation*. The second is that it would lead to a withdrawal of the Church from *public engagement in the affairs of the nation*.[41] I turn now to the first and treat the second in the next chapter.

A frequently voiced anxiety about disestablishment is that it would amount to an abandonment of the Church's sense of its *pastoral responsibility towards the nation as a whole*. Here we are speaking of what Wesley Carr calls 'earthed' rather than 'high' Establishment, chiefly its presence in the parishes and dioceses. Carr describes this role as 'generated by pastoral and theological response to what is presented to the Church rather than what derives from it' – by the Church's encounter with what is outside it rather than with the demands of its inner life.[42] William Whyte states the point rather more starkly: 'Rather than granting privilege, establishment now exacts a price from the Church, preventing it from abandoning a nation that often appears to have abandoned it. Establishment ... requires the Church of England to serve the people of England.'[43]

It is not immediately apparent what it might mean for a Church to 'serve' a community that has 'abandoned' it. At least, it is abundantly clear that the nation is no longer exactly clamouring for the Church's service.[44] The active membership of the Church of England now constitutes less than 2 per cent of the population, and a steadily declining number show up when they feel the need for some significant rite of passage.[45] This explodes any claim that the Church of England is the 'church of the nation' in any demographic sense. Over the last 50 years millions of English people have simply voted with their feet, to the point that 'the nation' has apparently lost any special sense of collective identification with the Church of England, however much they may continue to appreciate the aesthetics of its physical estate.[46] But since this compelling sociological point has no decisive bearing on the question of legitimate jurisdiction, I will not make more hay with it here. My case would hold *even if the vast majority of English people were committed Anglicans*.

A central concern behind the 'national pastorate' case is that a disestablished Church would lapse into 'congregationalism';

or, for some, lapse further into it than it already has. Writing in 2002, Paul Avis judged that congregationalist attitudes were already 'rampant' in some parishes.[47] The worry is that the Church would come to see itself as serving only the spiritual needs of its currently active members, disavowing responsibility for the much larger number of English people who still look to the Church for some kind of spiritual sustenance or orientation, even though they are not themselves active participants. William Fittall (then Secretary General of General Synod and the Archbishops' Council) suggested in 2008:

> Establishment serves as a constant and healthy reminder to the Church of England that it should resist the temptation to become simply a membership organisation for the like-minded or to focus its attention solely on people or communities expected to provide the most favourable response.[48]

He did not pause to explain why the Church might need such a 'reminder' or whether the instrument of law was the right one for such a purpose.

In the same vein, in 1983 John Habgood defended Establishment as implying a 'responsibility for the nation as a whole, and in particular for those whose religion is mostly inarticulate and submerged'. Moreover, he suggested provocatively, members of established churches have different 'instinctive reactions' towards non-members: 'For members of non-established churches there is always a prior question to be asked: What are my grounds for being concerned with this or that person? For members of established churches, the sense of responsibility is instinctive and natural.' He added, implausibly: 'I say this not in any way in criticism of other churches.'[49] Even Tom Wright, formidable advocate of a radical conception of the kingdom of God as a counter-movement to secular society, has claimed:

> Establishment means, among other things, that the church is there for everybody. Of course that means that sometimes nobody bothers [but] it also means that much of the society

regards the church as its own. To cut the link, to insist that the church is only there for its fully paid up members, would be to send a signal to the rest of the world that we were pulling up the drawbridge, that we were no longer there for them.[50]

Again, the key claim is that, as a 'national Church', the Church of England must continue to represent the interests of the large number of 'nominal' or 'cultural' Anglicans (or just Christians) who seek its aid, serve as custodian of their possibly inchoate spiritual aspirations and stand ready to minister to their spiritual needs, however episodic.[51] Thus Habgood fears that disestablishment would cause 'the alienation of large numbers of people whose residual allegiance to the Church of England is bound up with the perception that in some obscure way it represents "England"'.[52] He did not reflect on whether disestablishment might, on the contrary, provoke some fresh thought in the minds of some of these people about what membership meant, perhaps leading to their allegiance becoming less 'residual'.

The Chadwick Commission might, perhaps, have been on to something in 1970 when it claimed that Establishment was still appreciated by the nation: 'the people of England still want to feel that religion has a place in the land to which they can turn on the too rare occasions when they think that they need it.'[53] The claim was rather less convincing 40 years later when Martyn Percy spoke, without embarrassment, of the Church of England as a 'National Spiritual Service'.[54]

Much of the anxiety has centred on fear about the future of the parish system as the heart of earthed Establishment. I share the view that the Church should continue to attach a high value to parish churches as strategically important sites of embedded local ministry available to all comers. So it does not follow, as David Harte suggests, that critics of Establishment 'commonly tend to an exclusive view of the nature of the Church' or that they see inclusiveness as 'threatening'.[55] Indeed, one of the supposedly most 'congregationalist' wings of the Church, Evangelicalism, tends to be quite widely networked in local communities and succeeds in bringing at least as many outsiders into its activities, both social and evangelistic, as other wings. Critics of that movement might not come out of a comparative audit of local engagement as well as they might suppose.

Whatever their ambiguous history, parishes remain a precious heritage of the Church's historical identity as the Church of the nation and they should not be lightly abandoned, however hard it may be to sustain some of them. An acrimonious debate on just this issue was triggered in mid-2021 by the (mistaken) perception that the Church (at least its 'corporate managers') now regards traditional parish ministry led by trained stipendiary clergy as a 'limiting factor' in church growth.[56] This triggered the launching of a 'Save the Parish' campaign, the intentions of which seem entirely laudable even if premised on a misreading of official intentions.[57] Parishes should remain at the centre of whatever missional and pastoral strategies the Church eventually settles on, even as it moves progressively towards a 'mixed ecology' model of mission in which parishes operate as bases for, or partners with, alternative expressions of mission such as fresh expressions and church plants.[58] One compelling reason is that, as Grace Davie notes, evidence from the Church Growth Research Programme suggests that 'single church units under one leader are more likely to grow than churches that are grouped together'. While this does not rule out amalgamations, team ministries or group benefices, it does imply that 'a local focus is essential'.[59]

The parish can, of course, also remain open to generous partnerships with other locally based religious or other communities. Elaine Graham, for example, cites appealing examples of Anglican parishes helping build 'social capital' in a multicultural, post-secular context – what she calls 'religion from below'.[60] Most of the Church of England's constructive contributions in this respect could and should be maintained. While I find it misleading for Graham to refer to these as examples of 'the formal legacy of establishment', they are nevertheless highly desirable outcomes of earthed Establishment. In a similar vein, Jenny Leith argues that the Church today could seek to embody a distinctive ethos marked by the attractive idea of a 'non-competitive belonging to particular place'.[61]

Earthed establishment, however, continues to labour under burdens imposed by the law of the land.[62] One of these is a duty to provide regular services in the parish church. This, admittedly, is hardly experienced as burdensome since parish churches are all too keen to do this anyway. But it is an overstepping of the limits of the law all the same. Other arrangements, however, can be seriously irksome. Parish churches are obliged to provide baptisms, weddings and (where the church has an open graveyard) burials to pretty much anyone residing within their boundaries (there are narrow exceptions). In addition, all parishioners, whether members of the Church or not, can still vote on the appointment of churchwardens (although this is rarely a problem in practice).[63]

These legal duties are also backed by powerful, if not always well-informed, cultural expectations on the part of parishioners. Clergy can encounter considerable hostility if, for example, they decline to baptize infants on the grounds that the parents have, in their judgement, not yet shown sufficient clarity or sincerity over what is the Church's founding sacrament.[64] There is some disagreement over whether parental rights to baptism are ultimately enforceable at law. Parish clergy are under a canonical, but not a statutory, duty to baptize any infant in the parish presented to it, and it has been claimed that a bishop supporting a parish church's decision to decline a baptism could not be overridden.[65] Either way, these can be unwelcome burdens. Clergy also face injured indignation if they hesitate to preside over the weddings of parishioners who seem entirely innocent of the Christian meaning of marriage.[66]

On my proposal, after disestablishment any legal obligations in these matters would cease. Decisions about administering sacraments or other spiritual services fall exclusively within the authority of the Church itself. It would then be entirely up to the Church to decide how open or closed such policies should be. The Church might, after all, itself retain some or all of its existing canonical duties on such matters, but canon law would no longer be the law of the land. Parishes already exercise a fair bit of discretion in such matters anyway and might continue to do so. The national Church might wish to issue further pastoral guidance on the point, which I hope would encourage a willingness to serve as many comers as possible.[67]

But severing any *legal* obligations is the first necessary step to sending another important signal – that the Church has the authority to make its own decisions on such matters and is not to be viewed as an indiscriminate dispenser of spiritual services to anyone who happens to reside in the parish. For example, whatever one's particular theology of baptism, it is at least the sign that someone has publicly committed themselves to the life and disciplines of a community that seeks to follow Jesus Christ. It is not a meaningful experience – indeed it would be spiritually compromising one – for those who (or whose parents) have not made that commitment. Declining to baptize the infants of parents who have not yet reached the point where they are ready to make it, is not to 'exclude' them from the Church, to 'put up a drawbridge'. It is to invite people to cross the bridge knowingly, not ignorantly – to indicate the nature of the community into which baptism incorporates them. Local parishes might then find themselves with a challenging but creative opportunity to engage in the 'public explanation' of the Church's missional and pastoral policies. Such a conversation would allow churches to explain that they are indeed fully welcoming of anyone who happens to be resident in the parish, but are not 'owned' by them by virtue of the accident of historic residence or recent property acquisition.

So there is no reason whatsoever why the Church should all of a sudden 'pull up the drawbridge', the 'day after disestablishment'. Wesley Carr claims that 'earthed establishment' cannot exist without 'high establishment', for 'connections between different dimensions in a society exist covertly and need to be from time to time publicly confirmed'. But he concedes quickly that this is 'an untested (and probably forever untestable) hunch'.[68] Indeed so. On the contrary, citing the example of the Church's response in cases of tragic events, even defender of Establishment William Fittall concedes that 'at local level, the instinctive recourse to parish churches and cathedrals for services following local tragedies is *not intrinsically bound up with the legal status of the Church*.'[69] The point applies generally to all the Church's ministries. All its estimable resources in the realm of what Elaine Graham calls 'religion from below' could remain essentially intact after disestablishment.[70] The Church could thus continue to serve, as much as it desired and was able, as a site of welcome for those looking to it to perform religion 'vicariously' on their behalf.[71]

John Habgood feared in 1983 that the Church's sense of pastoral responsibility to the whole nation 'would probably not survive in the long run' without legal backing.[72] But if that were so, surely that commitment would already be threadbare. As Kenneth Leech puts it:

> As someone who has lived and/or worked in inner city areas for the whole of my life, I find this a strange claim. If the Anglican presence is only sustained by a legal structure, is it worth anything? ... Were it to be disestablished, the Church of England might well lose some of its more expensive buildings and much of its status, but what it might gain in credibility would be enormous.[73]

A disestablished Church could also maintain its important role, witnessed impressively in the process behind the production of *Faith in the City*, of building its national vision out of powerful locally rooted concerns rising up from the parishes.[74] Ben Quash thus rightly affirms Anglicanism as a 'polity of presence' in which 'embodied, contextual and personal' knowledge grows at the local level and is transmitted upwards to regional and even national levels.[75]

As Simon Barrow puts it, 'nothing that makes for a "church at the service of the nation", in the non-proprietorial sense of that phrase, is essentially or immutably bound up with the present constitutional status of Anglicanism.'[76] After disestablishment, the Church would be entirely free – and strategically ideally placed – to keep its doors open to anyone in England seeking its spiritual help. The question of its pastoral priorities and local mission strategies would be for it to decide entirely on its own terms. The severing of the Church's historic constitutional ties to the state need not make any significant difference to its commitment to 'earthed establishment'.

Disestablishment would also have no direct bearing on whether the Church would seek to maintain a presence across the whole of England. Whether or not it proved able to do so would be a matter of whether it could sustain a vision for comprehensive territorial ministry and whether its financial and human resources allowed it to do so – a central issue in the debate triggered by the 'Vision and Strategy' process. There is, of course, no guarantee that such resources will continue to be forthcoming. A reference to the Church of Scotland is instructive here since it faces the same issue of maintaining a comprehensive parish ministry.[77] In 2008, the Kirk launched a review of Article III of the Articles Declaratory, which asserts, 'As a national Church representative of the Christian Faith of the Scottish people it acknowledges its distinctive call and duty to bring the ordinances of religion to the people in every parish in Scotland through a territorial ministry.' Notwithstanding its shrinking resources, in 2010 it called on the General Assembly to reaffirm its 'commitment to be a national church with a distinctive evangelical and pastoral concern for the people and nation of Scotland'.[78] The Kirk could make such a commitment without being prompted to do so by any of the legal duties laid upon the Church of England.

However, confronting the reality of declining resources, and taking stock of rapidly declining attendance, David Fergusson had already, in his 2004 book *Church, State and Civil Society*, called for an amendment of Article III to distance the Kirk from the claim that it is 'the proper religious expression of Scottish national identity'.[79] In view of the daunting challenges it faced, he argued that 'the time has come to move forward to a church life that must inevitably be more voluntarist, congregational, countercultural in part, and engaged in new patterns of mission.'[80] Honest Anglicans south of the border will acknowledge that this is already the situation facing much of the Church of England. Like it or not, this is our missional context.[81] But the appropriate response to this state of affairs is not to cling on to archaic and theologically objectionable legal burdens, on the assumption that these could assist the Church to maintain its pastoral commitment to all. Rather it is to search yet more energetically for creative ways to continue to minister to as many parishes as possible, and to as many in any parish as possible, without the aid of law. As Peter Cornwell puts it, 'it is not the spirit of openness which the disestablishmentarian challenges but the argument that it depends on the particular laws which bind the Church of England to the state.'[82]

There is another iteration of the national pastorate anxiety that must also be named: the fear of 'sectarianism'. The worry is that the newly 'liberated' congregations – those upon whom disestablishment would, it is supposed, confer greater powers to erect barriers to 'outsiders' – might become not only insular but 'sectarian'. To those unfamiliar with internal Church of England politics, the term 'sectarian' often serves as code among some Liberal (or 'middle of the road', or 'open') Anglicans for the Evangelical and Traditionalist Anglo-Catholic wings of the Church, at least their supposedly flintier strands.[83] Many such Liberals flatter themselves as being entirely free of sectarian tendencies. By contrast, conservative Evangelical or conservative Anglo-Catholic congregations tend to favour more demanding understandings of Church membership and hold more specific expectations regarding members' belief and behaviour than do others. They may wish to insist that parents wanting their children to be baptized should first make a personal profession of faith and demonstrate that by becoming regular Church attenders, or they may be reluctant to remarry divorced persons. Such practices happen already, of course, but the worry for some is that disestablishment would exacerbate them. Thus William Whyte, commenting on the prospect that disestablishment might also imply disendowment (thus stretching the Church's capacity to maintain a parish everywhere in England), asserts confidently that 'Establishment ... is a bulwark against sectarianism.'[84] He does not pause to define 'sectarianism' or explain how exactly disestablishment would feed it. In the same vein, a key reason why Wesley Carr defends Establishment is that it stands as a constant reminder that 'there can be no such thing as "pure religion"'[85] – 'purity' here serving the same derogatory function as 'sectarian'.[86] The ELS Working Party takes note of the 'continual' charge that disestablishment would turn the Church of England into a 'sect', responding with the brusque reminder: 'This is hardly true of either the Church of Ireland or the Church in Wales.'[87] Nor, of course, is it true of other non-established churches. 'The established church has in truth no monopoly on the spirit of openness', as Peter Cornwell puts it.[88]

I want to suggest that the whole 'sectarian' charge trades lazily on a problematic sociological definition of 'sect' as a separated minority of purists, keeping their distance from mainstream 'churches' and wider society in order to protect the holiness of their internal life.[89] This sociological usage of 'sect' was challenged already in 1918 by B. J. Kidd, later Warden of Keble College, who offered a more adequate theological definition: 'a local Church does not become a sect by ceasing to be co-extensive with the nation. A sect is a body of Christians which has departed from the Faith, or the Order, of the Catholic Church.'[90] On the basis of that definition, one might reasonably ask which wing of the Church of England has actually departed further from the Church of England's *existing* Faith or Order and thus is guiltier of the charge of 'sectarianism'.[91] All things considered, the 'sectarian' charge is best laid to rest by all sides. Colin Buchanan rightly calls it 'mischievous propaganda'.[92]

Yet we cannot put the question to bed just yet. Some worry that without the binding power of Establishment, the feared unleashing of 'sectarianism' would actually *imperil the unity* of the Church. David Harte holds that Establishment 'benefits the Church by discouraging its fragmentation into a collection of sects'.[93] Sceptics might claim that we have virtually arrived at that point already. Given that the odds on *Living in Love and Faith* being able to hold the Church together over same-sex relationships are, as I write, no more than even, the possibility exists that any new controversial debate in the Church could further exacerbate divisions. John Habgood suggested in 1983 that, if disestablishment were initiated by the Church it would be highly divisive, whereas if initiated by the state it could serve to unite the Church. For him that was another compelling reason to defend Establishment.[94] I am sceptical about his second claim, but I agree that the risk of the first is probably higher than it was 40 years ago.

How should proponents of disestablishment respond? Theo Hobson throws down a pointed challenge that we do well to ponder. On the one hand, he also laments growing 'sectarianism', offering no false reassurance on the prospects for unity after disestablishment. But against many of his fellow Liberals, he claims that Establishment is a theologically inauthentic way to keep the Church together.[95] For the Church, he claims, is 'locked in a terrible, terminal dilemma'. It has 'always depended on establishment for its unity, its coherence, its order, its *identity*'. But now that Establishment has been exposed as hollow, 'a convincing and compelling form of Christianity cannot afford to be defined in this way'.[96] The Church should not defend Establishment in order to keep sectarianism at bay but rather abandon its legal privileges and take the risk of facing an admittedly uncertain future in faith and hope.

Whether or not we fully endorse Hobson's diagnosis of the Church's state of health, what we can take away from his argument is this warning: if the Church can only retain its internal unity by clinging on to something as theologically problematic as Establishment, its prospects are dire anyway. Defending Establishment would only defer the inevitable break-up. My chief argument throughout the book has been that Establishment is theologically problematic irrespective of possible consequences such as these. But I would still propose that the risk of furthering division is not an argument against disestablishment. Rather it is a challenge to summon up deeper reserves of ecclesiological courage and integrity in order to sustain the Church's fragile unity – to show that while the Church's 'dilemma' is indeed deep, it is far from 'terminal'. The challenge is to forge a new articulation of Anglican identity able to combine theological integrity with agreed boundaries of plurality forged out of respectful dialogue – as *Living in Love and Faith* is attempting to do on sexual ethics. If that process fails, that may be an indication that disestablishment could yet further hasten division. But in that case, the Church will already be on the road to schism and Establishment would not have been able to contain it. For some, 'integrity' will indeed mean departure. I would respect such a move, while profoundly regretting it. But we cannot with integrity look to constitutional ties to the state to avert such a prospect. A unity sustainable only by a fearful clinging on to a theologically objectionable sixteenth-century arrangement is not worthy of respect. On the other hand, might it even be possible that disestablishment could, after all, concentrate fractious minds on how much would be lost if the Church were to splinter into tribes, all the while proclaiming a gospel of 'reconciliation'? If we are talking about 'sending the wrong signal' to a sceptical society, that would surely be one of the worst of all possible signals.

The larger argument I have been developing in this section is that, whether or not the Church adopts a more 'inclusive' or 'restrictive' view of its pastoral responsibilities (and thus lapses into 'congregationalism' or 'sectarianism') does not and should not depend on any duties sustained by law. One can put the point in the form of a question: on what *theological* grounds could it ever be legitimate to rely on the provisions of the law of the land to advance an argument about 'inclusiveness' or 'openness' that belongs *within the Church itself* – even if, indeed especially if, it is one you are afraid of losing? Defending Establishment *with this end in mind* is to do exactly that. To such people I would say: if you, like me, want a broad, 'non-sectarian' Church, one that maintains an 'open door' to those outside the Church who might occasionally look to it for spiritual succour, then argue for that through the avenues of the

Church itself, at national and local levels, not by relying on the boosters of a compromised constitutional history. To continue to lean on the law of the land for help on such a question is in effect to ask the state, however obliquely, to take a substantive and controversial position on the doctrine of the church and the doctrine of mission, both of which fall squarely within the Church's 'spiritual jurisdiction'. It is palpably beyond the state's proper authority to maintain legal arrangements that serve to shore up one side of this debate over another, and beyond the Church's proper authority to avail itself of the aid of the state on such matters.

Conclusion

This chapter has assessed three widely invoked defences of Establishment and found them wanting. The first, the 'concession to secularism' argument, fails to distinguish between what Rowan Williams calls 'procedural secularism' and 'programmatic secularism' and to recognize that the former does not entail the latter. Rather, procedural secularism – and its corollary, a religiously impartial state – are theological imperatives, at least once the New Testament theology of church and state outlined in Chapter 2 is embraced. Procedural secularism implies disestablishment, but would make the British state *more*, not less, consonant with such a theology. The Church should affirm procedural secularism. Equally, it should continue to resist programmatic secularism and to work for a better realization of 'equitable public pluralism', thereby ensuring that religious organizations generally enjoy a more secure public standing than they currently do. Disestablishment might well be weaponized by opponents to further a programmatic secularist agenda. But this prospect should not cause the Church to dig its heels in. Rather it should commit to disestablishment and prepare to make the best of the unique opportunity it would open up for the public explanation of its identity and mission.

The second defence, the 'anti-neutrality' argument, rightly claims that the actions of states cannot be morally neutral and that the state's implicit moral commitments are, in turn, shaped by larger world views that might be more or less conducive to 'liberal' principles. But it implausibly concludes from these claims that it is within the jurisdiction of the state overtly to favour one such world view. I have argued that this is theologically problematic in that it requires the state to exceed its proper jurisdiction, and because it harbours unnecessarily demanding expectations regarding the 'coherence' of state policy.

The third defence of Establishment is that disestablishment would amount to the Church's retreat from its 'national pastorate' role. I have argued that, on the contrary, the Church can continue to be pastorally solicitous of all comers, within parishes and elsewhere, without the distracting legal constraints and cultural expectations bequeathed to it by Establishment. This side of its national mission would involve letting go of irksome legal duties to administer spiritual services indiscriminately, allowing it greater spiritual freedom to imagine more theologically and pastorally authentic ways of engaging in parish- or diocese-based mission. This could involve exciting new iterations of 'earthed Establishment', such as along the lines of Jenny Leith's vision of 'non-competitive belonging to particular place'.

The next chapter addresses the second part of the 'national mission' anxiety, the worry that disestablishment would cause the Church to retreat from its responsibility for national *political* engagement.

Notes

1 *The Persistence of Faith: Religion, Morality and Society in a Secular Age* (London: Weidenfeld, 1991), p. 68.
2 *Church, State and Establishment* (London: SPCK, 2001), p. 78.
3 'God and Caesar, Then and Now', Jubilee Reflections at West-

minster Abbey: A Series of Lectures on God, Church, Crown and State, 22 April 2002, p. 10.

4 Letter in *Church Times*, quoted in Matthew Grimley, 'The Dog that Didn't Bark: The Failure of Disestablishment Since 1927', in Mark Chapman, Judith Maltby and William Whyte, eds, *The Established Church: Past, Present and Future* (London: T&T Clark, 2011), p. 45.

5 Evangelical Alliance, *Faith in the Nation: Report of a Commission of Inquiry to the UK Evangelical Alliance* (London: Evangelical Alliance, 2006), p. 57.

6 James Macintyre, 'Interview: Rowan Williams', *New Statesman*, 18 December 2008.

7 Jeremy Morris, 'The Future of Church and State', in Duncan Dormor, Jack McDonald and Jeremy Caddick, eds, *Anglicanism: The Answer to Modernity* (London: Continuum, 2003), p. 180.

8 In Lucy Winkett's version of this argument, Establishment serves to keep the right kind of religion – moderate, tolerant religion – in the public square. The effect of disestablishment might be that religion would operate 'in darker corners, perhaps in more toxic atmospheres'. Thus: 'My advice to the politicians about religious leaders – keep us where you can see us' (Linda Woodhead and Lucy Winkett, 'The Duel: Should the Church of England be Disestablished?', *Prospect*, 26 March 2016, www.prospectmagazine.co.uk/magazine/the-duel-should-the-church-of-england-be-disestablished, accessed 28.10.2021). Whether or not that is good advice, it does not require the apparatus of Establishment to bring it about.

9 'Notes on *Church and State: A Mapping Exercise*', in R. M. Morris, ed., *Church and State: Some Reflections on Church Establishment in England* (London: UCL Constitution Unit, 2008), p. 10.

10 *Faith in the Public Square* (London: Bloomsbury, 2012), p. 2.

11 *Faith in the Public Square*, p. 27. It is not 'the empty public square of a merely instrumental liberalism, which allows maximal private licence' (p. 27).

12 Andrew Copson and David Pollock, 'Religion and the State in an Open Society', in Morris, *Church and State: Some Reflections*, p. 58.

13 Peter Cornwell already complained in 1983 that 'The [public] status of canon law has made it impossible for the church to articulate its own discipline [on remarriage]' (*Church and Nation* (Oxford: Blackwell, 1983), p. 68).

14 We can also speak of the 'secularization' of marriage in a more technical, but quite proper, sense. In the modern world, matrimonial jurisdiction formerly held by the Church came to be transferred to the state. This was the 'secularization' of marriage, but this did not mean the imposition of a secularist view of marriage on society: that came

much later and was not an inevitable outcome. The same can be said of the 'secularization' of poor relief, when the Poor Law Amendment Act 1834 created new secular bodies to administer such relief; or when new local authorities appeared in the late nineteenth century, superseding some of the Church's administrative roles (R. M. Morris, ed., *Church and State in 21st Century Britain: The Future of Church Establishment* (Basingstoke: Palgrave Macmillan, 2009), pp. 28, 30).

15 Simon Barrow, 'Unravelling the Rhetoric of Establishment', in Kenneth Leech, ed., *Setting the Church of England Free: The Case for Disestablishment* (Croydon: The Jubilee Group, 2001), p. 75.

16 'Why Christianity benefits Secular Public Discourse, and Why, Therefore, Anglican Bishops should sit in a Reformed House of Lords', *Theology* 117.5 (2014), p. 327.

17 In Chapman, Maltby and Whyte, *The Established Church*, pp. 1–25. A similar argument is advanced in Edward Norman, 'Notes on *Church and State: A Mapping Exercise*, pp. 9–13. See also Roger Trigg, *Religion in Public Life: Must Faith Be Privatized?* (Oxford: Oxford University Press, 2007).

18 I have argued that the fourth of these is not part of Establishment.

19 Nigel Biggar, 'Why the "Establishment" of the Church of England is Good for a Liberal Society', in Chapman, Maltby and Whyte, *The Established Church*, p. 25. Joan Lockwood O'Donovan also speaks of an 'Anglican Christian liberalism', in 'The Liberal Legacy of English Church Establishment: A Theological Contribution to the Legal Accommodation of Religious Plurality in Europe', *Journal of Law, Philosophy and Culture* 6.1 (2011), p. 29; as does Malcolm Brown, 'Establishment: Some Theological Considerations', *Ecclesiastical Law Journal* 21 (2019), pp. 333–4.

20 'Why the "Establishment" of the Church of England', p. 5.

21 'Why the "Establishment" of the Church of England', p. 5.

22 'Why the "Establishment" of the Church of England', pp. 5–6.

23 'Why the "Establishment" of the Church of England', p. 6.

24 'Why the "Establishment" of the Church of England', p. 6.

25 'Why the "Establishment" of the Church of England', p. 15.

26 'Why the "Establishment" of the Church of England', p. 19.

27 'Why the "Establishment" of the Church of England', pp. 21–4.

28 See John Coffey, *Persecution and Toleration in Protestant England 1558–1689* (Edinburgh: Longman, 2000).

29 See Jonathan Chaplin, *Faith in Democracy: Framing a Politics of Deep Diversity* (London: SCM Press, 2021), chs 4, 5.

30 'Establishment', p. 331.

31 'Establishment', p. 331.

32 'Opportunity Knocks: Church, Nationhood and Establishment', in Chapman, Maltby and Whyte, *The Established Church*, p. 32.

33 'Incarnation and Establishment', *Fulcrum*, 27 December 2008, www.fulcrum-anglican.org.uk/articles/incarnation-and-establishment/, accessed 28.10.2021.

34 See, for example, Chris Rowland, 'My Kingdom is Not of This World', in Leech, *Setting the Church of England Free*, pp. 9–26.

35 Barrow, 'Unravelling', p. 76.

36 See Alan Storkey, *Jesus and Politics: Confronting the Powers* (Grand Rapids, MI: Baker Academic, 2005).

37 *Church, State and Establishment*, ch. 2. Avis lists seven characteristics of a national church (pp. 15–16), but then concedes that the idea 'does not depend on legal establishment' (p. 16).

38 *Church, State and Establishment*, pp. 6–7.

39 *Church, State and Establishment*, p. 16.

40 *The Idea of a Christian Society and Other Writings* (London: Faber & Faber, 1982 [1939]), pp. 72–3.

41 John Milbank and Adrian Pabst have good things to say about both: 'The Anglican Polity and the Politics of the Common Good', *Together for the Common Good*, https://togetherforthecommongood. co.uk/leading-thinkers/the-anglican-polity-and-the-politics-of-the-common-good, accessed 28.10.2021. But neither depends on retaining those aspects of 'Anglican polity' that secure privileged constitutional links to the state.

42 'A Developing Establishment', *Theology* 102 (1999), p. 4.

43 'What Future for Establishment?', in Chapman, Maltby and Whyte, *The Established Church*, p. 194.

44 This is a key concern of Theo Hobson, *Against Establishment: An Anglican Polemic* (London: Darton, Longman and Todd, 2003). Hobson claims that the permissive revolution of the 1960s 'emptied establishment of its cultural significance' (p. 16). Grace Davie offers a more nuanced view in *Religion in Britain: A Persistent Paradox*, 2nd edn (Oxford: Wiley-Blackwell, 2015). See also Callum Brown, *The Death of Christian Britain: Understanding Secularisation 1800–2000*, 2nd edn (London: Routledge, 2009).

45 In 2009, average weekly attendance was 1,089,000 but by 2019 had fallen to 854,300 (Statista, www.statista.com/statistics/369080/ church-of-england-attendance-by-service-uk/, accessed 28.10.2021).

46 This argument was powerfully deployed by the Anglo-Catholic critic of Establishment Valerie Pitt in a 'Memorandum of Dissent' to the report of the Chadwick Committee (*Church and State: Report of the Archbishops' Commission* (London: Church Information Office, 1970), pp. 68–79). It casts doubt on Malcolm Brown's wistful hope

that Establishment 'affirms that there is a particular story around which the people of the nation can cohere' ('Establishment', p. 33).

47 *Church, State and Establishment*, p. 16. Wesley Carr uses the same term, in order then to flatter the ministry of cathedrals as, by contrast, 'bulwarks of a more open approach' ('A Developing Establishment', p. 3). A similar argument was already being deployed in the 1960s by Liberal Anglicans. See Grimley, 'The Dog that Didn't Bark', p. 48.

48 'Perspectives from within the Church of England', in Morris, *Church and State: Some Reflections*, p. 76.

49 *Church and Nation in a Secular Age* (London: Darton, Longman and Todd, 1983), pp. 96–7. His subsequent remarks about Nonconformists are frankly condescending (pp. 97–8).

50 Wright, 'God and Caesar, Then and Now'. Most of the lecture affirms the thrust of Chapter 2 above. But when Wright gets to contemporary application, he suddenly endorses elements of the 'Christian state' idea critiqued in that chapter. He notes that this part of his lecture is indebted to Ian Bradley, *God Save the Queen: The Spiritual Dimension of Monarchy* (London: Darton, Longman and Todd, 2002). This explains the following lines: 'Earthly rule is a kind of sacrament ... Monarchy at its best is a symbolic reminder that the power-games of this world do not stand alone, but in a curious and many-sided relation to a transfiguring love and power which exists in a different dimension. In a constitution like that of Great Britain, monarchy is meant to be an angled mirror in which we see round the dark corner to that other dimension of reality, and realise the provisionality of all earthly power' (pp. 8–9). I think there is a disconnect between the two parts of the lecture.

51 On the idea that the Church of England is 'owned' by the whole nation, see Roger Scruton, *Our Church: A Personal History of the Church of England* (London: Atlantic, 2012), a work of elegant prose saturated with English nationalist nostalgia.

52 *Church and Nation in a Secular Age*, p. 100.

53 *Church and State: Report of the Archbishops' Commission*, pp. 65–6.

54 'Opportunity Knocks', p. 31.

55 'The Church of England and the State: A National Church for a Plural Nation', *Law and Justice* 168 (2012), p. 25.

56 This was occasioned by misinformed responses to an admittedly poorly phrased communication regarding a new 'Myriad' plan to plant new churches in parishes, to be partly led by laypeople. See Ian Paul, 'Can the C of E plant new churches and retain the parish system?', *Psephizo*, 26 July 2021, www.psephizo.com/life-ministry/can-the-c-of-

e-plant-new-churches-and-retain-the-parish-system/, accessed 28.10. 2021. It came against the background of suspicions regarding a new national process launched in 2020, 'Vision and Strategy', already thought to be a threat to the parish system (www.churchofengland.org/sites/ default/files/2020-11/GS%202180%20Vision%20and%20Strategy. pdf, accessed 28.10.2021).

57 See https://savetheparish.com/. The concerns have some validity. See Frog Orr-Ewing, 'Do We Need to Save the Parish?', *Psephizo*, 16 August 2021, www.psephizo.com/life-ministry/do-we-need-to-save-the-parish/, accessed 28.10.2021.

58 See https://freshexpressions.org.uk/. For a critique, see Andrew Davison and Alison Milbank, *For the Parish: A Critique of Fresh Expressions* (London: SCM Press, 2010).

59 Davie, *Religion in Britain*, p. 109, n. 4.

60 See 'The Establishment, Multiculturalism and Social Cohesion', in Chapman, Maltby and Whyte, *The Established Church*, pp. 132–3.

61 Jenny Leith, 'The Place of Civic Belonging: The Dangers and Possibilities of Anglican Polity', *Religion, State and Society*, special issue, P. Gorski and M. D. C. van der Tol, eds, 'Who may Belong? Nationalism, Conservative Religion and Identity in German, Dutch and Anglo-American Politics' (forthcoming 2022). A similar vision is echoed in Barrow, 'Unravelling', p. 80.

62 These are listed in Julian Rivers, 'Disestablishment and the Church of England', in Michael Schluter, ed., *Christianity in a Changing World: Biblical Insight on Contemporary Issues* (London: Marshall Pickering, 2000), pp. 74–7, and Harte, 'The Church of England and the State'.

63 'Members' of the Church of England are 'baptised persons giving general allegiance to the ordinances and liturgy of the Church of England' (Rivers, 'Disestablishment', p. 74).

64 Adult candidates can be required to show genuine commitment before baptism (Harte, 'The Church of England and the State', p. 31).

65 Colin Buchanan, *Cut the Connection: Disestablishment and the Church of England* (London: Darton, Longman and Todd, 1994), p. 164.

66 There is also the question whether the Church should continue to perform the function of marriage registration at all. The Ecclesiastical Law Society's 'Working Party on "Disestablishment" Report' suggests that a disestablished Church might here be placed on the same basis as other churches. Currently, Church of England priests are automatically entitled to register marriages. Under the new arrangement, each parish would receive a licence from the Registrar General to permit clergy to act as registrars. This would then allow them to decide whom to marry

(George Spafford, Roger L. Brown and Ben Nichols, *Ecclesiastical Law Journal* 6 (2002), p. 267). In such a case, I would argue that this right be exercised generously. There are, however, good reasons quite apart from disestablishment why the Church should relinquish the registrar role entirely. See Jonathan Chaplin, 'Time to Marry – Twice', *Ethics in Brief* 18.2 (Cambridge: KLICE, 2012), https://kirbylaingcentre.co.uk/wp-content/uploads/2021/01/18.2EiBChaplin.pdf, accessed 28.10.2021.

67 The ELS Working Party proposes that the Church would probably need a new system of defined membership, especially with regard to voting rights, and most likely based on the current electoral roll. This would then allow for 'contractual obligations between members of the Church' ('Working Party on "Disestablishment" Report', pp. 266–7). This would not reduce membership, *theologically conceived*, to mere 'contract', only clarify its legal form. The Church could still adhere to a rich covenantal and sacramental ecclesiology.

68 'A Developing Establishment', p. 5.

69 'Perspectives from within the Church of England', in Morris, *Church and State: Some Reflections*, p. 77. Emphasis added.

70 'Establishment, Multiculturalism and Social Cohesion', pp. 124–40. The Church's contribution to chaplaincies in various institutions, alongside other faith providers, could also be seen as an extension of parish ministry and there is no reason why this could not continue after disestablishment. See Ben Ryan, *A Very Modern Ministry: Chaplaincy in the UK* (London: Theos, 2015).

71 I am alluding to Grace Davie's notion of 'vicarious religion' (*Religion in Britain*, pp. 81–8). Here I have in mind two of the four components Davie identifies: 'Churches and church leaders perform ritual on behalf of others; church leaders and churchgoers believe on behalf of others' (p. 81).

72 *Church and Nation in a Secular Age*, p. 98.

73 Letter to *The Guardian*, quoted in Hobson, *Against Establishment*, p. 39.

74 Davie, *Religion in Britain*, p. 93.

75 'The Anglican Church as a Polity of Presence', in Duncan Dormor, Jack McDonald and Jeremy Caddick, eds, *Anglicanism: The Answer to Modernity* (London: Continuum, 2003), pp. 38–57.

76 'Unravelling', p. 87.

77 As indeed do many historically territorial national churches in Europe. See Davie, *Religion in Britain*, p. 94.

78 *Special Commission anent the third Article Declaratory of the Constitution of the Church of Scotland in Matters Spiritual*, May 2010.

79 *Church, State and Civil Society* (Cambridge: Cambridge University Press, 2004), p. 184. The call was rejected in 2010 (Doug Gay,

Honey from the Lion: Christianity and the Ethics of Nationalism (London: SCM Press, 2013), p. 181).

80 *Church, State and Civil Society*, p. 186.

81 On the sociology of that context, one increasingly marked by a pluralistic and competitive religious 'market', see Davie, *Religion in Britain*, chs 7, 8.

82 *Church and Nation*, p. 42.

83 For some it is not code: Martyn Percy speaks explicitly of 'evangelical or catholic sectarianism' ('Opportunity Knocks', p. 31).

84 'What Future for Establishment?', in Chapman, Maltby and Whyte, *The Established Church*, p. 192.

85 'A Developing Establishment', p. 5.

86 The 'sectarian' charge was first voiced by champions of the sixteenth-century Elizabethan Settlement, which they and their successors framed as a 'middle way' between the 'extremes' of Calvinism and Catholicism. It was also invoked in 1981 in the parliamentary debate on the Prayer Book Protection Bill that was introduced out of a fear that the new *Alternative Service Book* would entirely displace the 1662 Prayer Book (Cornwell, *Church and Nation*, pp. 25–8, 30, 34–5). This was a desperate late attempt to invoke 'lay governance' of the Church through Parliament.

87 'Working Party Report', p. 266. Morris cites a Welsh bishop already in 1946 charging his clergy to minister to everyone in their parishes (*Church and State in 21st Century Britain*, p. 125).

88 *Church and Nation*, p. 42.

89 The distinction controls the entire narrative of Andrew Brown and Linda Woodhead, *That Was the Church, That Was: How the Church of England Lost the English People* (London: Bloomsbury, 2016). The paperback edition (2017) added a 'Coda – Note for Students' in which the 'church–sect' distinction – here rendered as that between a 'societal' and a 'congregational' church – is made explicit (pp. 223–32; see also ch. 4). The book is an extended, caustic lament that the Church has failed to embrace the radical social changes occurring in English society and will only survive if it does so. Although the book is largely innocent of theology, that thesis rests on unarticulated but highly controversial theological assumptions beyond the scope of my book. I largely concur with Andrew Goddard's critical review in *Fulcrum*, 19 August 2016, www.fulcrum-anglican.org.uk/articles/that-was-the-church-that-was-a-review/, accessed 28.10.2021. Their book only has a passing mention of 'effective disestablishment', which is depicted as involving the embrace of a 'full-hearted' congregationalism, with 'no duties or ties to the wider, indifferent society around it' (p. 216). I have argued that ending high establishment need involve no such withdrawal. Woodhead

has elsewhere expressed support for disestablishment, although for the different reason that the Church has 'drifted into irrelevance' and no longer functions as a 'nationalised religion' (Woodhead and Winkett, 'The Duel').

90 Quoted in Colin Podmore, 'Self-Government Without Disestablishment: From the Enabling Act to the General Synod', *Ecclesiastical Law Journal* 21 (2019), p. 516.

91 For example, when the Church accepted women's ordination in 1992, the Anglo-Catholic bishop Graham Leonard said that it had now become a 'sect' (Hobson, *Against Establishment*, p. 36). With a different concern in mind, Peter Cornwell asked in 1983 whether, if Roman Catholic and Independent churches were 'sects' on the definition proposed by defenders of Establishment, the Church of England was not in exactly the same boat: we have had such a status 'thrust upon us by a pluralist society' (*Church and Nation*, p. 34).

92 *Cut the Connection*, p. 78.

93 'The Church of England and the State: A National Church for a Plural Nation', *Law and Justice* 168 (2012), p. 25.

94 *Church and Nation in a Secular Age*, p. 111.

95 'In a permissive society, the established Church is necessarily a permissive Church: otherwise, it advocates social policies at odds with the law of the land and becomes a reactionary sect. This is why many liberals fear disestablishment, despite knowing in their hearts it is right: it would jeopardise the Church's commitment to the liberal values of the cultural mainstream. The fear is understandable, but it is not an excuse to cling on to establishment. Fear should not determine our conception of the Church' (*Against Establishment*, p. 37).

96 *Against Establishment*, p. xiii. Emphasis original.

6

Disputing Establishment:
Disengaging from the Nation?

A free church could be a selfish church, using its freedom
to escape from responsibility to society ... Yet if we serve
the nation with the integrity of the gospel, we are less likely
to find ourselves amongst the crowd of court prophets than
with the prophet Amos.
(Peter Cornwell)[1]

The first part of the 'national mission' defence of Establishment, considered in the last chapter, is that disestablishment
would amount to the Church withdrawing from pastoral
responsibility for the whole nation and cater only for insiders. I
have argued that this defence is unpersuasive. The second part
is that disestablishment would bring about a disengagement
from the affairs of the nation. It would cause a narrowing of
the Church's horizons, leaving it preoccupied with its internal affairs and allowing its historic commitment to civic life to
atrophy. A disestablished Church would no longer speak 'to
the nation' but be tempted to talk only to itself.

It is difficult to determine from advocates of this fourth
defence of Establishment exactly which of the specific steps
towards disestablishment I identified in Chapters 3 and 4 are
thought to imply such a renunciation; they are rarely specific on
the point. For example, it is not easy to see how a repudiation
of the Act of Supremacy and associated Tudor statutes, of the
Crown's power of appointment over senior Church officers,
or of Parliament's right of veto over Church Measures, could

be validly construed that way. Such changes would merely (mildly) strengthen the Church's ability to govern itself, free from state oversight. But they would in no way impair the Church's ability to address whatever national issues it chose to take up. They would not, for example, clip the wings of Lambeth Palace, the Mission and Public Affairs Council (the Church's lead national agency in this area) or discourage other organs or representatives of the Church from speaking out on national issues. The Church would remain entirely able to intervene in public affairs by means of statements from individual bishops or the House of Bishops, reports or resolutions of General Synod, diocesan synods, Archbishops' commissions and so forth. And it is difficult to imagine outsiders, or the media, abruptly deciding to ignore such interventions 'because now the Church is disestablished'. Outsiders mostly ignore them anyway, but why would changes to 'high Establishment' make them any less likely to pay attention? And, more to the point, why would the Church want its national interventions to profit from the improper advantage of arcane constitutional privilege? Perhaps the most plausible concern is over the possible impact of the withdrawal of bishops from the House of Lords, where the fear might be that the public would construe this as a signal that the Church was retreating from its engagement in national policy debates. But as I have already suggested, the departure of bishops from the Lords would in no way inhibit the Church's many other avenues of public speech. If a reformed House of Lords retained the possibility of faith leaders being appointed, the Church's voice, clerical or lay, could still be heard in that context anyway, albeit on a more equitable basis.

Those advancing the national political engagement objection to disestablishment often follow it, slightly apologetically, with the disclaimer that, of course, this is not to imply that *other* churches in England necessarily fail to engage in national affairs or suffer from the feared introversion. And that is just as well, since such a claim is obviously false. One of the most influential attempts by a church over the last quarter of a century to speak to the nation was the Roman Catholic Church's 1996 document, *The Common Good and the Catholic Church's Social Teaching* (dubbed at the time as 'the only game in town' by envious Anglicans). The document was widely appreciated as a serious contribution to debate about the ethical principles that should inform public policy. In this and several other interventions in recent decades, the Roman Catholic Church in England has amply demonstrated its commitment to constructive engagement with the public affairs of the nation. These concern not only so-called 'moral' issues like sexuality or bioethics (for which it routinely comes in for sharp criticism from liberal voices),[2] but also social issues such as homelessness, debt, refugees and poverty (where it usually elicits liberal support). The Methodist Church's track record of public interventions also leaves no doubt as to its commitment to national engagement, and this commitment is reaffirmed in its 2004 *A Report on Church, State and Establishment*.[3] It and other Nonconformist churches, while having far fewer resources in this area than Anglicans, have succeeded in making high-quality interventions in national affairs, often now through the Joint Public Issues Team, which represents four Protestant denominations.[4] If the Roman Catholic Church and Nonconformist churches can speak effectively to the nation without the benefits and burdens of Establishment, why could not the Church of England? The point is the same as in the national pastoral responsibility case: whether or not a church is committed to engagement in national affairs is first and foremost a question of how it understands its own mission and where it is prepared to put its resources, not of whether it retains any special ties to state institutions. Even if it continues to see one of its vocations as 'unifying the nation', as Malcolm Brown hopes,[5] it could do this just as well if it were disestablished. Indeed, it could do it better, since by losing its established status, it would be better placed to explore ecumenical cooperation with more churches.[6]

As even the strongly pro-establishment Chadwick Report conceded in 1970: 'No amendment of the laws could alter the vocation to a national mission.'[7] It is true that those churches whose theology is focused largely on personal behaviour and which lack a vision of the public scope of Christian faith will not attempt public engagement. And, regrettably, there are Anglican parishes, of all stripes, that exhibit such a narrow vision (due to introversion or lack of resources). Establishment seems not to have forestalled that possibility. But Anglicanism as a whole has long held out such a vision, of which one central pillar has indeed been a (properly construed) 'incarnational' theology of social engagement. This has been undergoing significant renewal in recent years.[8] The fear that the changes to high Establishment I am proposing would cause it to relinquish that deeply embedded theology of public engagement seems completely groundless.

It may even be possible that a disestablished Church could continue to offer the more public and political elements of what Grace Davie calls 'vicarious religion': to 'embody moral codes on behalf of others' and to 'offer space for the "vicarious" debate of unresolved [public] issues'.[9] I am somewhat sceptical regarding the former, but Davie alludes to a plausible example of the latter. This is Rowan Williams' reading of the Occupy London protest against global capitalism that ended up camped out on the steps of St Paul's Cathedral for several weeks in 2011, eliciting national attention (and dividing the Cathedral Chapter). Williams writes:

> It has sometimes been said that the Church of England is still used by British society as a stage on which to conduct by proxy the arguments that society itself does not know how to handle. It certainly helps to explain the obsessional interest in what the Church has to say about issues of sex and gender. It may help to explain what has just been going on around St Paul's Cathedral in the past fortnight.[10]

There may be truth in that. I would judge, however, that the Church would be able to serve such a 'proxy' function more authentically if it were not itself an integral part of the state apparatus against which such protests are targeted, and still more so if it could provide such a 'stage' on an ecumenical, or even inter-faith, basis.

What is more, the Church's deep rootedness in English history for many centuries has bequeathed to it innumerable customary place-based linkages to civic life at many levels of society and government. A friend has described to me how his location in a parish church, situated at the heart of a medium-sized, multi-faith city and engaged in substantial community reconciliation projects, had over many years afforded many opportunities to cultivate relational capital conducive to the church's mission. It is true that the Church of England's historical embedded-ness in the nation's culture and institutions have bequeathed it a significant advantage in generating such capital. My point is that this advantage would be largely unaffected by the dis-mantling of high establishment. For example, Robert Morris has noted that, after disestablishment, 'the *civic* status of [the Church in Wales] remained little changed and its overall posi-tion could be said to have improved.'[11] At the national level, too, the Church's historic assets alone would continue to secure it a strategic place in public affairs. We can confidently pre-dict, for example, that Westminster Abbey is going to remain rooted to the spot, right next to Parliament and around the corner from other institutions of state. I am assuming here that it had not, as a royal peculiar, been transferred wholly to the state's jurisdiction or fallen victim to a punitive disendowment settlement, depriving the Church of such a plum location. But even if it had, St Paul's Cathedral is just down the road, located at the heart of the nation's financial system.[12]

Anglican clergy will surely also continue to get invited to, preside over or offer prayers at local civic occasions such as Remembrance Day services. These could and should certainly be shared more equitably with other churches or faith groups. The complaint is recorded in the Methodist *Report* that some Anglican clergy continue to assume pride of place in offering spiritual service at local civic events rather than sharing such opportunities with other local churches as a matter of course.[13]

If, however, such invitations were to dry up over time it will not be because of some remote change at the constitutional level of which few local practitioners will be conscious. Rather, it will be because of changing perceptions of the Church's role by local officials, or because of a regrettable, but entirely avoidable, withdrawal from such a role by local parishes and dioceses.

I should note briefly that disestablishment would raise the question whether parishes would continue to maintain special links to military regiments or local army cadets corps. Such relationships might indeed come under scrutiny and it would be up to the Church nationally and locally, and the military agencies themselves, to decide whether and how to continue them. Some such bodies would find themselves thinking about the question for the first time. The logic of the religious impartiality of the state suggests the need to end any formal relationships between the Church and such agencies, implying the removal from churches of military symbols. Parish churches could be encouraged to engage the relevant agencies in a constructive conversation about what form of spiritual or chaplaincy support they might wish to continue receiving, if any.

A distinct argument sometimes deployed by those mounting the 'national engagement' defence is that Establishment 'keeps the Church close to the realities of politics'. It forces it to confront the complex contingencies of political decision-making, disabusing it of abstract moral absolutes. Establishment, so it is held, exercises what John Habgood calls 'a devastating effect on prophetic certainties'.[14] Or, as William Whyte puts it more censoriously: 'Instead of hiding in comfortable opposition, complacently criticizing from the sidelines, the formal link between Church and State emphatically establishes that it is the job of the Church to live in the real world.'[15]

There are two obvious problems with this view. The first is that it is puzzling why the Church should feel any need to have its 'prophetic certainties' blunted by an enforced proximity to the corridors of power. Why can't it calibrate its own prophetic stance itself? And isn't it entitled to do so free from pressures to conform to the expectations of an outside body? The second is its clericalism: it simply ignores the contribution of the Church's *own lay members* who are active in 'the real world' of politics on a daily basis and who could, if the clergy cared to inquire, tell them a great deal about the complex contingences of politics – much more than they could ever learn from loitering around elites in the Westminster bubble. Peter Cornwell turns Whyte's point on its head: 'the church present in its laity is more deeply immersed in particular situations and thus less likely to escape into woolly generalizations.'[16] The idea that the anachronistic apparatus of Establishment is required in order to instruct the Church in the ways of politics is frankly rather desperate. As a matter of fact, however, senior clergy *do* often seek the advice of laypeople in a host of ways. Whyte's worry about insularity is dated and overblown. Indeed, one of the reasons why the voice of bishops or other religious leaders in the Lords is often respected is that they are closer to the realities of people in their own communities than are many government ministers and officials.

If the Church were to embrace the challenge of disestablishment, how then should it frame its new understanding of its relation to the state? Article VI of the Church of Scotland's Articles Declaratory expresses the thrust of what, suitably clarified, updated and 'Anglicized', the Church of England's church–state theology could look like, the 'day after disestablishment':

> This Church acknowledges the divine appointment and authority of the civil magistrate within its own sphere, *and maintains its historic testimony to the duty of the nation* acting in its corporate capacity to render homage to God ... The Church and the State owe mutual duties to each other, and acting within their respective spheres *may signally promote each other's welfare* (emphases added).

As intimated earlier, I would only wish to propose that 'the duty of the nation acting in its corporate capacity to render homage to God' be understood in terms of practical deeds of justice rather than any explicit official statements of deference to God or the Christian faith.

If, regrettably, a disestablished Church of England no longer gave 'historic testimony to the duty of the nation ... to render homage to God' – if it abandoned its duty of engaged public theology – it would solely be the result of its own neglect. Nothing in what I have proposed would in any way prevent the Church from continuing to make the national political interventions it currently does (with the exception of its having fewer, if any, Lords Spiritual). Whether it was actually *listened to* by the public or government would then depend wholly on the intrinsic credibility and persuasiveness of its interventions and the degree to which they could be shown to be supported by Church members. But that is already the case – and why would the Church want it otherwise? For example, even without the constitutional privileges enjoyed by the Church of England, the Church of Scotland has regularly been able to maintain such historic testimony to the state. It has done so, for example, in the strategic contribution it made in the 1990s to the constitutional debates leading up to Scottish devolution and, again, in its interventions in the debate over independence in 2014.[17] So have the non-established Anglican churches of the UK – the Church in Wales, the Scottish Episcopal Church and the Church of Ireland (which includes Northern Ireland) – albeit with vastly fewer resources than the Church of England.

Could a disestablished Church be more 'prophetic'?

I have argued, then, that the Church could still remain effectively committed to national political engagement after disestablishment. But I have not yet examined the substance of the distinct argument that disestablishment would also 'liberate' the Church to be more 'prophetic' – more courageous or radical in its political interventions. Whether or not it aspires to adopt a prophetic voice in its public communications, and how it does so, are very important to its sense of its own mission – and, Christians will argue, to the state's as well. Here is one apt definition of a church's national mission: 'a quality of the church's whole life giving it a critical and prophetic self-consciousness in relation to the totality of the national life in which it is involved'.[18] Note that this does not imply that the Church should routinely be issuing denunciations of whatever the state happens to be doing. Rather it captures the idea that the Church should jealously retain its capacity for critical detachment from the nation's identity and interests, allowing the Church to determine its own theological mind on national affairs without being pre-emptively cowed by expectations of loyalty and deference to that identity or those interests. The Church's prophetic interventions could speak to all national issues, whether 'progressive' or 'conservative'.

My judgement is that, while it was once clearly the case that Establishment stifled the Church's prophetic voice, the picture is less clear today. There is evidence on both sides of the ledger. Already in 1985, the Church was able to produce *Faith in the City*, which (notwithstanding its much-lamented theological flimsiness[19]) was searchingly critical of the Thatcher government's urban policies, evoking forceful reactions from Tory politicians. Today its readiness to offer pointed critiques of the state in general or of the policies of a particular government seems not to have diminished.[20] Certainly, many would wish that these were more penetrating, more theologically coherent and more consistent (and more ecumenical). But a particularly promising example in this regard is *Who is my Neighbour?*, the pastoral statement put out by the bishops ahead of the 2015 election.[21] This set forth a robust and constructive social theology against which, inter alia, it exposed the shallowness of much British electoral and party politics and pointed to persisting structural distortions of states and markets and their threats to civil society. It would be encouraging if this kind of document were to serve as a platform for a fuller, developing articulation of the Church's public theology. I hope it does not suffer the same fate of some of its predecessors and get hastily forgotten, leaving the Church with the need to reinvent the wheel the next time it feels compelled to speak out. The Church needs to commit itself to building up a cumulative, developing body of public theology rather than finding itself having to respond piecemeal to whatever are the latest demands to 'say something'. Individual leaders have indeed made notable contributions,[22] but what is needed is a flow of widely endorsed official offerings from the Church collectively.[23] That will require significant changes of attitude and procedure at many levels of the Church, not least a greater commitment to episcopal collegiality and a less tribal posture on the part of groups in General Synod. It should make these changes anyway, but disestablishment will throw the Church more fully on to its own resources and make them even more imperative.

All that said, when one sitting archbishop (Rowan Williams) can write a *New Statesman* article accusing the government's austerity measures of being undemocratic;[24] when another (Justin Welby) can declare that he wanted the Church to 'compete' a notorious payday lender 'out of existence' by creating its own credit unions;[25] or when the Church argues that 'imposing for essentially ideological reasons a new meaning on a term as familiar and fundamental as marriage would be deeply unwise',[26] it becomes harder to make the 'muted voice' charge stick – whatever we make of those particular stances. I nevertheless submit that disestablishment would at least help to *create the conditions* in which the Church might be able to imagine more radical possibilities of political engagement and, perhaps, discover reserves of courage it did not realize it had. Because a disestablished Church would no longer need to feel obliged to perform a deferential 'chaplaincy function' to the state, it would find itself freer to take critical distance from organs or actions of the state it judged, by its own lights, to be theologically problematic.

To see how such inhibiting pressures are still operative, I now want to consider four recent examples where the Church's established status seems to have had the effect of blunting its capacities for courageous challenge to the state. In one, the

Church did all the rights things but still found itself in the wrong place; in another, its established status lured it into blessing a questionable state policy at odds with the Church's own developing mind; in a third, a well-intentioned attempt to exploit its established status foreclosed its capacity to speak bravely; in a final case, the inevitable tensions in its role as 'national Church' left it, literally, speechless.

The Thatcher funeral: pastoral succour or partisan complicity?

There was never any question that the Church of England would be expected to preside over the funeral of Baroness Thatcher in 2013.[27] At the time, many argued that in doing so it was acting as the national Church at its very best. Transcending the ideological fractures that her passing reopened, the Church was able to offer pastoral succour for a grieving nation, affording sacred space within which it could pay suitable tribute to one of its towering political figures. We may respect that reading of the event, but another is more compelling: that the Church was inadvertently implicating itself in what was inescapably a partisan political performance from which it should have taken distance.

This was not due to the shortcomings of any individual participant or even of the liturgy itself. Every Church official played their part with exemplary solemnity, sincerity and respect. The elegant choreography of the occasion was flawless – the Established Church still does ceremonial aesthetics better than most other national institutions. The Christian character of the service – much of the contents of which were apparently chosen by Baroness Thatcher herself – also came through clearly enough in the Scripture readings, prayers and poetry, and in a finely crafted and theologically resonant sermon from the Bishop of London. In subtle contrast to the dominant eulogizing tone prior to the event, the bishop gently reminded the great and the good assembled there that 'Margaret Hilda

Thatcher' was, finally, 'one of us', that all humanity is united in death even if it is divided in life.

Quite properly, the bishop declared that a funeral was not the occasion to assess Thatcher's political legacy. He sought to speak as pastor to grieving family, friends and colleagues and he did so with grace, sensitivity and humour. He even seized on the potentially hazardous opportunity to correct the pervasive misrepresentation of her most frequently cited aphorism, that 'there is no such thing as society'. He rightly pointed out that this was not a repudiation of all notions of social solidarity or care – Thatcher professed herself very much in favour of those aspirations, at least at the level of civil society – but only of the idea that we should turn to some reified abstraction called 'society' (which invariably meant the state) to fix all our problems. That is a claim consonant with much Anglican social theology.

So it was not any individual failing or liturgical defect that placed the Church in a compromising position. Rather, it was the inescapable public symbolism of the event itself. I doubt the Church had any real say in the basic decision as to what category of funeral Baroness Thatcher was to receive. It was the big beasts of the political establishment – starting with Tony Blair and Gordon Brown, later followed eagerly by the then Conservative leadership – who for their own ideological reasons concluded that Thatcher merited a 'ceremonial funeral' (essentially a state event, one stop short of a 'state funeral'). This was an accolade granted only to Sir Winston Churchill among modern Prime Ministers. Those ideological reasons were, in effect, to reaffirm that 'we were right to embrace the core of Thatcherism – there was no alternative'. But the Church should not have given its implicit blessing to such a controversial and contestable declaration. Here, the pastoral was inescapably wedded to the political, whatever the subjective intentions of Church leaders.

The Church should surely have been aware that elevating Baroness Thatcher to the same level as Churchill was an inherently divisive and partisan act. Even if the party elites (at least Labour and Conservative ones) may have signed on to it, much of the nation did not and could not. Immediately after Thatcher's death, the Prime Minister, David Cameron, suggested, grandiloquently, that she had 'saved' the nation. Now we know what we mean when we say that Churchill had 'saved' the nation. While victory in the Second World War would have been impossible without overwhelming military support from the USA, and without the (unsung) sacrifice of millions of Soviet troops on the eastern front, nonetheless Churchill's decisive and courageous national leadership soared far above any party concerns. So it could be argued that Churchill earned his ceremonial funeral because he was a truly unifying national figure, in war if not in peace.

The same cannot be said of Margaret Thatcher. Her premiership was intentionally and militantly partisan from the start. The political objectives she pursued and the methods by which she prosecuted them were profoundly and knowingly divisive – that must surely be conceded even by those who enthusiastically endorsed them. She relished opposition as a validation of her own messianic self-image (an observation later applying equally to Tony Blair and now to Boris Johnson).[28] Whatever we think of the Falklands Islands/Malvinas victory, it did not amount to 'saving the nation' (though it may have helped save Argentina from dictatorship). Moreover, we should not overlook the fact that under Mrs Thatcher's leadership the Conservative party never won more than 44 per cent of the popular vote – which is to say that at least half the voting nation consistently repudiated what she stood for.

But, some will say: is it not right at least to celebrate her extraordinary courage, determination and single-mindedness, to praise her for successfully 'imposing her will' on her generation? If so, why should the Church not host such a celebration? But the mere imposition of will, we might have hoped some Church leader would say (not in the service itself, of course), is a pagan not a Christian virtue – more Nietzsche than Jesus. The Christian gospel does not praise mere power but only the just purposes to which it ought to be subservient. 'Towering figures' are only as admirable as the virtuous ambitions they pursue. To the many millions who found Thatcher's policies profoundly unjust, and who personally experienced them as deeply destructive, her imposition of will was nothing to celebrate.

None of this is yet to say that, from the standpoint of Christian political thought, those ambitions or policies were in fact wrong. That would be an entirely different argument, one which is beside the point of the claim I am here making. But it is to say that Thatcher is an incurably divisive figure whom it is not possible to honour in such a uniquely privileged state ceremony without implicitly conferring one's blessing on her political legacy. If you doubt that, suppose that Tony Benn – as far to the left of the political centre as Thatcher was to the right – had imposed his will on the nation as Prime Minister for over a decade and redrawn its entire landscape (that 'we were all Bennites now'). Can we imagine the political and ecclesiastical establishments being so eager to put him in the same company as Churchill?

For the Church to preside over a funeral for a bereaved family, however famous the deceased, is one thing, and something it should almost always be prepared to do, accommodating the family's wishes as far as possible. But endorsing the official elevation of a profoundly partisan political figure whose legacy still deeply divides the nation is quite another, and something to which it should have devoted much greater critical reflection.

That the political establishment felt itself duty-bound to perform a final act of ritual public deference denied to any other peacetime British Prime Minister is proof of how profoundly Thatcher had cast a mesmerizing spell on an entire generation. It is not for the Church to instruct the state that it cannot stage such an event. But it is, or should be, for the Church to decide whether and how it wants to fall in line with it – to decide whether it is willing to offer its spiritual ministrations to a political establishment with an evident, and contestable, ideological agenda. Might the Church not have registered to the state (privately at first, and long before the time) its unease at being pressed into political service in this way and then quietly advised that it was in the nation's interest that Baroness Thatcher be treated the same way as all other peacetime Prime Ministers? If, in response, the political establishment was determined to have its way, might the Church not then have gathered up its courage and respectfully recused itself from presiding over such a service? The political expectations arising from the Church's Established status, however, appear to prevent the Church from even posing such a question to itself.

Nuclear weapons – banning or blessing?

On 3 May 2019, the Dean of Westminster Abbey, the Very Revd Dr John Hall, presided over a service to 'mark' the fiftieth anniversary of the UK's 'continuous-at-sea' nuclear deterrence programme.[29] This was one of a series of invitation-only events initiated by the Royal Navy. It was attended by Prince William, Commodore-in-Chief of the Royal Navy Submarine Service, who also read a lesson from Ephesians 2.13–20, which opened with the words, 'in Christ Jesus you who once were far off have been brought near by the blood of Christ. For he is our peace.' A central theme of the service was that God is our protector and that only Christ brings true peace.

Nearly 200 Anglican clergy signed a statement protesting against the event, reminding the Abbey that, as recently as July 2018, General Synod had passed a motion asserting that 'nuclear weapons, through their indiscriminate and destructive potential, present a distinct category of weaponry that requires Christians to work tirelessly for their elimination across the world.'[30] Nick Megoran, from the University of Newcastle, also pointedly reminded the Abbey that, only a year earlier, it had held a service marking the fiftieth anniversary of the assassination of Martin Luther King, a firm opponent of nuclear weapons: 'Drawing attention to the abbey's striking statue [of King], John Hall said: "We hope again to learn from [his] example ... and to commit ourselves afresh to keeping the dream alive of justice for all peoples under God and of peace in the world.'" Megoran observed that the Church 'cannot possibly claim to be learning from King's example if it is sanctifying the deployment of weapons of mass destruction'.[31]

The Dean responded to criticisms by suggesting that 'the service will be neither one of thanksgiving nor in any way a celebration of nuclear armaments' – despite the fact that 'service of thanksgiving' and 'celebrate' are exactly the terms in which the Royal Navy described the event in its own announcement.[32] There was thus a fundamental public ambiguity about what the event really signified. On the one hand, the order of service described it as a service to 'recognize' the deterrent;[33] and in his address the Dean asserted that 'we cannot celebrate weapons of mass destruction' but that we did owe 'a debt of gratitude' to those who maintain them.[34] Yet in his Bidding, he gave thanks to God that the deterrent 'has had the effect of maintaining peace and security between the nations'. In his address, he also rejected the claim of critics that General Synod had 'voted against nuclear weapons' and suggested that 'Synod did not call for unilateral nuclear disarmament but asked Her Majesty's Government to respond positively to the 2017 UN Treaty on the Prohibition of Nuclear Weapons.' He was, he affirmed, 'proud to be holding [the service] here in the Abbey'.[35]

What General Synod said is quite clear. While Hall is technically correct that it had not specifically 'voted against nuclear weapons', this hardly conveys its full intent. In 'welcoming' the 2017 UN Treaty (in a motion passed by 260 to 26), Synod was *in effect* embracing a call for such weapons to be banned, while leaving open the precise steps needed to bring this about.[36] Later, 31 bishops, including both archbishops, explicitly endorsed that position, writing to the *Observer* on 30 November 2020 that they 'warmly welcome and applaud the recent ratification' of the Treaty by some nations (it came into force in January 2021), and 'very much regret' that the UK government had not done so.[37]

The Church of England has in fact long been divided on whether and, if so, how to abolish nuclear weapons. There is a broad consensus against the legitimacy of their *use*, but continuing differences on the morality and feasibility of possessing them as a *deterrent*. The positions cited above, however, seem to herald a wider shift occurring in the Church towards support for banning nuclear weapons and away from deterrence. In any event, all sides know that the issue remains deeply controversial in the Church and that the Church seems currently to be undergoing another period of serious reflection on it. Given this state of affairs, the decision by Westminster Abbey to preside over the 2019 service was, at least, deeply disrespectful of the Church's current journey of discernment on the matter. The decision evoked deep discontent in the Church and scorn among many outside it.

Whatever one makes of it, the Abbey's decision to host such a service reveals something about the unresolvable tensions into which Establishment thrusts the Church. In this case, the tension is between, on the one hand, the Church's – and the state's – assumption that the Established Church must be available to serve a 'chaplaincy function' to organs of state such as the military, and, on the other, the Church's need to find its own common mind on the question and convey that boldly and consistently to the state. The chaplaincy function assumption is baked into Establishment (even if not enshrined in law). It is why the Church is routinely expected to preside compliantly over national occasions such as royal weddings and funerals, or military commemorations such as this, irrespective of whether these might be spiritually compromising or profoundly divisive in the Church. The thought that the Church might decline to do so, or only on the condition that it *itself* set the terms of a service over which it was presiding, is virtually unimaginable for leaders of both Church and state.

The inevitable result is the contortions, indeed self-deceptions, seen in the cathedral's attempt to defend its role. The Abbey denied it was a celebration or thanksgiving for the nuclear fleet but the navy was in little doubt on the point. Whatever the

Church told itself it was doing in presiding at such an event, what it was *objectively* doing was blessing the British state's possession of nuclear weapons. It could be perceived in no other way by wider society. On occasions like this, the chaplaincy function of the Church is not neutral public service. As Megoran observes:

> Events such as this at Westminster Abbey are deeply political interventions in public life. Commanding significant media attention, they narrate a story about who and what Britain values. This is only heightened when politicians and royalty attend. That is why [the] service matters to everyone, and not just to Anglicans. Trident renewal, approved by MPs in 2016, is deeply controversial. By holding this service the church is – possibly inadvertently – providing legitimation of a controversial choice that is morally, legally and politically dubious.[38]

The Church is not always entirely subservient to state expectations on such occasions.[39] For example, in 1983, Archbishop Robert Runcie incurred the wrath of the Prime Minister, Margaret Thatcher, and other Tory politicians, as well as sections of the media, when he insisted that the service of thanksgiving for victory in the Falklands Islands/Malvinas war renounce triumphalism and include prayers for fallen Argentinian servicemen and women as well as British ones. As Cornwell puts it: 'the Church of England declined to turn the service commemorating the Falklands Islands campaign into an occasion of nationalistic triumphalism and insisted that an act of Christian worship should remain recognizably Christian.'[40] The Archbishop of York, John Habgood, sought at the time to harness that moment of critical distance behind a defence of Establishment, opining that 'Only the Church of England could have insisted on counter-balancing the nationalistic thrust of the Falklands celebration, precisely because of its relationship to the nation.'[41] He did not ask whether the Church should even allow itself to be in a position in which it is assumed it will preside over such an event. Dean Hall seemed not to have posed the question in 2019 either. Cornwell's phrase, 'the Church of England *insisted*', is one that we should have heard far more frequently in the Church's dealings with the state.

Ambivalence about amnesty

My third example is one where Establishment seems to have allowed the Church, with the best of intentions, to manoeuvre itself into a position in which its ability to speak boldly against an unjust state proposal was compromised. It illustrates in a rather different way how the Church's proximity to the state arising from Establishment can sometimes draw it into actions, however well meaning, that end up stifling what many will feel should have been its prophetic voice. In July 2021, Anglican Archbishop John McDowell, Archbishop of Armagh and Primate of All Ireland, issued a trenchant response to the British government's proposed amnesty for killings taking place in Northern Ireland prior to the Belfast Agreement of 1998.[42] The effect of such an amnesty would be to close off further prosecutions of such killings on the part of all sides in the conflict, including those done by British security services, which many saw as the government's real concern. Archbishop McDowell argued that a general amnesty – which was what he judged the government's proposals amounted to – would be contemptuous of the thousands of victims' families who had long been yearning for at least a measure of truth about such killings.[43] It would be a 'morally empty response':

> In a repeat of a dismal pattern, once again political interests in Great Britain have been used as the criteria for settling policy in Northern Ireland. Imperfect as they may have been, the carefully worked-out provisions of the Stormont House Agreement have been set aside by one of the parties to the Agreement. Of course, that means a further erosion of trust

in those who have been entrusted with just and fair government. To believe that any process of reconciliation can be advanced by a measure that betrays the trust of victims, and of most ordinary citizens, indicates a profound ignorance of human nature and human suffering, and of the particular conditions of society in Northern Ireland.[44]

One might have thought that such a statement would have elicited robust support from the Church of England, for two reasons. One is that the Church might have been expected to endorse theologically the judgement that a sustainable peace in Northern Ireland cannot be traded off against justice for the victims of the Troubles. The other is that this would have been a natural gesture of solidarity towards the head of its neighbouring province in Ireland. No such statement was forthcoming.

I strongly suspect that this was because Lambeth Palace had, in November 2020, facilitated what was supposed to be a secret meeting to consider possible options around amnesty.[45] Hosted by the Archbishop of Canterbury, the meeting was described by its initiators, Jim Roddy (Derry city-centre manager) and the Revd Harold Good (a former president of Ireland's Methodist Church), as a 'seminar'. The gathering discussed an options paper on amnesty, co-authored by the Queens University Belfast academic Kieran McEvoy and a human rights organization, the Committee on the Administration of Justice. Roddy and Good said it was a continuation of long-standing conversations on legacy issues (a claim I have no reason to doubt). The paper recommended implementing the proposals of the 2014 Stormont House Agreement.[46] The meeting included a range of political figures, among them representatives of the British and Irish governments, military and academic figures and former paramilitaries.[47]

Conspicuous by their absence, however, were representatives of victims' families (such as Innocent Victims United) and veterans' groups, causing widespread anger. Danny Kinehan, Northern Ireland's Veterans' Commissioner, was present but reported being surprised at the absence of such groups.[48] When victims' groups declined to attend a planned follow-up meeting in December 2021, complaining of lack of 'openness and transparency', the meeting had to be postponed.[49] Political parties were also not invited, causing additional resentment (although Sinn Fein later claimed that Sean Murray had been there as its representative, evoking Unionist outrage).[50] Inevitably, reports of the meeting quickly leaked, exposing the Church to unwelcome publicity and making it appear (rightly or wrongly) to be doing the British state's business.

The difficulty in this case is different from that involved in the Westminster Abbey service, revealing another kind of tension inherent to Establishment. In this case, by presuming to be able to serve as 'neutral host' to a conversation on what was inevitably a deeply controversial issue, the Church necessarily denied itself the freedom to take distance from the state's eventual proposals. The assumption that the Church is in a position to act as such a neutral host for this kind of political conversation is one that arises naturally from its self-image as the Established Church of the nation (again, England, Britain, the UK?). That image is also evidently shared by members of the political establishment (among others), making them eager to exploit the opportunity such a gathering seemed to offer. From the state's standpoint, the Church here serves simply as a well-positioned convenor of processes that the state wishes to pursue for its own reasons. Lambeth Palace, moreover, is a convenient, commodious and (it vainly hoped) confidential venue. But the political establishment has little interest in whether the Church's performance of such a function might be damaging for the Church's own integrity.

I do not at all question the Church's best intentions in offering to convene such a gathering, nor its competence to do so.[51] But I judge that in this case the Church's leadership failed to anticipate the silencing effect that acting as host of such a gathering might have. Did it not foresee that, were the British state to come out with anything like the amnesty proposal it eventually did (and that seemed possible, given its earlier policy indications), the Church might have wanted to retain the freedom to speak 'prophetically' against it? This is especially so because of the Church's close affiliation to a state that had already been found guilty of serious crimes in Northern Ireland (as disclosed, for example, in the independent *Report of the Bloody Sunday Inquiry* in 2010[52]). And, not least, it would also have left it free publicly to stand shoulder to shoulder with, and defer to the leadership of, Archbishop McDowell, its principal partner in Ireland and someone who is rather closer to the issues at stake than leaders of the Church of England.

Brexit: nothing to see here?

The final example I will explore – Brexit – is one of institutional speechlessness. Examining this will allow me to elaborate further my earlier remarks on how the Church's public theology as a whole could be better calibrated after disestablishment. During the entire Brexit process, the Church of England made no official, collective intervention in what was to become the most agonizing and damaging national debate since, at least, the early years of the Thatcher government. As the nation ripped itself apart over whether to leave the EU and, if so, on what terms, the Church – the body that presumes to fulfil the role of national Church – had nothing collective to say on the fundamental issues at stake. Several individual bishops, the archbishops and other church leaders, clerical and lay, made occasional statements, often helpful.[53] Then, in August 2019, over 20 diocesan bishops declared their opposition to a no-deal Brexit, incurring the wrath of many pro-Leave Church members and politicians. After the final decision to leave was made, the Church did issue calls for national 'reconciliation'.[54] But a Church that during the 2015 election had had the wherewithal to publish a serious piece of public theology (*Who is my Neighbour?*), somehow barely a year later found itself officially mute on a much more momentous national event.

The most common explanation for the Church's official

silence was that the Church did not want to take an official position on such a deeply divisive question – that, precisely as the national Church, it wanted to maintain a stance of pastoral hospitality to the whole nation. Bishops themselves are explicitly enjoined to serve as a 'focus for unity' in their dioceses. But, first, this injunction has not prevented many of them over the years, individually or collectively, from issuing divisive statements on a whole range of questions, whether universal credit, immigration or same-sex marriage. Inclusive pastoral hospitality is an exemplary virtue for a national Church. But it need not be, cannot be and often has not been incompatible with taking robust stances on major political issues, sometimes at the cost of heightened divisions in and beyond the Church. Second, the assumption behind the concern about preserving unity is that the Church, had it intervened, would have been expected to come down on one side of the referendum question itself: to have straightforwardly recommended 'Remain' or 'Leave'. But what was needed from the Church was not such a partisan intervention but a serious, theologically informed *diagnosis* of the deeper causes at work in Brexit and an exposition of a broad (Anglican) theology of nationhood, statehood, international relations, sovereignty, democracy, solidarity and justice. Had the Church opted to offer such a diagnosis, it would (had it looked) have found ample reserves of Anglican and other kinds of public theology available to assist it.

There was, it turns out, another very specific reason why it opted not to take this course. Malcolm Brown, the Church's Director of Mission and Public Affairs, has offered a candid account of how the Church came to that decision.[55] He suggested that the bishops' collective silence reflected 'more profound thought than may have been apparent':[56] 'The crucial question, which staff at Church House debated privately with a number of bishops, Synod members, academics and others in the lead-up to the referendum was "Is Brexit a fundamentally theological question?"'[57] The assembled company, he noted, acknowledged the seriousness of the implications of Brexit for domestic and foreign policy and for the lives of ordinary people, recognizing that a pastoral response to the latter was going to be important. But the larger conclusion from the conversation was as follows:

> Christian churches – and good societies – can flourish in a variety of polities. If the core Brexit question was, as we surmised, whether the UK's culture and identity would, in future, tend more towards European solidarity, or look across the Atlantic to a new English-speaking union, then there were arguments pointing in both directions. Europe offered us allies who share monarchical systems and some form of established or state church. But the Christian heritage of the USA is also crucial to that nation's identity. The implications for the kind of society we may become are profound, and each view would entail secondary theological issues (about how to handle plurality, about economics, welfare and the individual, to name only a few). But to make the question, in effect, *a status confessionis*, on which Christian identity turns and which separates the faithful and the heretics, felt absurd. In short, if one could be a loyal follower of Christ while welcoming Brexit, and no less a true disciple while yearning to remain in the EU, the Church of England would not take sides.[58]

I find this way of reaching a decision on whether to speak into such a momentous national debate deeply surprising. It is troublingly elitist, theologically lightweight and disappointingly insular.[59]

First, how could it have been thought acceptable to reach a decision of such enormity in a private meeting of a handful of bishops and their invited guests? Is not this surely the kind of question that must be opened up to the larger forums of the whole Church in order to truly discern where 'the mind of the Church' might be tending (if anywhere)? The retort might be: 'But we had no time.' That response would in itself be an admission that the Church had failed to do any serious thinking on the EU – since its inception, the most momentous political project undertaken by the UK's continental neighbours.

But in that case, the Church should have had the honesty to say: 'We admit we are unprepared to offer any theologically serious guidance on Brexit, and, as a Church committed to national engagement, we deeply regret that. Given that lack, a select meeting of bishops and other will seek to craft a pastoral response to the challenges thrown up by the referendum, which we will publish and open up for discussion.'

Second, this account of the meeting suggests a surprising dearth of theological and ethical thinking. For a start, the platitudinous observation that Christian churches can flourish in various polities was not at issue. Brexit was not about the flourishing of *the Church* but of *the nation*. But when the prospects for Britain's 'culture and identity' are addressed, the question is framed as whether they will fare better if the nation adopts a European or an Atlantic orientation. This poses the question as if it were exclusively one about *Britain's* national interests, ignoring whether what was equally at stake were the interests of our European neighbours and of the wider world that might well be affected by the EU losing one of its largest members. There is no neutral way to put that question: either you think a nation may make its own interests decisive in its relations with others, or you accept that nations are under a norm of solidarity towards others that must temper those interests – not least towards its immediate neighbours, especially those with whom it has been bound in a far-reaching pact of solidarity for nearly 50 years. Is that not a serious matter of political theology on which a Church with a national mission ought to have had some clear opinion? But then, bizarrely, the question is framed as whether Brexit is a 'secondary theological issue' or a fundamental question of Christian identity (a *status confessionis*), one that 'separates the faithful and the heretics'. But that is a hopelessly binary way of dividing up fundamental questions of political (or any branch of) theology. In any case, if our membership of the EU was, at least, an important 'secondary' theological issue, and given the massive importance of the issue to a hurting nation and the desire of the Church to continue to claim the role of national Church, why not actually do some work on it? To point out that one can be a faithful Christian and vote either way in the referendum is, again, platitudinous. The Church rarely suggests that specific political choices like these become *tests of Christian faithfulness*. That is why I have suggested that what was required was not a partisan statement in favour of Remain or Leave but a theologically informed diagnosis intended to offer English Anglicans and any others listening in, deeper resources of reflection and wisdom to inform their own thinking and voting on a complex and contested question.

I have pointed out the political insularity revealed in the gathering. No less striking is its ecclesial insularity. Did any of the assembled experts draw attention to the fact that, while the Church of England itself may not have done much thinking on the EU of late, many of its European neighbour churches had been doing so for decades? Were participants reminded that a leading source of inspiration behind the emergence and contemporary sustenance of the EU was the movement of Christian Democracy flourishing in several European nations in the post-war period and, at its best, inspired by deep reserves of Christian political wisdom?[60] Ironically, a substantial statement on the EU issued by the Council of European Churches happened to appear in June 2016, days before the referendum.[61] It is not clear exactly when the Church's meeting took place, but did anyone attending it know or subsequently come to know of this document and think it worth learning from? In this regard, the outcome of the meeting mirrored precisely the long-standing and debilitating insularity about European affairs affecting much of English society. In that regard, the Church of England was at that point indeed a 'national Church' in precisely the wrong sense.

It is true that almost no other UK churches made any substantial statements on Brexit, not even the Roman Catholic Church, which, given its historic continental affiliations, might have been expected to do so.[62] So an immediate rejoinder to my critique would be that the non-established status of those churches had not in itself afforded them any greater capacity to speak prophetically on such issues. It is true that being non-established does not guarantee a church's commitment to national engagement. I suggest, however, that the Church of England's Established status was indeed a material factor in *its* silence on Brexit. That status places upon it a powerful sense of obligation that it is not simply a church with a national vision but a national Church, one that in some sense must seek to *represent* the whole nation, or at least *be hospitable to* all comers, members or not, whatever their political views. But on many important but divisive political questions, it is untenable for any one church to fulfil both aspirations simultaneously. And to aspire to do so is inhibiting of the Church's own message: any church faithful to the gospel is as liable to find itself at odds with 'the mind of the nation' on any national issue as it is concordant with it.

Attempting to sustain such a posture thus confronts a national Church with a constant and inescapable dilemma: risk making inevitably divisive (even if non-partisan) interventions on such matters, or remain silent in the interests of being 'representative' and 'hospitable'. The Church of England's track record here is, inevitably, erratic and inconsistent.[63] In *Faith in the City* it opted to speak the truth about urban deprivation as it saw it, absorbing the cost of the divisions inevitably fuelled.[64] In Brexit, the Church confronted an issue more complex and divisive than any it had faced for a long time. It chose to opt for what it thought was a stance of national *pastoral inclusiveness* across England rather than one of courageous national *political engagement* (although it was not, of course, inclusive for Scotland or Northern Ireland, which voted against Brexit). That option left it culpably speechless at a moment of great national trauma. I suggest that, had it been disestablished, it would have known itself to be significantly freer to confront boldly the nation's pathologies (voicing both 'progressive' and 'conservative' concerns), without labouring under the burden of the incompatible expectations sustained by Establishment. The Church's approach to deciding whether, and if so how, to be 'prophetic' when speaking into national affairs needs to be freed from the conflicting and inevitably compromising expectations arising from Establishment. Disestablishment would open up more psychic space for the Church to calibrate its national interventions – prophetic or otherwise – according to its own lights and without the distracting expectations sustained by the presumption that it can be 'chaplain to the nation'.

Conclusion

I have argued that the Church of England can amply retain its commitment to a 'national mission' even after disestablishment. There is no reason why it should not maintain its long-standing practice of national political engagement after it has let go of the special ties to the state sustained by Establishment. It could also better discharge this role if its public interventions displayed greater depth, coherence and consistency – a point that applies even under existing arrangements but which would assume greater importance after disestablishment. There are plenty of signs that it retains a vision for such a goal and evidence that, at times, it is able to put it into practice. Fulfilling such a role more faithfully would involve renouncing the presumption that it is entitled or equipped to represent the whole nation, be hospitable to all its citizens, or act as neutral host in conducting national debates (even in private). It cannot represent the whole nation because no church can ever presume to do that and because the vast majority of English citizens no longer consent to it doing so. Nor should it attempt to do so: the gospel itself will sometimes compel it to adopt oppositional and divisive postures towards the nation. A disestablished Church would involve 'not a withdrawal from the world, but rather a withdrawal from mechanisms of political control in order to re-engage more forcefully and critically with the ways of the world'.[65] Beyond Establishment, the Church of England could fully remain a church *for* the nation, even it was no longer officially acknowledged by the state as the church *of* the nation.

Notes

1 *Church and Nation* (Oxford: Blackwell, 1983), p. 79.

2 Including Anglican liberals: Mary Warnock wrote *Dishonest to God: On Keeping Religion out of Politics* (London: Bloomsbury, 2010) mostly with Catholic members of the House of Lords, and their 'interfering' cardinals and bishops, in mind.

3 *A Report on Church, State and Establishment* (Peterborough: Methodist Church, 2004), paras 31, 96.

4 The Church of Scotland, the Methodist Church, the Baptist Church and the United Reformed Church, www.jointpublicissues.org. uk/, accessed 30.10.2021.

5 'Establishment: Some Theological Considerations', *Ecclesiastical Law Journal* 21 (2019), pp. 340–1.

6 The broader implication of disestablishment for ecumenism in England is a major theme I have not addressed in the book. My sentiments on the matter are beautifully expressed by Peter Cornwell in *Church and Nation*: 'The sure mark of true ecumenism is the conviction that we are turning with joy to Christ to receive from his hands even more than he has, in his mercy, given us in our separation' (p. 98).

7 *Church and State: Report of the Archbishops' Commission* (London: Church Information Office, 1970), p. 11.

8 See, for example, Malcolm Brown et al., *Anglican Social Theology: Renewing the Vision Today* (London: Church House Publishing, 2014); Stephen Spencer, ed., *Theology Reforming Society: Revisiting Anglican Social Theology* (London: SCM Press, 2017).

9 *Religion in Britain: A Persistent Paradox*, 2nd edn (Chichester: Wiley-Blackwell, 2015), pp. 81–2.

10 Quoted in Davie, *Religion in Britain*, p. 83.

11 R. M. Morris, 'Introduction: Mapping the Issues', in R. M. Morris, ed., *Church and State in the 21st Century: The Future of Church and State* (Basingstoke: Palgrave Macmillan, 2009), p. 10. Emphasis original.

12 The St Paul's Institute is already exemplary in engaging with the City on ethical and theological matters. The Church generally has more to learn in this area, of course. See Eve Poole, *The Church on Capitalism: Theology and the Market* (Basingstoke: Palgrave Macmillan, 2010).

13 *Church, State and Establishment*, paras 44, 45.

14 *Church and Nation in a Secular Age* (London: Darton, Longman and Todd, 1983), p. 193.

15 'What Future for Establishment?', in Mark Chapman, Judith Maltby and William Whyte, eds, *The Established Church: Past, Present and Future* (London: T&T Clark, 2011), p. 193.

16 *Church and Nation*, p. 66.

17 For one statement of a contemporary Presbyterian account of such 'testimony', see Doug Gay, *Honey from the Lion: Christianity and the Ethics of Nationalism* (London: SCM Press, 2013), ch. 8. See also, for example, *A Right Relationship with Money: The Church of Scotland's Commission on the Purposes of Economic Activity* (2012), www.churchofscotland.org.uk/__data/assets/pdf_file/0009/9765/Economics_Commission_email_and_web_version.pdf, accessed 30.10.2021.

18 This is Anthony Dyson's definition of a church's 'spiritual independence: '"Little Else But the Name" – Reflections on Four Church and State Reports', in George Moyser, ed., *Church and Politics Today: The Role of the Church of England in Contemporary Politics* (Edinburgh: T&T Clark, 1985), p. 305.

19 See, for example, Nigel Biggar, *Theological Politics* (Latimer Studies 29/30) (Oxford: Latimer House, 1988).

20 Based on a survey of the previous 20 years, especially of bishops in the House of Lords, Andrew Partington and Paul Bickley concluded in 2007 that 'the attitude of the Church of England towards the state has been overwhelmingly critical' (*Coming off the Bench: The Past, Present and Future of Religious Representation in the House of Lords* (London: Theos, 2007), p. 44).

21 *Who is My Neighbour? A Letter from the House of Bishops to the People and Parishes of the Church of England for the General Election 2015* (London: Church of England, 2015).

22 To cite just a few from the last decade: Justin Welby, *Reimagining Britain: Foundations for Hope* (London: Bloomsbury, 2018); John Sentamu, ed., *On Rock or Sand? Firm Foundations for Britain's Future* (London: SPCK, 2015); Rowan Williams, *Faith in the Public Square* (London: Bloomsbury, 2012).

23 The former Board of Social Responsibility, for all the criticisms it has received, produced a decent number of these. See Giles Ecclestone, 'The General Synod and Politics', in Moyser, *Church and Politics Today*, pp. 107–27.

24 Rowan Williams, 'The government needs to know how afraid people are', *New Statesman*, 9 June 2011, www.newstatesman.com/uncategorized/2020/05/ns-archive-coalition-government-archbishop-canterbury-rowan-williams, accessed 30.10.2021.

25 Miles Brignall, 'Archbishop of Canterbury wants to "compete" Wonga out of existence', *The Guardian*, 25 July 2013, www.theguardian.com/money/2013/jul/25/church-england-wonga, accessed 30.10.2021. Welby has served on the parliamentary Banking Standards Commission.

26 'A Response to the Government Equalities Office Consultation – "Equal Civil Marriage"' (London: Church of England, 2012), 'Summary'.

27 This section is an edited version of 'The Church of England and the Funeral of Baroness Thatcher', *Fulcrum*, 26 April 2013, www.fulcrum-anglican.org.uk/articles/the-church-of-england-and-the-funeral-of-baroness-thatcher/, accessed 30.10.2021.

28 For an amateur poetic rendition of Johnson's messianism, see Jonathan Chaplin, 'Liberator', *PoliticsMeansPolitics*, 29 August 2019.

29 'Duke of Cambridge marks Royal Navy anniversary', *Westminster Abbey*, 3 May 2019, www.westminster-abbey.org/abbey-news/continuous-at-sea-deterrent, accessed 30.10.2021.

30 The full motion reads: 'That this Synod, mindful that a faithful commemoration of the centenary of the 1918 Armistice must commit the Church afresh to peace building; and conscious that nuclear weapons, through their indiscriminate and destructive potential, present a distinct category of weaponry that requires Christians to work tirelessly for their elimination across the world:

(a) welcome the 2017 UN Treaty on the Prohibition of Nuclear Weapons and the clear signal it sends by a majority of UN Member States that nuclear weapons are both dangerous and unnecessary;

(b) call on Her Majesty's Government to respond positively to the UN Treaty on the Prohibition of Nuclear Weapons by reiterating publicly its obligations under Article VI of the Nuclear Non-Proliferation Treaty and its strategy for meeting them; and

(c) commit the Church of England to work with its Anglican Communion and ecumenical partners in addressing the regional and international security concerns which drive nations to possess and seek nuclear weapons and to work towards achieving a genuine peace through their elimination', https://www.churchofengland.org/sites/default/files/2018-07/Voting%20results%20-%20Item%2013%20%28July%202018%29.pdf, accessed 3.3.2022.

31 Nick Megoran, 'It's disgraceful that nuclear weapons are being celebrated at Westminster Abbey', *The Guardian*, 2 May 2019, www.theguardian.com/commentisfree/2019/may/02/nuclear-arms-westminster-abbey-jesus-weapons, accessed 30.10.2021.

32 'Submariners celebrate 50 years of success of Navy's ultimate mission', *Royal Navy*, 18 January 2019, www.royalnavy.mod.uk/news-and-latest-activity/news/2019/january/18/190118---submariners-celebrate-50-years-of-mission-success, accessed 30.10.2021.

33 Specifically, to recognize 'the expertise, innovation and skill of the thousands of people who have designed, built, supported, and crewed the submarines on more than 350 patrols; it pays tribute to the extraordinary effort that has been required to maintain the deterrent without

a minute's break for fifty years'; see the service book here: www.west
minster-abbey.org/media/12354/continuous-sea-deterrent-service.pdf,
accessed 30.10.2021.

34 The Very Revd Dr John Hall, 'Address given at a service to
recognise fifty years of Continuous At Sea Deterrent', *Westminster
Abbey*, 3 May 2019, www.westminster-abbey.org/abbey-sermons/con
tinuous-sea-deterrent, accessed 30.10.2021.

35 Hall, 'Address given at a service to recognise fifty years'. Cathedrals enjoy considerable autonomy from dioceses. Such decisions are
taken by Dean and Chapter, not bishops.

36 This went considerably further than the thrust of a Mission and
Public Affairs Council paper, 'The Ethics of Nuclear Weapons' (GS
2095, June 2018), published ahead of the July Synod and responding
to the UN Treaty on the Prohibition of Nuclear Weapons. The paper
offered a useful overview of the evolving state of official Church opinion
on Britain's nuclear deterrent up to then and set out a variety of ethical
positions on how to assess the 'Ban Treaty'. While noting the diplo-
matic success of the Treaty, the paper raised significant doubts as to its
feasibility and does not endorse it (paras 78–84). The paper's summary
(paras 48, 64) of the Board of Social Responsibility-commissioned
report, *The Church and the Bomb* (London: Hodder, 1982), also mis-
states both the report's key recommendations on 'unilateral' nuclear
disarmament and General Synod's response to it in 1983. For a more
accurate account, see John Elford, 'The Church and Nuclear Defence
Policy', in Moyser, *Church and Politics Today*, pp. 176–200.

37 'Bishops' letter on UN Nuclear Weapons Treaty', *Church of
England*, 13 November 2020, www.churchofengland.org/news-and-
media/news-and-statements/bishops-letter-un-nuclear-weapons-treaty,
accessed 30.10.2021. In March 2021, eleven leaders, including the
Archbishop of York, from seven denominations and from Churches
Together in Britain and Ireland, also denounced the government's
decision to increase the number of Trident warheads. See 'Statement
from Church leaders on the UK Government announcement on war-
head numbers', Archbishop of York, 16 March 2021, www.arch
bishopofyork.org/news/latest-news/statement-church-leaders-uk-govern
ment-announcement-warhead-numbers, accessed 30.10.2021.

38 Megoran, 'It's disgraceful'.

39 In 2003, Archbishop Rowan Williams stood against the Blair
government on Iraq, warning that an invasion without UN authoriza-
tion would be unjust. See Neil Tweedie, 'Rowan Williams attacks
government over Iraq war', *Daily Telegraph*, 9 October 2009, www.
telegraph.co.uk/news/uknews/defence/6283914/Rowan-Williams-attacks-
Government-over-Iraq-war.html, accessed 30.10.2021.

40 *Church and Nation*, p. 29.

41 *Church and Nation in a Secular Age*, p. 110.

42 Hattie Williams, 'Archbishops angered by Johnson's Northern Ireland amnesty', *Church Times*, 15 July 2021, www.churchtimes. co.uk/articles/2021/16-july/news/uk/archbishops-angered-by-johnsons-northern-ireland-amnesty, accessed 30.10.2021.

43 For many reasons, of the 3,500-plus killings that took place during the Troubles, one-third were still being investigated in 2018.

44 'Statement by the Archbishop of Armagh on Legacy issues', *Diocese of Connor*, 16 July 2021, https://connor.anglican.org/2021/07/16/statement-by-the-archbishop-of-armagh-on-legacy-issues/, accessed 30.10.2021.

45 Julian O'Neil, 'The Troubles: Organisers defend NI legacy event in London', *BBC News*, 5 December 2020, www.bbc.co.uk/news/uk-northern-ireland-55201483, accessed 30.10.2021.

46 Stormont House Agreement, https://assets.publishing.service.gov.uk/government/uploads/system/uploads/attachment_data/file/390672/Stormont_House_Agreement.pdf, accessed 30.10.2021.

47 According to a BBC report, they included, for example, representatives of the British and Irish governments, the senior republican Sean Murray, the loyalist Winston Irvine and Judith Thompson, until recently the commissioner for victims and survivors (O'Neil, 'The Troubles'). See also Adam Kula, 'Irish State involved in secret legacy talks "as partners of the UK"', *News Letter*, www.newsletter.co.uk/news/politics/irish-state-involved-secret-legacy-talks-partners-uk-3058740, accessed 30.10.2021.

48 'Legacy: Veterans Commissioner questions Lambeth Palace talks', *BBC News*, 3 February 2021, www.bbc.co.uk/news/uk-northern-ireland-55919555, accessed 30.10.2021.

49 A UUP MLA said: 'Without a shadow of a doubt Jim Roddy and Harold Good were not doing this for anything other than good reasons … But the execution of that was extremely poor. The cast of people invited to that, the manner in which it was convened, the less than open manner in which we all found out about it, the follow up about what was discussed and how the invites were issued created more confusion.' 'Lambeth Palace legacy talks: Victims' campaigner refuses to attend future meetings', *Belfast Telegraph*, 10 December 2020, www.belfasttelegraph.co.uk/news/northern-ireland/lambeth-palace-legacy-talks-victims-campaigner-refuses-to-attend-future-meetings-39847777.html, accessed 30.10.2021. See also Allan Preston, 'Archbishop of Canterbury Lambeth Palace legacy talks postponed after criticism from victims' group', *Belfast Telegraph*, 10 December 2020, www.belfasttelegraph.co.uk/news/northern-ireland/archbishop-of-

canterbury-lambeth-palace-legacy-talks-postponed-after-criticism-from-victims-group-39846513.html, accessed 30.10.2021.

50 Mark Rainey, 'Troubles victims angered by "secret" Lambeth Palace talks on legacy issues', *News Letter*, 4 December 2020, www.newsletter.co.uk/news/crime/troubles-victims-angered-secret-lambeth-palace-talks-legacy-issues-3057572, accessed 30.10.2021.

51 Two of its representatives present, Archbishop Justin Welby and Canon David Porter, have exemplary 'peacebuilding' track records, the latter in Northern Ireland itself.

52 'Report of the Bloody Sunday Inquiry', *Gov.uk*, 15 June 2010, www.gov.uk/government/publications/report-of-the-bloody-sunday-inquiry, accessed 30.10.2021.

53 Most bishops who spoke up favoured Remain, though, contrary to a widespread perception, the great majority did not speak at all. See Malcolm Brown, 'Brexit-shaped Britain and the Church of England', in Jonathan Chaplin and Andrew Bradstock, eds, *The Future of Brexit Britain: Anglican Reflections on British Identity and European Solidarity* (London: SPCK, 2020), pp. 193–203. Nevertheless, many on the Leave side berated the Church for appearing to be pro-Remain. See the contributions by Sam Norton, Adrian Hilton and Suzanne Evans in *Future of Brexit Britain*.

54 Press Association, 'Archbishop of Canterbury calls for "reconciliation" to heal Brexit divisions', *Premier Christian News*, 14 December 2018, https://premierchristian.news/us/news/article/archbishop-of-canterbury-calls-for-reconciliation-to-heal-brexit-divisions, accessed 30.10.2021. See also the chapters by Graham Tomlin and Robert Innes in Chaplin and Bradstock, *Future of Brexit Britain*.

55 'Brexit-shaped Britain'. I am entirely happy to assume that this account of the meeting is reliable. I have no access to any other insider information.

56 'Brexit-shaped Britain', p. 194.

57 'Brexit-shaped Britain', pp. 194–5.

58 'Brexit-shaped Britain', p. 195.

59 Here I intend no personal criticism at all of Malcolm Brown, who at this point in his essay writes only as a scribe of the meeting. On the contrary, I am very grateful to Malcolm for agreeing to contribute such an enlightening chapter for *The Future of Brexit Britain*. We allowed him only 4,000 words, so his account of the meeting may not convey all its nuances.

60 In fact, I think it is almost certain that some of the assembled company must have tried to press issues such as these. I can think of at least two senior figures who by virtue of their roles in the Church could

not have been left off the invitation list and who would have argued thus. If so, they evidently lost the argument.

61 'What future for Europe? Reaffirming the European project as building a community of values. An open letter of CEC to churches and partner organisations in Europe and an invitation to dialogue and consultation', 21 June 2016, www.ceceurope.org/wp-content/uploads/2016/06/1GB2016_Doc15-Open-letter-Future-of-Europe.pdf, accessed 30.10.2021.

62 An exception is the Church of Scotland, which published a thoughtful document, 'Our Place in Europe', in May 2016. It came out in favour of Remain.

63 For an account of the deeper historical reasons for the lack of a coherent social theology, see the 'Response' by Ben Ryan in Chaplin and Bradstock, *Future of Brexit Britain*, pp. 261–3.

64 In the debate over *The Church and the Bomb*, by contrast, General Synod refused the principled radicalism of that report and fudged the ethics of nuclear deterrence. That, at least, is my view, but my argument at this point does not hang on my being right on this point of interpretation.

65 This is Jeremy Morris's apt summary of the thrust of Kenneth Leech, ed., *Setting the Church of England Free* ('The Future of Church and State', in Duncan Dormor, Jack McDonald and Jeremy Caddick, eds, *Anglicanism: The Answer to Modernity* (London: Continuum, 2003), p. 175).

Conclusion:
Life Beyond Establishment

[T]he Church [of England] has never made any unforced concessions of its status.
(Robert Morris)[1]

[C]ut the connection and 'let the Church of England be free'.
Soon.
(Colin Buchanan)[2]

This book has argued that Establishment amounts to a theologically problematic confusion of the spheres of authority
of Church and state and that the Church should itself seek
to terminate it. This is both to recover non-trivial areas of
autonomy that should have been reclaimed long ago and to
relinquish unwarranted privileges that it should be willing to
surrender as a matter of constitutional fairness. The New Testament's theology of the relation of the church to political orders
points clearly to a state that refrains from making judgements
about religious truth and adopts a posture of impartiality
towards the diverse faiths represented in its territory. Establishment is founded on biblically and theologically untenable
notions of the Christian nation and the national Church. These
in turn rest tacitly on Old Testament assumptions about the
corporate religious agency of covenanted nations, assumptions
that are radically superseded in the New Testament. The legacy
of these ideas remains embodied in constitutional provisions
such as the sacral coronation, the public–legal status of Church

law, the monarch's supreme governorship of the Church and his or her obligation to maintain England (and Scotland) as Protestant nations, the remaining authority of Parliament over Church law-making and the privileged presence of the Lords Spiritual. Each of these arrangements amounts to 'special forms of privilege and responsibility' conferred on the Church of England that breach the principle of state religious impartiality and church autonomy in ways that still matter. I argue that – if Morris's assessment above is correct – the Church should break the habit of a lifetime and voluntarily relinquish these special forms. It should do this not as a PR exercise designed to shore up its fragile public standing but as a manifestation of its own commitment to a better theology of church and state.

That is my fundamental argument for disestablishment. I have sought to shore it up with exposés of four principal arguments mounted in defence of Establishment. There are undoubtedly others, but these seem to me the most frequently cited. The first is that disestablishment would be received publicly as a 'concession to secularism', a retreat of faith from the public square. I have argued, first, that disestablishment would be a *concession to the right kind of secularism* ('procedural secularism', and its logical concomitant, a religiously impartial state) and that the Church itself ought to make such a concession. Second, however, I argue that the Church should seize the reins of the public debate about disestablishment and show why its goal is to reset, not scale back, the presence of faith in the public square and to free the Church to pursue its own mission with greater authenticity. That would demand robust advocacy of what I have called 'equitable public pluralism' so that a disestablished Church 'lands' in more hospitable political and legal territory than many churches and faith communities currently enjoy. Trends threatening to undermine such hospitality are growing and explain the degree of anxiety evoked among Church leaders at the prospect of disestablishment. So an early task of a disestablished Church, in partnership with other churches and religious organizations, would be to redouble its efforts to resist the *wrong* kind of secularism.

The second common defence is that, since states cannot be neutral with regard to society's overarching world views, disestablishment would open the door to the establishment of some non-Christian world view (or, in Nigel Biggar's terms, at least a world view less able to defend 'humanism'). My response is to claim that while states cannot attain moral neutrality in their actions, they can and must aspire to impartiality on matters of ultimate religious (or other) truth. They do need widely endorsed *political* principles (such as the rule of law or democratic process) but they are not authorized to favour one set of *ultimate truth-claims* over others. They must practise 'confessional' silence. Yet they are not thereby condemned, as Biggar implies, to intolerable internal 'dissonance' if they do.

The third and fourth arguments I critique are the two parts of the 'national mission' argument – that disestablishment would amount to an abandonment of the Church's commitment to the spiritual welfare of the whole nation. The Church of England, I claim, can fully sustain such a commitment after disestablishment. It can, first, at the local level continue to be pastorally receptive to all comers without the distracting legal constraints and cultural expectations sustained by Establishment. Those worried that disestablishment might unleash yet further 'congregationalism' or 'sectarianism' in the Church should argue their case within the Church itself, without leaning on archaic laws to assist them. We do not need to look far to see an example of non-established churches remaining committed to a national pastoral mission: the Church in Wales has been so committed since 1920 and the Church of Ireland since 1871. Second, the Church can at the national level maintain its longstanding commitment to public engagement without retaining the special ties to the state sustained by Establishment. I also argue that disestablishment could at least create the possibility that the Church might discover greater reserves of theological integrity and moral courage, thereby allowing it to speak more 'prophetically' on a range of national issues without being pre-emptively cowed by the expectations deriving from its national 'chaplaincy function'.

Where might support for disestablishment be found within the Church today?[3] One of the reasons why disestablishment has been 'the dog that didn't bark' is that the issue cuts across the three principal wings of the Church: Anglo-Catholicism, Evangelicalism and Liberalism. Most adherents to each wing have traditionally supported Establishment, if only by default, or been indifferent on the question. Equally, supporters of disestablishment have found themselves scattered across the three wings, with the result that it has not been possible to enlist the organizational machinery of any of them behind a campaign. It is worth briefly recalling some episodes in the history of such affiliations.

Anglo-Catholicism originated in the Oxford (or Tractarian) Movement, launched by John Keble's 'Assize Sermon' of 1833, 'National Apostasy'.[4] The sermon was an explosive reaction to the reforming British government of the 1830s, notably its support for Catholic emancipation and Irish disestablishment. Keble took these to be a betrayal of traditional Anglican primacy. He was, on the one hand, entirely justified in protesting that it was the state, not the Church, that had determined a reorganization of Irish dioceses and provinces – another late flexing of Erastian muscles on the part of the British political class. On the other, Keble had been quite happy to support Establishment so long as it defended Anglican primacy. If, however, the state threatened it, Anglicans were bound to seek to recover the 'freedom of the Church' from state control in order to defend their spiritual integrity. Later Anglo-Catholics – notably J. N. Figgis – transformed this self-interested motivation into a generalized pluralist argument for 'free churches in a free state', one that is entirely congenial to disestablishment, and to a broader model of equitable public pluralism. So it is no accident that the leading protagonists of Church reform in the twentieth century were Anglo-Catholics in Church and Parliament. Anglo-Catholic Christian socialists offered another distinctive case for disestablishment, arguing that the intimate ties to the state sustained by Establishment had rendered the Church incapable of challenging the wider political and economic establishments that stood in the way of Christian socialist aspirations. It is this strand of Anglo-Catholicism that is most likely to lend support for such a cause today.[5] Yet I would hope that others in this wing could also appreciate that what they wish to preserve in the Catholic tradition today gains nothing from Establishment and is more likely to be secured in a disestablished Church.

What are the prospects for Evangelical support for disestablishment? Andrew Atherstone's account suggests that, since the nineteenth century, prominent Evangelicals have defended Establishment not on the basis of any well-articulated church–state theology but because they thought Parliament a better defender of orthodox Protestantism than the Liberal- and Catholic-dominated bench of bishops; or, since 1970, than a similarly unsympathetic General Synod.[6] This self-interested stance precisely mirrors that of the early Tractarians: we will defend Establishment if it works in our favour. Yet Evangelicalism has also produced the most formidable recent exponent of disestablishment, Colin Buchanan. His book *Cut the Connection* is still one of the most thorough and impassioned statements available.[7] Buchanan's case should likely still appeal to Evangelicals who retain a strong missional sense of the distinctiveness of the Church within the world and its calling to submit wholly to 'the Lordship of Christ', rather than to the expectations of a secularized society and state. Given what many key Evangelical leaders claim about gospel, church and world, one might expect this to be most of them. Those who have valued Establishment, as Atherstone puts it, as a 'gospel opportunity' (a 'good boat to fish from'), might at least be open to persuasion that it has now become a hindrance to the proclamation of the gospel.

Liberal stances on Establishment have evolved over time and, like the other two wings, have not been unanimous. Some Liberal Catholics may, I fear, remain broadly sympathetic to John Habgood's patrician argument in *Church and Nation in a Secular Age*. More radical Liberals could, however, be expected to endorse the case for disestablishment as a statement against the political co-option of the Church. But this will be the case only if their desire that the Church take prophetic distance from the state were to outweigh their anxiety about sectarianism. Those on the fence might consider Theo Hobson's argument, discussed above, that the apparatus of Establishment is hardly the most spiritually authentic way to secure an 'open Church'.

I cannot predict whether a significant constituency in favour of disestablishment might emerge from these diverse sections of the Church (or from the large number of unaffiliated members), or whether the cause might, after all, remain 'the dog that didn't bark'. But we need to know what might happen if it did emerge. Suppose the Church at large, for the first time, became open to a serious debate over disestablishment, how should it then proceed? While the following suggestions must remain tentative, I owe it to readers at least to indicate the broad direction of travel that disestablishment might involve.

The necessary first step would be for the Church itself to clarify fully its own mind whether, and if so, how far, to move 'beyond Establishment'. To do that it would need to devote adequate resources of time and expertise to reflecting deeply on the questions raised by existing arrangements. It should therefore commission a fully representative expert body whose task would be to formulate a new theology of church–state relations and, if a consensus emerged, suggest initial proposals towards disestablishment. Lawyers and officials would be on tap, not on top. The outcome of these deliberations should then be submitted to a widely accessible consultation process – a Church 'citizens' assembly' (perhaps one in every diocese). The desired outcome would be a fresh, critical, theologically driven statement on disestablishment (or, if opinion does not go that far, at least a much better theological defence of Establishment than it has ever mounted before). Decisions would in due course have to be debated and decided in General Synod. I have proposed that in such a deliberative process the Church should take its cue from the jurisdictional theology of the Scottish Articles Declaratory, though there are many rich Anglican sources on which it might also draw. No complete reinventing of the wheel would be required.

The next step – which might be concurrent with the first – would be to open a wider ecclesial dialogue on the question. The first ports of call here would be other Anglican provinces in the UK and Ireland and, crucially, the Church of Scotland, whose own constitutional status is implicated in English Establishment.[8] There is clear evidence that the Church of England would find ample sympathy among English Free Churches for many of the moves towards disestablishment I have proposed. For example, the Methodist Church's *Report on Church, State and Establishment* in 2004 indicated an openness to the Scottish model, while also not excluding a more thoroughgoing disestablishment on the model of the 'voluntary society' in which all trace of privilege is removed.[9] In 2008, at a Constitution Unit conference on Establishment, the United Reformed Church representative Geoffrey Roper reported the emergence of a 'consensus of Free Church ecumenists that they would be happy for any emerging united Christian church to have the standing the Church of Scotland has in that country'. While rejecting any state role in church appointments, they 'would be happy with a pastoral role for the nation and a chance to express Christian voices on community issues'.[10] The Roman Catholic Church would, at least, sympathize with the ending of Protestant succession, and likely much more.[11]

The third step would be to initiate a conversation with representatives of other faith communities in England. The goal would be both to solicit their opinion and advice and to clarify to them that steps towards the disestablishment of the Church of England should not be read as a retreat of faith from the public square but only a resetting of the Church's place within it, in order to free it to be more faithful to its own lights in its public witness, in a context of a more secure equitable public pluralism. The Church should reassure such communities of their commitment to standing with them in upholding a dignified place for religion in public life and combatting ignorance about and discrimination against them.

That is the point at which a formal dialogue with the state – government and Parliament – should start. Of course, the Church should from the outset formally notify these bodies of its intentions to move in the direction of disestablishment and then keep them informed of the progress of its own thinking and the findings of conversations with others. But the Church should keep its distance from formal state conversations until it has achieved a sufficient level of clarity and commitment in its own mind. That might take years rather than months. If it invites politicians or officials into its deliberations prematurely, before it has, so to speak, learned to walk unaided, there is a serious risk of it pre-emptively capitulating to state expectations (which would certainly be forthcoming). In such conversations the Church should unambiguously declare its preferred direction of travel towards disestablishment and indicate a series of steps it thinks would facilitate the process, while, of course, soliciting state advice on how these might proceed. This would amount to what Colin Buchanan terms a 'negotiated separation on the Church's initiative'.[12] The state might judge that it needed something like a Royal Commission to explore implications from its side. Given the dependence of Establishment on fundamental statutes such as the Act of Supremacy 1559, the Act of Settlement 1707 or the Statute of Westminster 1931, weighty primary legislation from the side of the state would be required. The Church should, of course, offer all cooperation to such a body, while safeguarding the independence of its own deliberative processes and holding to its most important negotiating objectives.

I doubt that an initiative from the Church would be simply rebuffed by the state, even if it were not immediately welcomed with open arms. The 2004 Methodist *Report*, while noting a lack of political interest in the question at the time, judged that, 'should the Church of England itself demonstrate a clear majority in favour of radical change … it is hard to believe that Parliament could not be persuaded to act.'[13] The Church should keep in mind that, while the most recent governmental statements on Establishment have been cautious, Parliament itself might take renewed interest in the question. In 2012, the Commons Select Committee on Political and Constitutional Reform, in a report on the Succession to the Crown Bill, noted that 'the proposal does ... raise questions about the future of the Crown in the Church of England, *which the House may wish to consider in due course*.'[14] There could yet be a revival of parliamentary interest, and Chris Loder's intervention in 2021 shows that the Church might not find such interest wholly congenial. The bold assertion of the right of parliamentary control over the Church voiced by Frank Field in 1985 may yet be voiced again:

> [A]s the Church continues to press for further de jure self-governance, continues to espouse postures that challenge traditional understandings and, not least, recruits into its leadership men (*sic*) who adopt apparently novel positions on doctrinal matters ... so certain sections of conservative opinion within Parliament will seek vigorously to resist.[15]

But whatever official or parliamentary attitudes might turn out to be when the time came, it is essential for the Church to be thoroughly prepared for initiatives from the state's side rather than finding itself scrambling around for hasty compromises in the face of pressure for particular changes – or just ambushed by impatient and ill-informed politicians (however seemingly sympathetic). As Morris puts it, 'The problem for the churches about doing nothing or refusing to think things through is that they will be apt to be overtaken by events not of their own making.'[16]

It is beyond the brief of this book, and my expertise, to propose any kind of detailed legal blueprint for disestablishment. The overriding goal would be to reset the boundaries of authority between Church and state so that there is no longer any jurisdictional subservience of Church to state in 'ecclesiastical causes' and no longer any 'special forms of privilege and responsibility' afforded to the Church by the state. The means to such a goal would, as already indicated, include a variety of legal, political and structural changes. The proximate targets of these changes would include, at least, the following:

- nullifying what remains of the legacy of the Act of Supremacy 1559 and other linked Tudor statutes;
- ending Protestant succession;
- discontinuing the Church's role in the coronation service;
- abolishing the residual state role in Church appointments;
- ceasing parliamentary involvement in the Church's law-making processes, ending the right of the Church to initiate parliamentary legislation and abolishing the Ecclesiastical Committee;
- renouncing the element of privilege in the status of the Lords Spiritual;
- ending legal obligations on parishes;
- converting Church law (canon and Measures) to voluntary status.[17]

Establishment need not be and probably could not be dismantled in a single, sweeping act of state – perhaps to the chagrin of the more gladiatorial campaigners in state or Church. As Morris points out, disestablishment 'is not an all-out or all-in, zero sum choice but a combination of specific elements each of which may be treated separately ... It could be tackled in bite-sized chunks.'[18] Nor could it be achieved by the Church in some dramatic act of flouncing out – a 'Measure to end all Measures', as Buchanan calls it.[19]

In *Church and State in 21st Century Britain*, Morris and his co-authors set out a helpful and concise table summarizing the key elements of high Establishment and identifying the most likely means by which they could be ended.[20] For readers innocent of the technical details, two things stand out about this table. One is that the most important of the required actions are listed on a mere two pages; there are fewer than a dozen of them.[21] I mention this simply to show that disestablishment is nothing like as stupefyingly complex as some of its opponents would have us believe.[22] A spreadsheet setting out the process need only be as large as a classroom whiteboard. A team of creative legal minds in Church and state could draw up workable draft proposals without inordinate difficulty. The other thing that stands out is that several of these proposals (Morris et al. list six) could be initiated by the Church itself by means of Measures, even though some, as noted, would also need primary legislation introduced by Parliament. Thus, not only as a matter of dignity but also as a matter of law, the Church need not wait for the state to get the ball rolling. It could initiate the process itself from General Synod.[23] The various Measures involved would not need to be introduced all at the same time. The Church might identify a list of key priorities and, as it deliberated on its preferred journey, prepare suitable draft Measures addressing these matters. Notifying government and Parliament that it was embarking on such a process would, if such were needed, usefully concentrate minds in Westminster.

For what it is worth, I would suggest three steps the Church might take to launch the process (especially if the state were dragging its feet). The first would be a dramatic signal of its larger intentions. The Church should announce its intention voluntarily to withdraw its bishops from the House of Lords; or, at least, to reduce them to the number proposed in 2012 by the Joint Committee on reform of the Lords (12), with an agreement that the rest would lose automatic rights to sit following a wider reform of the Lords. This would not even need a Measure but would, of course, require negotiation with government and Parliament.[24] Second, following the accession of King Charles III (if that is the regnal name he chooses), the Church should introduce a Measure relinquishing the Church's role in future coronations and calling on the state to devise a new ceremony of civil investiture. That would require only relatively straightforward parliamentary legislation; and initiating the process in General Synod would, again, underline the seriousness of the Church's commitment. Third, as part of the second initiative, the Church should open discussions with Crown and government with a view to terminating the title of Defender of the Faith. This is, of course, finally a decision of the Crown, but the Church could indicate its preferred outcome. It would require no legislation but only an official announcement, once agreement had been reached with relevant stakeholders. I propose these particular initiatives because they seem to be the easiest to implement and because they would be guaranteed to stimulate wider public debate – for which the Church had better be prepared long before lighting the touchpaper. The 'harder yards' of disestablishment (ending Royal Supremacy, Crown appointments and Protestant succession; or repealing the Enabling Act) would take longer, but the ground would have been prepared and momentum generated.

These are my layman's proposals on how the Church itself might commence a process towards progressive disestablishment. There are likely other, perhaps better, ones. But however the process is embarked upon, there is no question that feasible options lie before the Church. The argument that the whole thing would be 'just too complicated' must be squarely faced down. It would inevitably take some time before the Church was of a mind to – and had the institutional bandwidth to – commit itself seriously to such a process. But if Church and state could summon the political will, obstacles could be steadily overcome. One could envisage, perhaps, a ten-year process commencing in 2024 and culminating in 2034, the 500th anniversary of the first Act of Supremacy – sending, one might say, a truly 'pregnant' signal.

It is likely that the Church would also have to countenance significant internal restructuring in the event of disestablishment. Given the widely dispersed nature of authority in the Church, that would be a demanding and controversial exercise, underlining the need for the Church fully to know its own mind before embarking on such a course. Some further administrative and legal streamlining and centralization is almost inevitable. Many would wish this to be kept to a minimum so as not to disturb too much the delicately pluralistic ecology of the Church's deliberative processes. That is to describe such processes rather flatteringly. The 2021 report of the Church's Governance Review Group concludes that the complexity of such processes has the effect of 'encouraging confusion, dupli-cation and accountability gaps' and is 'not sustainable or suitable for the Church's future mission'.[25] It would certainly be helpful if such moves were already under way before the Church embarked upon disestablishment, although disestab-lishment would necessitate further changes.

The danger is that, overwhelmed by other pressing matters – as it will always feel it is – the Church will simply continue to turn a blind eye to the issue. It would thereby leave itself vulnerable to being manoeuvred towards piecemeal or sudden disestablishment by a future government with other things on its mind and other agenda in play. If so, the Church would have squandered a unique historical opportunity to engage in a strategic public explanation of its identity and mission. The state will not care much about that and nor will most of the rest of society. But the Church should. For, as Paul Avis rightly asserts, the question of Establishment is fundamentally a ques-tion of mission.

Notes

1 'Half-Opening Cans of Worms: The Present State of "High" Establishment', *Law and Justice* 172 (2014), p. 22.

2 *Cut the Connection: Disestablishment and the Church of England* (London: Darton, Longman and Todd, 1994), p. 208.

3 A 2003 survey found 42 per cent of clergy and 35 per cent of laity supporting complete severance of church–state links (Guy Smith, Leslie John Francis and Mandy Robbins, 'Who Wants Establish-ment? A Comparison of Clerical and Lay Opinion in the Church of England', *Journal of Beliefs and Values* 24.3 (2003), pp. 349–65). In wider society, a 2011 survey found substantial minorities in favour of partial or full disestablishment (Ben Fulford and Nick Spencer, 'Public Opinion in Britain Towards the Disestablishment of the Church of Eng-land', *Journal of Anglican Studies* 13.1 (2014), pp. 30–9; Clive Field, 'Monarchical Religion', *British Religion in Numbers*, www.brin.ac.uk/monarchical-religion/, accessed 30.10.2021).

4 See Mark D. Chapman, '"A Free Church in a Free State:" Anglo-Catholicism and Establishment', in Mark Chapman, Judith Maltby and William Whyte, eds, *The Established Church: Past, Present*

and Future (London: T&T Clark, 2011), pp. 56–74; Matthew Grimley, 'The Dog that Didn't Bark: The Failure of Disestablishment Since 1927', in Chapman, Maltby and Whyte, *The Established Church*, pp. 39–55; Valerie Pitt, 'The Protection of Faith?', in Tariq Modood, ed., *Church, State and Religious Minorities* (London: Policy Studies Institute, 1997), pp. 36–9.

5 See several pieces in Kenneth Leech, ed., *Setting the Church of England Free: The Case for Disestablishment* (Croydon: The Jubilee Group, 2001).

6 Andrew Atherstone, 'Gospel Opportunity or Unbiblical Relic? The Established Church through Anglican Evangelical Eyes', in Chapman, Maltby and Whyte, *The Established Church*, pp. 75–97. See also Max Warren, 'The Functions of a National Church', in David Holloway, ed., *British Values and the National Church: Essays on Church and State from 1964–2014*, Latimer Study 19, 2nd edn (London: The Latimer Trust, 2015).

7 *Cut the Connection*. It is perhaps telling that this was not published by an Evangelical publisher.

8 For example, the Act of Union 1707 makes the Establishment of the Church of England a condition of union with Scotland.

9 The Methodist Church, *A Report on Church, State and Establishment* (Peterborough: Methodist Church, 2004), p. 104. Nigel Biggar finds the report less resistant to Establishment than I do. He correctly claims that Methodism embraces a variety of views on the subject but adds that the report 'does not observe that support for disestablishment predominates' (Biggar, 'Why the "Establishment" of the Church of England is Good for a Liberal Society', in Chapman, Maltby and Whyte, *The Established Church*, p. 24, n. 68). The document, however, reports that almost all comments offered by Methodists on Establishment in response to the Anglican-Methodist Covenant 'questioned or were hostile' to it (para. 111). The report commends several areas of significant reform to current arrangements (paras 113–18).

10 'View of a Critical Friend – From the United Reformed Church', in R. M. Morris, ed., *Church and State: Some Reflections on Church Establishment in England* (London: UCL Constitution Unit, 2008), p. 30.

11 In 2012, Cardinal Cormac Murphy-O'Connor indicated his support for disestablishment, while noting that it was not for the Roman Catholic Church to ask for it. Mark Greaves, 'Cardinal says disestablishment would benefit the Church of England', *Catholic Herald*, 24 August 2012, https://catholicherald.co.uk/cardinal-disestablishment-would-benefit-the-church-of-england/, accessed 30.10.2021.

12 *Cut the Connection*, p. 203.

13 Methodist Church, *Church, State and Establishment*, p. 109.

14 Morris, 'Half-Opening', p. 18. Emphasis added.

15 'The Church of England and Parliament: A Tense Partnership', in George Moyser, ed., *Church and Politics Today: The Role of the Church of England in Contemporary Politics* (Edinburgh: T&T Clark, 1985), p. 72.

16 R. M. Morris, ed., *Church and State in 21st Century Britain: The Future of Church and State* (Basingstoke: Palgrave Macmillan, 2009), p. 237.

17 This is what occurred in the Welsh Church Act 1914, in which 'all the laws of the Church were in effect converted into the rules and trusts of a voluntary society' (Chadwick Report, *Church and State: Report of the Archbishops' Commission* (London: Church Information Office, 1970), p. 48). In England it would involve, inter alia, repealing the Enabling Act 1919. Morris notes that this could be a highly complex process since repeal would also require a replacement Act, probably legal incorporation and law codification. He thus cautions against early repeal of this Act (*Church and State in 21st Century Britain*, pp. 228–9).

18 'Half-Opening', p. 17. Iain McLean and Scot Peterson, however, propose a single bill removing bishops from the House or Lords, abolishing lay patronage, repealing the Enabling Act, allowing the Church to legislate without reference to Parliament and converting the Church Estates Commissioners into trustees answerable to the Charity Commission. This would 'put the Church of England on a virtually identical footing to the Church of Scotland, so that both would be spiritually independent and autonomous, while retaining their place in the constitution of the United Kingdom' ('A Uniform British Establishment', in Chapman, Maltby and Whyte, *The Established Church*, pp. 141–57). I tend to agree with Morris that such a gargantuan proposal might simply be unworkable, or interminable.

19 Buchanan, *Cut the Connection*, p. 206.

20 *Church and State in 21st Century Britain*, p. 238–40.

21 They include, for example: repealing section 8 of the Act of Supremacy 1559 and other surviving remnants of the Tudor statutes (such as the Submission of Clergy Act 1533 and the acts governing episcopal appointments from 1533 and 1534); repealing part of the Act of Union 1706/07; repealing the Accession Declaration Act 1910; the possible introduction of new statutes ending Protestant succession, the exclusive Anglican role in the coronation, the privileged status of the Lords Spiritual, and converting ecclesiastical courts to the voluntary sphere; a public announcement of the end of the role of Defender of the Faith; and the political negotiation of new coronation and accession ceremonies.

22 The Ecclesiastical Law Society's 'Working Party on "Disestablishment" Report' notes that the Welsh Church Act 1914, which also dealt with complex matters of disendowment, only ran to 34 pages (George Spafford, Roger L. Brown and Ben Nichols, *Ecclesiastical Law Journal* 6 (2002), p. 269). English disestablishment would, however, be more complex.

23 Indeed, according to Morris, the government itself seems to have indicated in a 2008 White Paper that it looked to the Church to initiate certain changes to Establishment (*Church and State in 21st Century Britain*, p. 224).

24 It would require a technical parliamentary statute (Morris, *Church and State in 21st Century Britain*, p. 239).

25 Quoted in *Church Times*, 17 September 2021, p. 3.

Index of Names and Subjects